# ECOMYSTICISM

"A fascinating account of a crucial issue for our species, presented in an intelligent, articulate, and immensely readable way. I feel a close kinship in much of what he says."

ANTHONY STEVENS, JUNGIAN ANALYST
AND AUTHOR OF *THE TWO MILLION-YEAR-OLD SELF*
AND *THE ROOTS OF WAR AND TERROR*

"Carl von Essen mixes the personal, the scientific, and the ecological as he tracks the experiences of nature exemplified by the ways of the hunter, the warrior, the athlete, the mystic, and the scientist. As an angler, physician, scholar, and adventurer, he is uniquely qualified for these explorations. Read and be enlightened!"

STEPHEN BODIO, AUTHOR OF *ON THE EDGE OF THE WILD:
PASSIONS AND PLEASURES OF THE NATURALIST* AND
*EAGLE DREAMS: SEARCHING FOR LEGENDS IN WILD MONGOLIA*

"A significant statement in our present chemical era on the return of the physician to the role of the naturalist. To see ourselves through the lens of nature is to see that everything in nature is reflected in the life of the soul. And when we see this, God speaks to us and our consciousness is transformed."

EUGENE TAYLOR, PH.D., AUTHOR OF *WILLIAM JAMES
ON CONSCIOUSNESS BEYOND THE MARGIN*

# ECOMYSTICISM

## The Profound Experience of
## Nature as Spiritual Guide

CARL VON ESSEN, M.D.

Bear & Company
Rochester, Vermont • Toronto, Canada

Bear & Company
One Park Street
Rochester, Vermont 05767
www.BearandCompanyBooks.com

Text paper is SFI certified

Bear & Company is a division of Inner Traditions International

Originally published in 2007 by Lindisfarne Books, Great Barrington,
   Massachusetts, under the title *The Hunter's Trance: Nature, Spirit & Ecology.*
Revised edition published in 2010 by Bear & Company

**Library of Congress Cataloging-in-Publication Data**
von Essen, Carl, 1926–
   Ecomysticism : the profound experience of nature as spiritual guide / Carl von
Essen.
      p. cm.
   Rev. ed. of: The hunter's trance.
   Includes bibliographical references (p.      ) and index.
   ISBN 978-1-59143-118-3 (pbk.)
   1. Nature—Religious aspects. 2. Environmentalism—Religious aspects. 3.
Mysticism. I. Essen, Carl von, 1926– Hunter's trance. II. Title.
   BL435.E88 2010
   201'.77—dc22

                                                                    2010022332

Printed and bound in the United States by Lake Book Manufacturing
The text paper is 100% SFI certified. The Sustainable Forestry Initiative® program
promotes sustainable forest management.

10 9 8 7 6 5 4 3 2 1

Text design and layout by Priscilla Baker
This book was typeset in Garamond Premier Pro, with Avant Garde and Centaur
used as display typefaces

To send correspondence to the author of this book, mail a first-class letter to the
author c/o Inner Traditions • Bear & Company, One Park Street, Rochester, VT
05767, and we will forward the communication.

*For Manisha*

# CONTENTS

# PREFACE

It all began in childhood when I saw the wonder of life in streams and tidal pools, the magnificence of mountains and giant trees and starry skies. Later there came primal adventures of camping, trekking, hunting, and fishing. These explorations of spirit and body etched everlasting memories. I came to feel a kinship with life on this small earth and discovered these feelings were shared by fellow hunters, anglers, and mountaineers. But, over a lifetime now drawing to a close, disturbing revelations intensified that things were not going well with humanity's connection to Mother Nature. My concern grew as I heard other voices and saw in my worldwide travels increasing evidence of our destructive impact upon the wild.

A vision evolved that our spiritual bond with the natural world can be a potent path of action toward environmental healing. That vision, undoubtedly shared by many, took shape in *The Hunter's Trance: Nature, Spirit & Ecology*. As a physician and scientist, I felt it also important to explore mystical experience as it relates to our evolutionary, biological, and psychological connections with nature.

The burgeoning global ecocrisis, including what has been called the greatest environmental disaster in U.S. history in 2010, provided compelling reasons to revise and expand my book and to create a new title that clearly stated its aims.

# ACKNOWLEDGMENTS

Without the comments and suggestions of stern critics and generous supporters, this project would have faltered much more often than it did. Stephen Alter, Steve Bodio, Anthony Stevens, Eugene Taylor, and Edward O. Wilson provided authoritative comments that stoked my fire of determination to proceed.

Others, friends and colleagues, gave critical leavening to this diverse and diffuse topic. I am grateful to Joan and Herman Suit, the late Bruce Wallace, David Oswald, André Toth, Sister Elaine Prevallet, David Englund, Subhas Roy, Göran Olbers, Isabel Tellez, Mary Robson, Bishopryo Sanyal, Nancy Wilson, Peggy and the late Paul Eriksson, Nicholas Helburn, the late Joe Wray, and Bill Ventigmilia.

Stuart Weinberg, owner of the Seven Stars Bookshop in Cambridge, encouraged me to revise and republish *The Hunter's Trance*. I am grateful to my editors at Inner Traditions, Jeanie Levitan and Laura Schlivek. My wife, the author and Jungian analyst Manisha Roy, is always a beacon of support and inspiration.

*I walked into the forest, struck as always by the coolness of the shade beneath the tropical vegetation, and continued until I came to a small glade that opened onto the sandy path. I narrowed the world down to a few meters. Again I tried to compose the mental set—call it the naturalist's trance, the hunter's trance—by which biologists locate more elusive organisms. . . . The effect was strangely calming. Breathing and heartbeat diminished, concentration intensified. It seemed to me that something extraordinary in the forest was very close to where I stood, moving to the surface and to discovery.*

E. O. WILSON, *BIOPHILIA*

# INTRODUCTION

Early in his lifelong career as a nature photographer, Ansel Adams came to love the beauty and majesty of the California High Sierra. This is what he experienced in the summer of 1923, trekking through the rugged country east of Yosemite:

> I was climbing the long ridge west of Mount Clark. It was one of those mornings when the sunlight is burnished with a keen wind and long feathers of cloud move in a lofty sky. The silver light turned every blade of grass and every particle of sand into luminous metallic splendor; there was nothing, however small, that did not clash in the bright wind, that did not send arrows of light through the glassy air. I was suddenly arrested in the long crunching path up the ridge by an exceedingly pointed awareness of the *light*. The moment I paused, the full impact of the mood was upon me; I saw more clearly than I have ever seen before or since the minute detail of the grasses, the clusters of sand shifting in the wind, the small flotsam of the forest, the motion of the high clouds streaming above the peaks. There are no words to convey the moods of those moments.
>
> I dreamed that for a moment time stood quietly, and the vision of this actuality became but the shadow of an infinitely greater world, that I had within the grasp of consciousness a transcendental experience.[1]

Those words by Ansel Adams represent the essence of what I seek to convey in this book.

What has happened to the young climber? One minute he is trudging along a mountain ridge; the next, time stands still, light becomes extraordinary, every detail stands out as if etched, a memory is imprinted, and something is changed forever. Such a magical moment must have been charged with spiritual energy. Ansel Adams described his experience as transcendental, from the Latin *transcendere,* meaning "to climb across or beyond, to surpass the range or grasp of human experience, reason, or belief." The biologist E. O. Wilson, too, felt "something extraordinary" happening in the dark glade of the jungle of Surinam as he entered the trancelike state of the stalking naturalist or hunter. It was a sense of mystery. Its Greek root is *mystes,* the same as for mysticism, which in the ancient Greek tradition was the initiation into secret rites.

To many of us, such experiences arising from the nurturing splendor of our natural world give depth and meaning beyond a mundane existence increasingly beset by "civilization's" superficial and materialistic values. They can burrow deep into the soul and become a conduit to an expansion of a worldview, of a clearer understanding of self and our natural world. Let us explore this dimension of experience and discover some of its surprising and varied manifestations.

The word *mysticism* is often cloaked in connotations of spiritualism, occultism, obscure religious sectarianism, and fuzzy thinking. *Ecstasy,* from the Greek *ek* + *statikos,* meaning "a displacement, to stand apart from oneself," is now so misused that to many people it refers to the notorious drug of the same name. Writers nowadays avoid these words, replacing them with expressions such as *epiphany, bliss, rapture, oceanic feeling,* and *peak experience.* But I believe that the words *mysticism* and *ecstasy* deserve to be reconsidered with respect to their archaic roots and returned to their traditional meanings.

How rare are those soaring ecstatic moments such as the one Ansel Adams experienced? It appears from several studies that they are common. Fifteen hundred Americans in one survey by the *New York Times* were asked, "Have you ever had the feeling of being very close to a powerful spiritual force that seemed to lift you out of yourself?" About 40 percent of the respondents answered yes. Yet nearly all admitted never speaking about that feeling to anyone.

When I talk to fellow outdoorspeople, hunters, anglers, and mountaineers about such experiences, most of them nod, often with a glint of fond recollection in their eyes, a far-off gaze while they recall some unforgettable memory. But they do not generally volunteer to describe those moments. So, too, with the respondents in the *Times*'s survey. When asked, "Why not?" the common answer was, "It didn't seem to be the kind of thing people talk about."* How can one share them in everyday conversation? It is like baring the soul. Indeed, we often share, as Coleridge wrote, "cowardice of all deep feelings."[2]

The extraordinary ecstatic moment of Ansel Adams can certainly be considered a mystical experience. Can one completely describe it? Philosophers, sages, saints, and Zen monks may firmly state that this is not possible, that such an experience lies beyond expression in words. Nonetheless, volumes upon volumes have been written in that attempt—including, of course, this writing. Somehow the glory of these experiences generates an urge to share them with others—after overcoming our initial reticence.

In his monumental work *The Varieties of Religious Experience,* the great American philosopher and psychologist William James (1842–1910) described and defined some of the feelings that are associated with mystical experience. They ring true to the undercurrents I lovingly preserve from memories of spiritual adventures in nature. These feelings are, to me, *ineffable,* indescribable; *noetic,* true; *transient,* brief; and *passive,* unexpected, just as James indicated in his 1902 Edinburgh lectures.

---

*Marghanita Laski described in her groundbreaking book *Ecstasy* the circumstances leading to mystical experience in a survey of sixty-three volunteers. Greeley and McCready, in a larger sample ("Are We a Nation of Mystics?"), corroborated the universality of many characteristics of mystical experience, such as the sensation of unusual light, the alteration of the sense of time ("time stood still"), and the feeling of deep and profound peace.

William James specified the criteria for his term "mystical states of consciousness" as 1) ineffability: "The subject of it [the mystical state of mind] immediately says that it defies expression that no adequate report of its contents can be given in words"; 2) noetic quality, "They are states of insight into depths of truth unplumbed by the discursive intellect"; 3) transiency: "Mystical states cannot be sustained for long"; "Often, when faded, their quality can be imperfectly reproduced in memory, but when they recur it is recognized, and from one occurrence to another it is susceptible of continuous development in what is felt as inner richness and importance"; and 4) passivity: "[T]he mystic feels as if his own will were in abeyance, and indeed sometimes as if he were grasped and held by a superior power."[3]

Teresa of Avila, St. John of the Cross, and others had fervent ecstasies. How do such moments come to ordinary human beings? Do we have an inner site that can be lit by the transcendent spark of mystery, of a presence or power that has been given many names, but that one knows only tacitly, inside ourselves?

Somewhere in the soul there exists a burning light that flares up at certain moments of introspection. It is an inborn need to go beyond mundane experience, beyond eating, sleeping, and procreating, to find some "ultimate truth" that can give a deeper meaning to life. It is a search for something more than what we are, a need for an ultimate relationship, beyond family, clan, and community, with a divine presence. It is a thirst for transcendence, the over-belief, where mysticism and religion and transcendentalism and all other names for the deep well of our soul-search come together. It is a search for spirituality, the vital and animating essence of a person ("spirituality" comes from the Latin *spirare,* "to breathe"). Spirituality is the manifestation of over-beliefs that transcend "the further limits of our being" and brings us into another dimension, beyond the sentient world, into a mystical region, of which William James said, "I feel as if we have no philosophic excuse for calling the unseen or mystical world unreal."[4]

There are those who may not know or accept the concept of mystical experience. But for me it is the feeling that leaves me awed and speechless, knowing that some great power has touched my life. It is a sense of vastness, of a unity with an ultimate reality. As will be seen, this numinous state, extending through a spectrum of intensity, can be associated also with sublime creativity and physical achievement and can lead to unforgettable memories, to the creation of a work of art, a mathematical theorem, great athletic achievement, an architectural concept, or a complete change of one's life.

The subject of mystical experience has engaged scientists back to the origins of experimental psychology in the nineteenth century. Several have placed it into a basket of conditions often called "altered states of consciousness." These phenomena include hypnotic states, hallucinations, out-of-body, near-death, alien abduction, and crop circle cult experiences. Such "altered," "anomalous," "dissociative," or "exceptional" states of human experience have been parsed in numerous ways, including pathological, nonpathological, introvertive, and extravertive.[5] Much of this information and speculation still lies in a Pandora's box waiting for further elucidation. One difficulty, for example, is to distinguish "normal" from "paranormal" in phenomena such as the enhanced sense of light (photism) and the altered sense of time, both frequently encountered in mystical experience by apparently normal individuals. But I (and many others) believe that spontaneous spiritual encounters in nature are normal, healthy, and wondrous gifts that arise out of the consciousness of ordinary individuals.[6]

Neuroscientists seem to have great difficulty or reluctance in dealing with this area of human consciousness. In fact, a most respected scientist, Christof Koch, in his definitive work, *The Quest for Consciousness,* bypasses altered states of consciousness by stating, "A comprehensive theory of consciousness will ultimately have to account for these unusual phenomena."[7] So much for the subject of mystical experience, a phenomenon of consciousness that lies at the heart of all religion and spirituality. One can perhaps understand why mystical experience seems to be at the fringes of investigative psychology and neurobiology. It may lie at the fringes of our consciousness, an area that still challenges the powers of scientific study.

Some modern psychologists and others have created names such as "peak experience," "flow," and "relaxation response" for the moments that often appear related to the encounters that may be called mystical. From athletes and others come terms like "the groove," "the high," "the rush," "the zone," and so on. How do they fit together, if, in fact, they do? Are these experiences part of mystical revelation, in a spectrum like the colors of light from the mundane to the profound? Many think so, but they surely remain private feelings, rarely shared yet common to a large segment of humanity. Indeed, William James's metaphor, "Our lives are like islands in the sea," seems to ring forth with clarion clearness in the thoughts surging each minute of our waking days, each distinct, but, as from the "islands of Conanicut and Newport, (we) hear each other's foghorns . . . and the islands hang together through the ocean bottom."[8]

These foghorns of our consciousness symbolize the essence of life's meaning, the stage beyond survival and reproduction. The existential questions are asked; what do they signify, what do they mean? The neuroscientists Eugene d'Aquili and Andrew Newberg put it thus:

> Is spiritual experience nothing more than a neurological construct created by and within the brain, or does a state of absolute union (with the universe) that the mystics describe in fact exist and the mind has developed the capacity to perceive it? Science offers no clear way to resolve the question.[9]

This vital question deserves to be explored, for unquestionably the experience is real and potentially transforming of one's worldview, behavior, and the love that comes with such transcendent moments. We can gain much by trying to fathom the underlying mechanisms and conditions that lead to such experience, as I attempt in this book.

Does nature offers a more immediate and primal source of transcendence? I and many believe so, for nature is our immanent world, and transcendent experience springs from the sensory communication of a waterfall, a lion's roar, a lark's song, a single note of music, from the perfumes of a rose or the salt-encrusted edges of an ocean marsh, from the first glimpse of a mountain peak after weeks of trekking, or of a mushroom, or a tiny ant.

These spiritual voyages in the wild, even in the "civilized" outdoors, nurture and enhance the meaning of our everyday lives and provide a zest and elevation of spirit that is transforming. However, they need not all be experienced in the wild; it may not be necessary to retreat to the mountaintop or enter the forest. A musical concert, a work of art, the joy of sex, the pangs of childbirth, perhaps even the ecstasy of death may enhance the meaning of life. Does not nature encompass our sentient universe?

What is the scope of this book? First, I see no conflict between religious belief and nature spirituality. As Wallace Stevens wrote, "In the cathedral I felt one presence; on the highway I felt another"[10] But I do see the increasing need to strengthen humankind's emotional connection to our natural world. Supernatural powers are not needed to foster that bond. We now benefit enormously from the burgeoning scientific knowledge of what makes us and our fellow life tick, and of the origins and evolution of the universe. That knowledge offers the ability to see more clearly, without superstition, our place in the universe. The mystery that ultimately remains is that of our spirit, without which life is meaningless.

Mystical experience of nature can be of particular relevance to our troubled age, bringing deeper into our consciousness and emotions the logic that nature sustains humanity as humanity must, in turn, sustain nature. Rationality alone, however, cannot be our guide in the task of restoring our environment. A spiritual connection to nature must inspire the emotional commitment that is the *yin,* complementing the *yang* of intellectual understanding.

As an outdoorsman I have partaken in some of the spiritual adventures in nature of which I write. They grace me with unforgettable and profoundly numinous memories. The deepest of these experiences have been associated with the magic feeling of cosmic unity, imparting a radiant serenity and sublimity. The word *love* basically describes such feelings, and it is the love of nature that leads to the instinct to cherish it, beyond our mundane and materialistic needs. That emotional connection to nature, generated from the unforgettable memories of mystical experience, shapes an understanding of oneself and one's place in the world. It is a fundamental mechanism that connects us with our environment.

Yet, my calling as a physician with a perspective of over half a century has brought me to places where the wild once reigned but has been trampled down by the foot of humanity, by the relentless pressure of population increase and the seemingly unstoppable pollution of the biosphere. Nature has all but disappeared where large concentrations of population live, surely leading those individuals to suffer an erosion of the innate spiritual connection with their primeval roots. But we will see that there is an innate quality in us that has been called *biophilia,* a part of our psyche that may be smothered by urban dust, yet can be reawakened, particularly in younger years.

Does this phenomenon relate to our evolutionary relationship with all living things, with the physical environment of our Earth and the universe? Such an exploration requires that I cross fences that often confine thinkers and writers and travel into academic and literary fields that can provide the spectrum of knowledge needed for this broad and nebulous topic. Using the carte blanche of a medical diploma I shall take risks, I know, in trying to paint with a very broad brush a picture of nature mysticism, some of its manifestations in human experience and possible psychobiological mechanisms, and its relevance to environmentalism.

It is important to bring a critical approach to this misty subject. Much of what I present is based on the experiences of others and myself. The Sufi philosopher Pir Vilayat Inayat Khan has said, "What the scientist and the mystic have most in common is the importance they attach to experience. . . . Science has learned through experience to eschew dogma, and it is this very principle that is at the heart of the distinction between religion and spirituality."[11] The empirical observations and reflections on personal experience and their effects on our thinking and emotions are at the heart of my thesis.

Accordingly I will present at the beginning an exploration of the spiritual encounters by a spectrum of individuals who have close ties to nature. This phenomenological approach will give a clearer picture of the robust nature of mysticism that is for many an intimate part of the psyche.

First, however, in part 1, I invoke the Orphic trinity of Chaos, Gaia, and Eros to link our beginnings from the cauldron of creation to the ecological balance of our living and breathing biosphere, and thence to the love that should be engendered in humankind through nature spirituality. Revelations of evolutionary biology and psychology show that not only our genome but also our psyche may be connected with all of life going back billions of years. If consciousness has emerged from these primal origins it is possible that some of that experience is hardwired into our mind. Thus our spiritual as well as instinctive perceptions of the medium that enfolds us, wild nature, may have very deep roots.

From that beginning I move to the intimate numinous experiences of many individuals. They represent archetypes that are deeply connected in their activities with our natural world. In the chapter entitled "The Hunter," I describe a stalking meditation, the hunter's trance, which is deeply connected to our primal origins, arising from the hunting instinct yet associated with a mystical vision of the quarry, be it a prey or a scientific problem.

The way of seeing is described in "The Explorer" as an important part of imaginative creativity and links mystical and meditative experiences. The spiritual affinity for certain places, *topophilia,* is often associated with *biophilia,* our innate affinity with all life.

The archetypes of the Warrior and the Athlete represent primal conflict and competition, an evolutionary characteristic of life that includes humanity. Remarkably, there can be mystical experience in the midst of the brutality of conflict. Competitive and strenuous sports and other outdoor activities such as mountain climbing may lead to spiritual processes that can give profound meaning. A physiological component undoubtedly plays a role in many of these encounters.

From the robust spirituality of rugged contact with nature, the words and images of the Poet and Artist add to the depth, sublimity, and complexity of nature mysticism. Nature poetry is represented from the writings of three selected poets over successive eras: Wordsworth, Thoreau, and Ted Hughes. This medium is unique in being able to transmit some of the ineffable feelings associated with mystical experience.

Paleolithic cave paintings convey numinous feelings to the observer of ancient, sacred attempts to go beyond the self. In later eras the homage to stones and other natural objects showed the deep feelings our ancestors had for their environment, and they continue to this day as part of Taoism and Zen Buddhism in the veneration of "scholar's" rocks and other natural objects.

The natural roots of healing often have mystic qualities. As a physician I have seen and practiced some of the spiritual methods that are inherited from ancient shamanistic practices. In "The Healer" I show how modern medicine often loses perspective and power in emphasizing science at the cost of the spirit.

Processes of the mind that are involved in mystical experience, and the contributions of William James and others to our understanding of consciousness and mysticism and its relationship to creativity, are considered in part 2 to be a foundation for our nexus with nature. Modern advances in neurobiology and neuropharmacology can light the way to a better understanding of why these experiences are so powerful and unforgettable. How do external factors such as extreme stress, danger, and drugs influence mystical feelings? We know now that there are identical receptor sites in the brain for certain neurotransmitters and for externally originated plant opiates, as there are for other substances of plant or synthetic origin. Science may help bring tools to pry out the deep truths that lie just beyond our ken in the chapter "Wider Than the Sky."

I do not claim to be able to address all the problems and possible solutions to the increasing environmental crisis. Bookshelves groan from the weight of books dealing with these questions. But in part 3 I give concrete arguments for why and examples of how our spiritual relationship with nature must be nurtured and revived in order to bring us back, literally, to our senses, to preserve what is being destroyed by humankind's continued exploitation of the earth.

I conclude with the blunt declaration, "The future rests with us." Humanity's connection to nature is an important key to our salvation for we are in danger of demise if not extinction. A rational understanding of our potential fate will not be enough. The emotional commitment to each other as well as all life is also required. My answer is the mounting of a supreme effort in bringing to the youth of the world the opportunity to bond with nature, to learn (again) to love it. What is needed is the moral equivalent of war, the call to arms that William James described a century ago as necessary for our very survival.

As I have traveled the world, often on medical duties, I have witnessed the damage done around the globe by burgeoning populations, violence, urban sprawl, and disease; and my memories affect me profoundly. Yet I have another set of memories, of time spent in the outdoors, ranging from the mundane to the ecstatic, that comforts me today. I have felt a need for these two worlds of my memories to somehow join in a healing process. Now, like W. H. Hudson in his bedsit in London, writing his memories and novels of Patagonia, I sit in my Cambridge apartment to write of memories but also of the mystery that can give such profound ecstatic experiences in nature's realm.

The nature mysticism that I espouse in these pages is a state of mind, a calm and contemplative way of looking at our relationship with nature, not in the vertical transcendence to a remote and greater Being but in a horizontal vision, seeing ourselves as part of this thin and fragile biosphere, the source of life and our spiritual home.

PART ONE

*Heritage and Experience*

# I  THE BEGINNINGS OF NATURE AND SPIRIT

... at first Chaos came to be, but next wide-bosomed
Gaia, the ever-sure foundation of all the deathless ones
who hold the peaks of snowy Olympus, and dim Tartarus
in the depth of the wide-pathed Earth, and Eros, fairest
among the deathless gods, who unnerves the limbs and
overcomes mind and wise counsels of all gods and all men
within them.

HESIOD, *THEOGONY*

Suddenly from behind the rim of the moon, in long,
slow-motion moments of immense majesty, there emerges
a sparkling blue and white jewel, a light, delicate sky-blue
sphere laced with slowly swirling veils of white, rising
gradually like a small pearl in a thick sea of dark majesty.
It takes more than a moment to fully realize this is Earth
... home.

EDGAR MITCHELL, *THE HOME PLANET*

*The earth is not a mere fragment of dead history, stratum
upon stratum like the leaves of a book, but living poetry
like the leaves of a tree, which precede flowers and fruit—
not a fossil earth, but a living earth, compared with whose
great central life all animal and vegetable life is merely
parasitic.*

HENRY THOREAU, *WALDEN*

## Chaos

As eternity is said to be a blink of Brahma's eye, so is the span of life on
Earth a fleeting iota in cosmic history—and the existence of humankind a mere moment in the saga of life. Blessed as we are, however, by
advances in sciences such as chemistry, physics, biology, paleontology,
and cosmology, we have increasingly powerful methods to seek out our
tiny tendrils in the origins of the universe and of life. From that evolutionary ferment come opportunities of finding our psychic roots as well,
although we have yet to find fossils of the mind.

I begin this story with a remarkable hypothesis based on recent
explorations. In 1969 the Apollo 11 mission brought back lunar rocks
that have now been studied for decades. From that analysis, many scientists agree on the theory that a gigantic asteroid, estimated to be the size
of Mars, collided with the newly formed Earth about four and a half
billion years ago (BYA). This massive cataclysm, the so-called Giant
Impact, dislodged a large chunk of molten magma from Earth's surface that eventually condensed into the sphere that is now our moon.
As that cosmic collision occurred, Earth's axis may have been knocked
askew. Through these billions of years the axis of rotation has been
tilted about twenty-three degrees from the normal, relative to our sun.
Earth's tilt, we know, is responsible for the seasonal changes that are
so familiar to us now, but it also possibly led to the conditions for the
generation and evolution of the first forms of life. These conditions

could have included the fluctuating environments of temperature, water vapor, and carbon compounds that were needed for reactions to proceed to the eventual generation of reproductive life. Half a billion or more years later some forms of life appeared.* They could have emerged from the hot bubbling oceans that formed from the condensation of clouds of interstellar dust and gases. Eventually some organism evolved, perhaps three BYA, to become what is called our Last Universal Common Ancestor. Charles Darwin, when summing up his *Origin of Species,* concluded that "probably all the organic beings which have ever lived on this earth have descended from some one primordial form, into which life was first breathed."[1] Darwin seems to have been largely right according to our present understanding. It is now considered likely that the source of life—which led to our existence and to that of all living organisms today—was a single progenitor, a bit of protoplasm that came into existence in that chaos and possessed the remarkable ability to reproduce itself.[†2] That protocell contained a genetic code that reproduced itself most times exactly. We may all stem—every individual organism, from the smallest bacterium to the largest tree, from the simplest to the most complex, together through these billions of years—from that single event. In their book *Microcosmos,* evolutionary biologist Lynn Margulis and her son, the science writer Dorion Sagan, say, "From the paramecium to the human race, all life forms are meticulously organized, sophisticated aggregates of evolving microbial life. Far from leaving microorganisms behind on an evolutionary 'ladder,' we are both surrounded by them and composed of them. Having survived in an unbroken line from the beginnings of life, all organisms today are

---

*Recent reevaluation of patterns on ancient rocks challenge original estimates and suggest that life, at least as detected with paleological methods, began closer to 2.8 billion years ago.

†In a chapter entitled "The Origin of Life," which he wrote before 1932, J. B. S. Haldane theorized that all organisms alive now are probably descended from one ancestor. With modern techniques of DNA chemistry, Haldane's prediction is now surely confirmed. Christian de Duve (*Vital Dust*) and Lynn Margulis and Dorion Sagan (*Microcosmos*) have written easily understandable reviews of these exciting advances in evolutionary biology.

equally evolved."[3] Some of the relatively unchanged descendents of these earliest ancestral organisms known as archebacteria still survive around the superheated thermal fumaroles under our oceans.

At some point our ancestral cells developed characteristics that are today shared by all living cells: the ability to grow, reproduce, inherit, and mutate. A fifth characteristic, awareness, a quality that may lie at the very heart of the origins of what we know as consciousness, slowly developed the processes of intercellular communication and organization.[4]

These earliest ancestors survived by digesting the organic molecules in the ancient ocean broth. But time began to run out (measured in millions of years) for this early life. As the earth cooled, the energy available for the metabolism of these cells diminished. They multiplied and consumed what little organic matter there was in that stark environment. This amounted to a population explosion, eerily akin to the crisis we humans are facing today. Our ancestors simply ran out of food.

Somehow, as their sources of energy diminished, they evolved in a way that accomplished the truly revolutionary takeover of the earth's environment—the radical transformation of our atmosphere. The primitive protobacteria began to utilize the sun's energy to consume much more abundant inorganic chemicals, such as carbon dioxide and hydrogen sulphide. These cyanobacteria also metabolized the ever-present water and produced free oxygen as a waste product. The oxygen-producing chlorophyll-containing organelles of these primitive cyanobacteria became incorporated into eukaryotes, "modern" cells with distinct nuclei.*[5] Those cells led to the complex structures that today we call green plants. They used the sun's energy as the power source to metabolize water and carbon dioxide and to generate oxygen and carbohydrates. This astonishing event has led to the preservation and continuation of nearly all life as we know it on Earth. It allowed the evolution of more motile organisms, animals that needed large bursts

---

*In their article "The Beast with Five Genomes," Margulis and Sagan show that endosymbiosis did not end just there. Today many organisms have been found to have five or more genomes. Life is truly cooperating and interpenetrating.

of energy, such as running, fighting, and swimming, for their survival. Life had come to conduct an orchestra, as it were, of ferment, change, and evolution in the thin layer that is called the biosphere.

This biological revolution demonstrates that life, nearly at the very beginning of its existence on this planet, responded to the conditions of its environment by developing survival skills that have led through evolution to our own existence. The human psyche may be a direct descendent, too, of those events billions of years ago when cells struggled to adapt to their circumstances, and through the process of adapting, transformed the biosphere. Humanity is now in a process of transforming the biosphere, but in another and unfortunate direction.

The separation of a generally rooted and stationary kingdom of plants from the rootless, mobile kingdom of animals occurred early in our evolution. As extremely mobile animals, human beings have tended to ignore the development and remarkable properties of our genetic cousins that still by far dominate the earth in mass and regulate its atmosphere, our mutual staff of life. Plants have ruled the biosphere for billions of years.

The nineteenth-century German physician, physicist, and founder of experimental psychology, Gustav Fechner, reasoned that plants must have nervous systems "hidden perhaps in their strange, spiral fibers."[6] The time frame of movement by plants is vastly different, generally, from that of animals (with exceptions of such plants as mimosa and fly-catchers). Fechner noted that the walls of plant cells were perforated by "unspeakably fine filaments" that stretched out in every direction, evidently transmitting and receiving the impulses of sensation and reaction.[7]

He proposed that plants, too, have a consciousness and a soul, which man, in his ignorance and limited view of perception, does not generally appreciate. Fechner's analogical reasoning was translated into the pioneering experimental studies by the German botanist Raoul Francé and the Indian physicist Jagadis Chandra Bose on the physiology of plants, which showed that modern plants can communicate, organize, and think; that is, they indeed have nervous systems. These experiments showed that plants have forms of intelligence that we humans can barely comprehend. In *The Secret Life of Plants,* Peter Tompkins and Christopher Bird draw on the work of Bose and France when they say, "Evidence now supports the vision of the poet and the philosopher that plants are living, breathing, and communicating creatures, endowed with personality and attributes of the soul. It is only we, in our blindness, who have insisted on considering them automata. Most extraordinary, it now appears that plants may be ready, willing, and able to cooperate with humanity in the Herculean job of turning this planet back into a garden from the squalor and corruption of what England's pioneer ecologist William Cobbett would have called a 'wen.'"[8] Even the growth of the tiny rootlets (radicles) of a plant is seen to be the product of remarkable sensory and perhaps cognitive qualities. Charles Darwin devoted his powers of observation and deduction also to a study of plant growth and wrote, "It is hardly an exaggeration to say that the tip of the radicle . . . acts like a brain of one of the lower animals; the brain being seated within the anterior end of the body, receiving impressions from the sense organs and directing the several movements."[9] Today, research in plant intelligence continues in such new areas as plant neurobiology. Powerful new methods are enabling researchers to find that single cells have the ability to learn and store memory.

There is much to learn from the comparative study of the evolution of awareness, reactivity, and organization in both great kingdoms of our biosphere. According to the Yale biologist Edmund Sinnot, biological organization and consciousness are related processes: "The primary reason for the rise of higher types of psychological behavior, culminating in mind, seems to have been the necessity of speedy regulating reaction to insure the survival of motile organisms in a complex and changing environment."[10] He considered the trait of organizing as the distinctive character of all life. He saw slime molds, among the most ancient of organisms, as examples of this ability to organize, that is, to form colonies and to move. Sinnot wrote, "Biological organization and psychical activity are fundamentally the same thing."[11] His hypothesis was, "The whole conscious life of man . . . is simply a manifestation of an organized biological system raised to its loftiest levels."[12] Lynn Margulis and Dorian Sagan assert that this capability—to communicate and thus to organize—was the first step of the evolution of mind, a property that all complex organisms share, including humankind. In *Microcosmos* they say, "Again and again, the study of the microcosm brings home to us that human capacities grow directly from other phenomena. Nature has a certain subsuming wisdom; our aptitudes must always remain meager in comparison to the biosphere of which we form relatively tiny parts. But we are not discontinuous from the general path of evolution, from the flows and flux of matter, information and energies. Nor can human thought—the last refuge of those insisting on human 'higherness'—be isolated or dissociated from the prior accomplishments of life."[13]

The first sustainable organized systems of life that we can trace were the cyanobacteria that created mats of organisms apparently seeking better living conditions and growing into various shapes that are seen today in fossilized structures. Their existence three BYA indicates that indeed awareness, cooperation, and motility were necessary parts of survival close to the time of the very beginning of life.

Purposeful actions are clearly seen in modern slime molds, demonstrating a remarkable degree of organization that works for their survival and propagation. In their life history, the amoeboid slime mold cells grow and divide as individuals, close to but independent of each other, devouring rotting vegetation and animal feces. When the food supply diminishes, the cells transmit chemical signals to each other, the wave of communication flowing like a ripple through the water, triggering the cells to transform themselves into a colony, a "single, multicellular organism." This sluglike organism moves until it finds a more favorable location for survival and nourishment. It then develops stalks, sporangia, containing clusters of spores that are released, spread, and germinate into individual slime mold cells that begin this process over again.[14]

The ability of these amoeboid cells to organize into a single motile organism shows an inherent high level of awareness and intention. Sinnot would certainly consider this an ability of biological organization to carry out a "speedy regulating action" to ensure individual and collective survival. It represents a sort of thinking through a primordial communicating system of the simplest of eukaryotes.

From the fossil evidence of their archebacterial ancestors that lived billions of years ago, perhaps modern slime molds are a living example of the early steps in biological organization, an example of the continuous chain of evolution toward the human mind, a "pre-enactment," as Peter Dawkins puts it, of our present metazoan multicellularity, complexity, and behavior.

The behavior of other simple organisms in our living universe also helps to illuminate our understanding of this evolutionary process. The paramecium, a microscopic single-cell protozoan, displays rapid movements that are produced from its ciliated surface. Its motion may appear erratic but, as one of our greatest theoretical physicists and a Nobel Prize winner, Richard Feynman, pointed out, the behavior may not be random but purposeful. The conjugation of two paramecia to exchange nuclei and the behavior when dehydrating, due to environmental changes, into a "seed" seems indeed to represent complex processes. Feynman, ever the acute and astute observer and thinker, said, "Until we see how many dimensions of behavior even a one-celled animal has, we won't be able to fully understand the behavior of more complicated animals."[15]

Recent studies, however, show the remarkable learning capacities of single specialized cells, such as mammalian neurons. Any astute observer of our fellow beings, or a careful reader of the great ethnobiologists such as Lorenz, Tinbergen, von Frisch, Griffin, and Wilson, will appreciate the dimensions of complex behavior that relate to awareness and response and that extend widely through the animal world. The fascinating observations of ants and bees, particularly, should give us reason to question those who claim that consciousness is the supreme and singular characteristic possessed only by humanity.

The philosopher Karl Popper considered "mindlike properties" to exist in these early ancestors in order to cope with environmental dangers and to seek secure ecological niches.[16] This mindlike behavior, turns, at some point, into conscious behavior. As Sinnot suggests, it may be the continuous evolution of a property found in all life, in different degrees, from the very beginning to the present.

If the human psyche preserves elements that ultimately connect with the protozoa, then, as Carl Jung believes, it could be possible to "peel the collective unconscious, layer by layer" back to the psychology of the worm "or even the amoeba."[17]

William James wrote, "If evolution is to work smoothly, conscious-

*Fig. 1.1. William James in 1888, seen with the caretaker Paul Ross (left) near the barn of his new summerhouse in Chocorua, at the foot of the White Mountains in New Hampshire. He wrote in a letter to Henry James, "75 acres of land, mountain 3500 ft. high, exquisite lake a mile long, fine oak and pine woods, valuable mineral spring, two houses and a barn, all for 900 dollars or possibly less. . . . The more we live the more attached we grow to the country." (Sept. 17, 1886. Photo courtesy of the Houghton Library, Harvard University.)[18]*

ness in some shape must have been present at the very origin of things." In his closely argued chapter "The Mind-Stuff Theory," William James attempts to trace the continuity of consciousness through "an infinite number of degrees" from "the primordial mind-dust."[19]

## Gaia

It is little wonder that we have begun to view our place on planet Earth as precarious. Underneath is the cooled and hardened shell of our Earth, just eighty kilometers, about forty-eight miles, thick at the most, and less than six kilometers, about four miles, thick in places below the ocean floors. Thus we float on that thin shell over a gigantic core of increasingly molten magma, four thousand degrees centigrade in its center, on a veritable crust that shields us from extinction. Around us is the biosphere, a relatively thin sheet of water, land, and air that supports life. From the deepest parts of our oceans to the limits of sustainable life in the high atmosphere, it is no thicker than perhaps eighteen kilometers or eleven miles, the distance that an automobile can travel in eleven minutes at sixty mph, or a champion runner can achieve in less than an hour.*[20] Yet well over 90 percent of all life dwells in an even thinner layer, just six kilometers thick when bisected by the ocean level. That is just the distance for a brisk morning walk! If we imagine that Earth is reduced to the size of a large orange, then the equivalent thickness of the biosphere becomes approximately that of a sheet of thick writing paper.† The volume of the biosphere relative to that of Earth is less than one-tenth of 1 percent.

One astronaut, viewing the Earth's atmosphere from space, was "terrified by its fragile appearance."[21] "We all live in a subjective and fragile soap bubble," according to the pioneering German ecologist

---

*I calculate the biosphere a bit more conservatively than others: add the deepest part of the ocean (eleven kilometers) to the tip of Mount Everest (nine kilometers) and take away two (nothing lives on top of Everest).

†The Earth's equatorial diameter is 12,756 km. Assume that an orange's diameter is ten centimeters. If the biosphere were eighteen kilometers thick, then its counterpart around the orange would be 0.14 millimeters.

Jacob von Uexküll, who likened our biosphere to life in a terrarium, not, say, twenty meters high but actually nine kilometers high.[22] The tenuousness of this thin sheet is experienced, for example, when seismic events occur. These can be relatively small shifts in the earth's cooling crust, yet, as was seen in the Indian Ocean tsunami of 2004, they can also lead to events that swept away tens of thousands of human and other lives in a matter of minutes. Yet within this biosphere are incredible forces of life that have created millions of species and incalculable numbers of living organisms.

The concept that our earth is a living, homeostatic organism led the English biologist James Lovelock to give it the name Gaia, after the Greek name for the earth and its goddess.[23] Earlier, however, the priest and philosopher Teilhard de Chardin had postulated that intelligence pervading the cosmos had led the evolution of life on Earth into a "single, giant organism" that he called Demeter.[24] But even before these visionaries there came Aristotle and much later Gustav Fechner who conceived the very same thing.

In keeping with its name, the contemporary Gaia movement has sometimes taken on a religious significance, the concept a substitute for God, a new "planetary animism" that may lead to sentimentality and irrational activism rather than the common sense action needed by humanity, the renewal of a spiritual connection to nature, that can guide us to the difficult moral and practical choices. It is the stark choice of destructive consumerism versus constructive conservation because, "It is the natural world we are feeding into the ovens of overconsumption and technical arrogance."[25]

The urbanization of the world is certainly leading populations away from awareness of nature, not to speak of its sacredness. That source of mystical inspiration is increasingly denied to vast numbers. What is left in its place?

Remove humankind from her natural environment and psychopathology results. In Carl Jung's thinking, modern man remains archaic in his deepest psyche.[26] He continued, "The archetypal endowment with which each of us is born prepares us for the natural life cycle of our species, in the natural world in which we evolved."

## Eros

Around me, in a forest, in a handful of soil, in the rivers and ponds, are living cells, alone or joined as individuals of various sizes and complexities—a throbbing pulse of life, all related to me through that common ancestor, the veritable Adam of Creation, a speck of protoplasm. I feel at home and in tune. Ralph Waldo Emerson in his first book, *Nature,* wrote, "The greatest delight which the fields and woods minister is the suggestion of an occult relation between man and vegetable. I am not alone and unacknowledged. They nod to me, and I to them."[27] In Wordsworth's "Tintern Abbey," the poet speaks of the mystical kinship between nature and the human spirit and of the "power of harmony . . . as we see into the life of things."[28] That harmony relates to "the innate tendency to focus on life and lifelike processes" that the Harvard entomologist Edward O. Wilson defines as biophilia.*[29]

Because our evolution parallels that of all other present life, then our whole being, physical and psychic, has been associated with eons of proximity to it, and even to the incorporation of other life into our very cells. This association, as Wilson asserts, results in an inherited attraction to nature and fellow life. What we contain in our psyche are engrams (neural connections) for coexistence, but also for competition and exploitation. All our concepts of beauty, pleasure, fear, distaste, and attraction are based on the inheritance of these engrams. For example, the passionate feelings for life and nature of Richard Jeffries, the nineteenth-century English mystic, vividly express the deep roots of biophilia and its mystical connection:

---

*Biophilia* has been defined by the Harvard biologist E. O. Wilson as the innately emotional affiliation of human beings to other living organisms. Millions of years of human evolution (indeed, perhaps, billions of years of our entire evolution) affects our awareness, our consciousness of nature. Wilson says that "biophilia is inscribed in the brain itself expressing tens of thousand of years of evolutionary experience."

. . . touching the crumble of earth, and blade of grass, the thyme flower, breathing the earth-encircling air, thinking of the sea and sky, holding out my hand for the sunbeams to touch it, prone on the sward in token of deep reverence, thus I prayed that I might touch to the unutterable existence infinitely higher than deity.[30]

What would I or any other human being be without life around us, if only crows in a congested city or companionable dogs or sparse strips of vegetation, not only for physical survival but for spiritual nourishment? I watch homeless men and women, sitting in a nearby square, feeding pigeons. I feel their pleasure of contact with other living creatures. Look at the aquariums in doctors' waiting rooms containing graceful, colorful fish that give solace to anxious patients. There are now even "healing gardens" designed for the comfort and support of patients. For example, the Howard Uhlfelder Healing Garden sits atop the massive, impersonal structures of the Massachusetts General Hospital in Boston.

Contact with living beings is an obvious human need. A quarter of a million Americans are said to be bird-watchers, and millions watch whales each year.[31] If the inhabitants of the less affluent parts of the world had such opportunities, perhaps the course of world history might change. Now, however, there is a progressive "extinction of experience,"[32] a consequence of world population growth, ecological degradation, and urbanization.

Are not many human conflicts generated in the crowded concrete beehives of urban life? Human beings in such environments may funnel the aggressiveness that is part of our evolutionary survival mechanism into mutually destructive acts. Even the substitution of domesticated animals for wild fauna in our everyday world, according to the American naturalist and ecologist Paul Shepard, impairs the respect and understanding for our spiritual place in the natural world. And the ecologist and philosopher David Abram asks whether our modern intellect is not "rooted" in our forgotten intimate association with all the sensory images of nature that surround us.

That forgotten contact can be regained if our ancient engrams of evolutionary conjunction with wild nature still survive. There is no reason to believe that they have been lost over the brief evolutionary history of modern *Homo sapiens.* But Abram points out that inherited patterns must be adapted to our immediate orientation in the present world. The processing of sensory stimuli may atrophy from disuse. Thus we can see and hear with beautifully evolved sets of eyes and ears, but the messages to the brain may be blurred or simply lost, as possibly happens, according to Erik Jonsson, a Swedish engineer and outdoorsman, with our atrophied sense of orientation.

Most of us are oblivious to much of nature's language. "If we no longer experience the enveloping earth as expressive and alive," then our senses have gone somewhere else. It is "the written text" that now speaks to us instead. "The stones fall silent, the trees become mute, the animals dumb."[33] With the specter of global urbanization threatening to deny whole generations any animal contact save with pigeons and pets, I have a foreboding feeling that the collective psyche will continue to fragment with each succeeding generation cut off from nature. There is a process that the psychologist Peter Kahn calls "environmental degradation"—a loss of experience, thus a progressive depletion of the memory of our connection with nature.[*34]

The zoological park is, however, a tiny example of how humanity can nurture its tenuous connection with nature from its concrete warrens of urban existence. People need to see, smell, and possibly touch their fellow animal beings, in, for example, children's "petting" zoos. There are even "therapy" animals, meant to be held, petted, and loved by disturbed and disadvantaged individuals. Apart from the now important environmental roles of preserving threatened species and their genomes, the zoo provides this spiritual, albeit thin, link between wildlife and domesticated humanity. It is remarkable where one finds zoos. There are

---

*Kahn explores evolutionary psychological theory through a series of interviews of various groups of adults and children. He found that many young children were limited in their relationship with nature.

flea-bitten, decrepit zoos in remote cities of developing countries where urban sprawl, poverty, and overcrowding have blocked out all contact with nature. These dusty places, often poorly run with dismaying inhumane conditions for the animals, provide children particularly with the experience of the innate love we have for fellow life. (I will refer to children again and again as the carriers of our innate spirituality that need to be nurtured in the bosom of our remaining wilderness.)

It is sad, indeed, to need to capture and imprison wildlife for the sake of human pleasure. Sadder is the pressing need to capture them in order to preserve endangered species, endangered because of humankind's subconscious yet relentless elbowing aside of fellow inhabitants of this earth.

The loss of wildlife, not just the "charismatic" big mammals, but "all creatures great and small" and plants and trees, leads to a spiritually sterile world. The disappearance of the "wild others," as Paul Shepherd sees it, leaves nothing but our own image to explain ourselves, leaving an empty psychic space.[35]

True, millions of species have come and gone on this planet. What, really, is the difference if this or that animal or plant disappears forever? Will it be our turn soon?

We form ties of affection spontaneously with both plants and animals. These feelings can profoundly affect us. The poet Rilke wrote of flowers "faithful to earthliness," whereas mankind, weighty and pleased by his gravitas, presumes to instruct them—yet,

> *O how lightly he'd emerge*
> *From the depth they had shared, different into a*
> *     different day,*
> *Or maybe he'd stay; and they'd blossom and extol*
> *Him as someone converted, resembling now one of their*
> *     own,*
> *All the silent siblings in the breeze of the meadow.*[36]

How much life can teach us!

There is an ongoing debate about what *biophilia* means and if it exists. Is it inherited or acquired? Edward Wilson believes that it is fundamental, inherited need to affiliate with nature. It is clear, nevertheless, that much of humanity gains pleasure from nature, and the aesthetic of landscape is particularly strong. The "Wilderness Continuum" was conceived by the geographer Nicholas Helburn to describe the spectrum of landscape ranging from primal wilderness to the urban dwelling containing perhaps a single flower.[37] Our innate topophilia, the love of place, and biophilia drive the instinct of the human being to somehow reunite with and to love nature.

But cannot there be something beyond? If there is a wilderness continuum, can there be also a limitless, seamless sense of attachment to all creation? Beyond the spirituality of life there must be an innate spiritual feeling for all being, call it God, call it nature.

Is urbanization crushing out the last vestiges of topo- and biophilia? I sometimes think so when talking to city dwellers who are either totally enchanted with their concrete environment or beset by crowding, poverty, and strife.

This innate pleasure of viewing nature is seen in the work of the nature sculptor Andy Goldsworthy. His unique creativity is demonstrated in totally unexpected yet familiar constructions of natural objects that belong to their surroundings. Viewing a simple pile of rocks being submerged by the flood tide, a woven pattern of leaves or branches swaying in the breeze, or a structure of melting snow or ice gives me a deep, comforting pleasure.

Remarkably, even the abstract drip paintings of Jackson Pollock reflect nature's patterns. Fractals, the fragmented, irregular patterns in nature that are predicted by the new scientific field of chaos theory, are being rediscovered in natural settings. An analysis of Pollock's paintings reveals, according to the physicist-turned-artist Richard Taylor, typical fractal patterns.[38]

The aesthetic appreciation of fractals can be seen, for example, in the silhouette of a leafless tree, an image that the English mystic Richard

Jeffries loved, or patterns of moss, or seaweed on the beach, or clouds and sand dunes. Emerson, strongly moved by Goethe's thinking on the evolution and continuity of form, wrote, "All is in each. . . . A leaf is a compend of Nature, and Nature a colossal leaf."[39] These patterns are visually pleasing and can generate an evocative emotion similar to that experienced when viewing "great" art. We are thus surrounded by natural patterns that our sensory engrams have perceived for billions, not millions, of years, since our ancestors first developed the powers to see, smell, hear, and feel. The deep pleasure and harmonic vibration comes from piercing the veil of artificial form and seeing the essential reality of things.

The garden, an invention of humankind after leaving her primeval forest, is remarkably evocative of ancient roots. The Oriental garden, for example, is the contemplative garden, a place of healing and refuge, and homage to this earth. The Zen garden particularly brings out mystical feelings that can lead to the sense of unity with nature. This formal creation allows for an unhindered opportunity of meditation.

From a different perspective, however, the Oriental garden is a stunted and artificial substitute for nature. When viewed within the framework of certain traditions and cultures, it is beautiful and enriching to the spirit. When seen by a native of the Amazon forest, it may seem to be a view of nature in prison.

Cultural blinders thus restrict and direct our perception of the beauty of natural forms, of the inherent chaos that is in the real and spontaneous world. Yet in whatever form nature, imprisoned or not, exists—petting zoos, formal or miniature gardens, city pigeons—all represent the yearning of humanity for her aboriginal environment.

In summing up, it is seen, in contrast to the abundance of structural fossil remains dating back billions of years, that there are yet no fossils of the mind. Those involved in disciplines such as evolutionary psychology must explore our psychic past through analogy with comparative behavioral patterns and neural structures of other species. In examples such as the behavior of protozoa, slime molds, plants, and animals, there may be a "pattern that connects," suggesting that psychic evolution is analogous to somatic evolution in a continuous, seamless way since the beginnings of life.

Is it not possible, then, that the human spirit is linked, through billions of years of symbiotic patterns of sensation, instinct, and behavior, to our living world? The process of evolution that shaped the "complex interrelationship of all living and non-living things," according to Al Gore, may be understandable scientifically; "but the simple fact of the living world and our place on it awakes awe, wonder, a sense of mystery—a spiritual response—when one reflects on its inner meaning."[40] It is little wonder that humanity has inherited the ancient engrams of memory and cognition that arouse deep feelings when in the magnificence of our natural world. Such feelings evoke a love of nature that when manifest can bring us to our senses to preserve what is now being destroyed. The spirituality that nature can bring to individuals of many callings is presented in the series of chapters that follow.

# 2  THE HUNTER

*Hunting is the master behavior pattern of the human species.*

WILLIAM LAUGHLIN, *CULTURE:*
*MAN'S ADAPTIVE DIMENSION*

*For perhaps ninety-five percent of our history we have been primarily hunters.*

PAUL SHEPARD,
*ENCOUNTERS WITH NATURE*

## An Angler's Trance

I stood alone in the water near the bank from where I had emerged. All was still. The ripples from the disturbance of my boots smoothed into the blank mirror of water. With my quietness the stillness left. A bird called in the distance. Murmurs of distant rapids sounded. Creaks and crackles came from the growth along the riverbank. A bubbling of life seemed to emerge from every speck of earth, every drop of water, every breath of air. Roiling thoughts, beset by problems from where I had come, quickly faded. My attention turned to that moment of dawn upon a river tracking a quarry. The surrounding sky, hills, trees, and water merged in my inner vision to a brilliant panorama. In a moment the whole world entered my spirit together with the stars and galaxies still glimmering in the light of dawn and all the limitless space beyond.

My mind was now blank, yet each sense was sharply aware of all that was about me—every sound, every movement, and every smell. The earth slowly awakened—more scraping in the bush, birdcalls, hum of insects, and the faint rattle of leaves from a gentle movement of air. Smells of rotting vegetation and wild roses drifted by in the slow breeze. Time was forgotten. The sky lightened and the stars and galaxies faded from sight. There was a splash from the distant bank and a muskrat swam by, its whiskered seal head held erect, without the slightest notice of my still solitary figure.

A dimple appeared ahead on the placid water. I was aware of all, yet my eyes rested on that one spot. The dimple reappeared. After long experience, I knew not to think. I slowly raised the rod, ran out the line, and cast the curling line with its passenger, the feathered hook. I carried out the movement on command from an inner source that was always and solely the source of certainty. The fly gently landed one foot to the right and one foot upstream of the dimple pattern. There was a sudden swirl of water, the tranquillity of that pastoral picture disappeared, and the spell was gone.

I described this meditative state from my direct experience. It was as if I had honed a razor in my mind to an unimaginable sharpness of memory. Such moments, I say again, remain unforgettable memories, as if burned into the soul.

## The Alert Man

Until about ten thousand years ago (an iota of time in evolutionary terms), we were all hunters and foragers, living in daily intimacy with all surrounding life.[1] That evolutionary period of competitive success and brain enlargement, achieved through organization and the use of tools, has profoundly affected the engrams of our psyche.[2] The brain of our forebears rapidly enlarged over a relatively short time. By 100,000 years ago, that hallmark of our species, "a disproportionately enlarged brain size," was found in fossil cranial cavities.[3] It is small wonder then that hunting stirs deep recesses in our consciousness and brings up a sharp awareness of this connection. In those thousands of centuries when modern *Homo* developed, alertness was a prime necessity, for both attack and defense. That awareness can still result in a vibrant state where all senses become more acute, and time and space merge into a feeling of unity.

In his *Meditations on Hunting,* the Spanish philosopher José Ortega y Gasset describes the state of awareness in what we know as the hunter's trance:

> He (the hunter) does not look tranquilly in one determined direction, sure beforehand that the game will pass in front of him. The hunter knows that he does not know what is going to happen, and that is one of the greatest attractions of his occupation. Thus he needs to prepare an attention of a different and superior style—an attention that does not consist in riveting itself in the presumed but consists precisely in not presuming anything and avoiding inattentiveness. It is a "universal" attention, which does not inscribe itself in any point and tries to be on all points. There is a magnificent term for this, one that still conserves all the zest of vivacity and imminence: alertness. The hunter is the alert man.[4]

"Not presuming anything," as we shall see, is part of apophasis, the emptying of the mind. Ortega y Gasset associated the development of the capacities of observation and alertness in the ancient hunter with the evolution of the intellect.[5] The sensory processes among many traditional hunters are, to us, extraordinary. From those sentient qualities arise a deep understanding of the world around them, qualities that at some time, long ago, we "civilized" human beings must have also possessed. The ethnologist Richard Nelson felt this when describing the Alaskan Koyukon to possess a sense of another dimension in nature, "As if someone were telling us about the other side of the moon."[6]

Every aspect of life and environment (weather, geology, geography) has been part of the lives of these peoples for tens of thousands of years. Part of this knowledge, acquired by Ortega's archetypal Alert Man, is not just the mystical connection with the quarry but also with his environment.

Henry David Thoreau observed fellow fishermen on Walden Pond "as wise in natural lore as the citizen is in artificial. They never consulted with books, and know and tell much less than they have done. The things which they practice are said not yet to be known."[7]

In another example of the hunter's trance, a friend told me of this experience when stalking Wapiti elk in the Sawatch Range of central Colorado.

One day in May I set out at dawn, alone, to track a herd of elk up into the foothills of Mount Princeton. There was still plenty of snow and muddy terrain to follow the herds migrating to upland pasture. I came across fresh tracks of several elk, including one bull. The morning was bright and sunny with a slight wind in my face, assuring me of getting a reasonably close approach to my quarry. After perhaps an hour of slow and careful tracking, I came out on a long glade, fifty yards wide. If the elk were nearby they would detect my crossing the snowy and slushy meadow. It remained for me to be completely still and pay complete attention to the opposite hillside. I felt now their presence and somehow knew that they felt mine. As I stood there, the sense of time remarkably changed. What seemed like minutes I found later to be over an hour. At the same moment an intense feeling of the clarity of the scene swept over me. All my senses seemed to sharpen to an exquisite razor's edge. I heard the tiniest sounds of distant streams and rustling leaves as if magnified in a celestial amplifier. Everything seemed closer to me and I felt, amazingly, a sort of merger of myself with everything, a sense of belonging. I was connected with everything in that panorama, the grass, trees, rocks, insects, birds, the elk that I knew were quietly moving uphill, out of my sight. I felt a great rush of emotion, a joy of being alive, the chance to exist along with everything else. I will never forget that day. What happened to the elk? I never saw them.

The hunter's unfocused alertness, his trance, is similar to the attentive form of meditation practiced in Zen Buddhism.[8] The word *trance* means precisely what the Latin roots say: *trans* = "across" and *ire* = "go," in sum, "to move across" or "to pass over" the object. The Oxford English Dictionary goes on to define *trance* as "a state of mental abstraction from external things." The hunter, however, is certainly not disconnected perceptually from "external things." His whole being is directed toward a quarry; he is the Alert Man with "universal attention," unfocused, aware of all yet somehow filtering out what is extraneous or irrelevant. The blocking or diversion of those external and internal signals sharpens his senses.

This state of mind is not unique to the hunter. As will be seen, it is a phenomenon common to many who search. It is, as Ortega y Gasset maintains, a state of mind that is the ground for the creative process. The external world as perceived by the hunter is drawn into his inner vision, which leads to a feeling of union with all that is outside—in fact, the cosmos.

In my (outwardly) casual interviews with fellow hunters and anglers, I find a spectrum of comments on what constitutes the hunter's trance. Some describe a simple focus on tracking the quarry, akin perhaps to the tiger stalking and preparing to dispatch his prey. From others, I hear of feelings of unity with nature or the cosmos, of alterations in the sense of time and light, of unforgettable moments.

It is possible, if not probable, that human beings vary considerably in genetic and cultural heritage with respect to spiritual capacity. Similar events may be experienced in different ways, thus supporting the findings of investigators such as Greeley and McCready in their survey and the genetic studies of the neuroscientist Dean Hamer and his coworkers.

The Zen practice of *shikan-taza* resembles the hunter's trance in that the mind is brought to a heightened state of awareness, intensely involved in the object of its attention. It is part of the preparation for *bushido* or actual battle, but it could as well be part of the stalking hunt. Simultaneously, the participant can be peculiarly detached, but centered into the ground of his being. This acute sensitivity of awareness lies at the heart of a mystical state from which energy can flow into extraordinary physical and mental achievement. But as Zen practitioners know, as well as the stalking hunter, such concentration is only possible over short periods.

The traditional hunter, through the evolutionary patterns of millions of years, perceives every whiff of air, sound, movement as he stalks. This sensitivity to each subtle sign of nature is a direct precursor to intellectual awareness. Today, in much of the urbanizing world, we have lost the language of nature in return for the language of written words.[9]

This mystical connection sets apart the alert man in nature from his daily routine of existence. Edward Wilson adopts the hunter's trance to his discipline as naturalist:

> The naturalist is a civilized hunter. He goes alone into a field or woodland and closes his mind to everything but the time and place, so that life around him presses in on all the senses and small details grow in significance. He begins the scanning search for which cognition was engineered. His mind becomes unfocused; it focuses on everything, no longer directed toward any ordinary task or social pleasantry.[10]

This "scanning search" is a remarkable ability that *Homo sapiens,* at least, possesses. But see the focus of the eagle, the eerie concentration of the owl, the pointing of the setter. I wonder if we are unique. We are part of an evolution that stems from our primitive heritage, but is woefully neglected as our senses atrophy from lack of application.

It is the Far Outside that the naturalist Gary Park Nabhan also seeks, one's inner preparation for the hunt, tied through evolution to the drive to find, to discover, and, ultimately, to create. It is a meditative state preparing an individual for that second path. "It is the path found when one falls into the 'Naturalist's trance', the hunter's pursuit of wild game, the curandera's search for hidden roots, the fisherman's casting of the net into the current, the water witcher's trust of the forked willow branch, the rock climber's fixation on the slightest details of a cliff face." Nabhan asks, "Why is it that when we are hanging from the cliff—beyond the reach of civilization's safety net . . . we are most likely to gain the deepest sense of what it is to be alive?"[11]

Alertness and awareness hone the consciousness. And, where it is a matter of life or death, they are factors of evolutionary selection. Hunting, including foraging and exploration for new territory, has been perhaps a vital factor in the evolution of humankind's mind, speech, and much of his early culture.*[12]

The duality of mind and spirit is no longer considered valid. The English physicist Sir Arthur Eddington's "intellectual pursuits of science" and "mystical pursuits of spirit" are one and the same. Experience, the direct apprehension of being, the cornerstone of William James's thesis, is the source of physical, no less than mystical, significance "here . . . in the mind."[13]

Stalking a quarry evokes those qualities of alertness and connectedness that tune the brain to a fine pitch, a pure vibration of total aware-

---

*In his encyclopedic overview of our world, Guy Murchie shows how *Homo*'s brain has tripled in size in less than one million years, a dramatic change that has exceeded that of all other mammals.

ness. Watch a cat on the stalk in the garden, or if you are fortunate enough to be Jim Corbett, a tiger in its forest. The perfect concentration of that feline belies its total awareness of all about. See the ears quiver and turn with each sound. The quarry, if aware of its predator, may be equally alert in playing its role in the deadly game.

The stalking tiger, David Peat observes, is a pure example of perception and awareness.[14] Contrast this with the way most people live, their senses numbed and alienated from their environment. The quality of primal alertness can, however, be recaptured, for example, by hunters such as Jim Corbett.

I know a master hunter, a hunter of fish: "His slow and stealthy approach was that of a stalking Indian hunter. . . . The stalking approach . . . came from very primitive instincts. The concentration focused upon the quarry was absolute—the hunter's trance. A half-hour could elapse without movement or any thought, only total absorption upon the slightest activity from underwater. The mind was remarkably cleared of extraneous cerebral noise."[15] In his evocative book on nature and hunting, Christopher Camuto writes of "dream-like moments" occurring during the "transcendental concentration of the hunt."[16] The hunter's trance is thus a form of meditation, but in a dynamic and primal mode that evolved from evolutionary forces that existed millions of years ago.

Many professional hunters support the theory that there is an inborn instinct for hunting.[17] In *Woman the Hunter,* Mary Stange observes that men, women, and children, when newly introduced to the stalking of game, become "visibly changed, their pace becoming more stealthy and deliberate, their breathing and facial expressions altered." The hunting guide sees that those "who had never hunted before had all the instinctive movements that many people think they learn only through years of experience."[18]

The animal tracker Paul Rezendes regards stalking as a form of walking meditation, yet "all the while being incredibly attentive and aware of everything around you."[19] The hunter's pursuit of his prey may involve every resource—physical, mental, and spiritual. Jim Corbett's accounts of tracking and killing the man-eaters of the Himalayan Terrai convey the total involvement necessary when nearly equal adversaries contend. He was raised in the nature of northern India and absorbed the rhythms and sensations of forest and stream. The lore and myth of animals predominated in his growth. Thus a deep knowledge of all life around him clung to him.*[20] Corbett's solitary quests are prime examples of "stalking meditation," which Rezendes defines as the employment of the senses so acutely as to perceive every footfall, breath, and sound and the nuance of surrounding landscape, wind, and humidity, as examples. When in this acute state of concentration, the stalker moves from "the tiny perspective of self" to an "awareness with the eyes of the whole universe."[21]

When all conditions in our inner and outer selves are in harmony, the senses that connect us to the outside may lead, through neural pathways, straight into an inner realm of our consciousness, of which, as William James implied, we are normally scarcely aware. Seeing with that inner eye and with every sense of our nervous system allows us to perceive, equally for the thinker, hunter, poet, and artist, a grand and sweeping landscape that transcends our usual waking consciousness.

This happened one spring evening when the New England nature writer John Hay watched for hours a poppy closing its petals. That long and focused mental devolvement, a naturalist's trance, led Hay to a heavenly unity: "By then I had become part of a whole new cosmos, barely glimpsed, a new opening into space and time and into feeling. I had never thought of sense perception in a flower."[22] Hay had surely formed a spiritual bond with that solitary plant. The outer eye becomes the inner eye; awareness expands into a vast dimension, encompassing one's total being and all about.

---

*This legendary hunter describes how his deeply rooted instincts combined with acquired knowledge to deal with the notorious man-eating tigers and leopards he was assigned to kill. He found at least once how the tables were turned, when the supposed quarry, the Champawat man-eater, stalked him with nearly fatal results.

Annie Dillard, in her classic *Pilgrim at Tinker Creek,* stalks to observe, not to kill; yet she hunts with the same mind as our ancestral Alert Man:

> In summer, I stalk. Summer leaves obscure, heat dazzles, and creatures hide from the red-eyed sun, and me. I have to seek things out. The creatures I seek have several senses and free will; it becomes apparent that they do not wish to be seen. I can stalk them in either of two ways. The first is not what you think of as true stalking, but it is the Via negativa, and as fruitful as actual pursuit. When I stalk this way I take my stand on a bridge and wait, emptied. I put myself in the way of the creature's passage, like spring Eskimos at a seal's breathing hole. Something might come, something might go. I am Newton under the apple tree, Buddha under the Bo.[23]

When Dillard stands on the bridge, "emptied," it is of course the same as preparing for meditation. The mind is made receptive. Either deliberately or subconsciously, thoughts are quenched, and sensory input is enhanced through this clearing of neural pathways. Zen meditation and the other "altered states of consciousness" that I have presented all lead to an "emptying" or *via negativa* that open the mind to enhanced perception, be it of a quarry, a unity with the universe, or God.

Another hunter was Vladimir Nabokov, an avid lepidopterist. He vividly records his lifelong passion of capturing, killing, mounting, and classifying moths and butterflies in page after page of his autobiography. Perhaps as with other hunters and anglers, this hobby may have been partially a pretext, driven by the primitive undercurrent of the hunt, to embrace the mystical comfort of nature. Other great writers of that land have also lovingly described the Russian landscape, particularly before the revolution. Nabokov returns again and again to his childhood memories of Russia's forests, fields, and streams. As with others, the mystical experience included a sense of timelessness. As he wanders across the fields, stalking his winged prey, this feeling appears, and he exclaims, "This is ecstasy, and behind ecstasy is something else, which is hard to explain [even for Nabokov!]. It is like a momentary vacuum into which rushes all that I love. A sense of oneness with sun and stone."[24] He captures the feeling of apophasis, of an emptiness that is a boundless receptacle for creative energy, and the cosmic unity that is represented by love, the ground of being.

We need not, of course, stalk an animal quarry. Mushroom hunting may serve the purpose. Ultimately a solitary walk in the woods with no purpose in mind yet with primal alertness can lead to the same union with Mother Nature that has been so often described by writers and poets. It is likely, however, that evolutionary changes have inserted the hunting instinct into our genome. That instinct can serve to discover a new species, a new mineral, and a new part of this earth or beyond. In the novel *A River Runs Through It,* the protagonist's father reminds him, "All there is to thinking—is seeing something you weren't noticing which makes you see something that isn't even visible."[25] Thus Newton and the apple, Buddha under the Bo.

## The Archer and the Inner Game

It is not coincidental that archery, with other martial arts such as *bushido,* has been adopted in Zen and other Eastern philosophies as an exercise of the mind and body to approach the mystical state of satori. It can be imagined that the formalization of hunting and martial arts into disciplines of meditation and perfection of living began with rituals early in our evolution. Paleolithic cave art suggests that these states of union with the quarry extended beyond our historical reach.

The German philosophy professor Eugen Herrigel spent years in Japan learning the art of archery from Zen teachers. At the point of his achieving mastery of the bow, Herrigel felt a sudden jolt of concentration that seemed to remove the block or inhibition that had beset him for so long. It occurred spontaneously (the Jamesian "passivity"), and once that barrier was surmounted, Herrigel knew that the flight of the arrow to the true mark could be repeated with certainty (the Jamesian "noetic quality").

Indeed, the condition of alertness is key to Zen philosophy and to its forms of discipline and exercise. Although the hunter may not have such disciplined training, the conditions of the stalk and hunt requires him to practice and it follows spontaneously. The fine line where a transcendental experience appears is beautifully expressed when Herrigel makes that leap through the invisible wall. He wrote:

> With its help the soul is brought to the point where it vibrates of itself in itself—a serene pulsation, which can be heightened into the feeling, otherwise experienced only in rare dreams, of extraordinary lightness, and the rapturous certainty of being able to summon up energies in any direction, to intensify or to release tensions graded to nicety.[26]

Christopher Camuto, preparing for the hunt, experienced this leap of concentration. The critical point in his training in marksmanship was when "every muscle in your body shifts to serve that aim." His experience is like Herrigel's: "You can feel the body and mind come together, and the arrow flies straight to the spot without your having a conscious memory of releasing it." Ultimately he realizes that the bowman is a passive onlooker, "egoless," releasing the arrow, not shooting it, and when mind and body are perfectly coordinated the arrow will go exactly to its goal.[27]

This essence of Zen is illustrated in the hunter's (angler's) trance by the perfect cast to the hidden quarry, a mindless, yet intricately coordinated motion that is beyond instinct and beyond conscious purposeful action.

There is an "inner" game throughout the spectrum of arts and sports. Take for instance a highly technical form of mountaineering called "bouldering." Here the British climber John Gill describes the mystical dimensions of "inner" climbing, where the boulderer finds self-realization through kinesthetic awareness. Beyond the barriers of demanding technical moves, the agony, pain, and uncertainty, there remains the exhilarating and fundamental quality called inner climbing. "If one never proceeds beyond these barriers, no matter what the limits of one's technical competence, the ecstasy of artistic fulfillment is never captured."

Just as Herrigel repetitively practiced archery until an invisible wall was suddenly transcended, so can this magic occur to the boulderer. Gill continues, "To saturate the mind with kinesthetic awareness is to enter a state of reality in which grace and precision define the world."*[28] The boulderer, too, sees the rock as a quarry, one to which he is physically and spiritually bound.

As we will see, the neural pathways of the limbic system may play a major role in this and other mystical experiences. What remains beyond reductive analysis is the particular affinity of the hunter with the inanimate and inorganic world from which we have evolved. This is the true mystical connection with Gaia.

The hunter's trance is thus a total mental and physical concentration whereby extraneous signals, internal or external, are quenched or diverted, enabling the psyche of the hunter to perceive his quarry and its world with a supernormal alertness. The merging of that world into the mind allows the subject to experience a comprehension that extends beyond the everyday dimensions of perception. It is in fact a form of meditation that probes the subconscious. The subject thus feels a harmony, a unity, a merging of self with object, the quarry and its sur-

---

*Bouldering draws, out of a rugged, competitive sport, the "inner" game, similar in many respects to the "inner" games of tennis, golf, chess, bridge, etc. The achievement of technical skill, whether kinesthetic or intellectual, can be ecstatic.

roundings. The shaman's trance, just as the hunter's trance, is a form of meditation, which forms a direct communication between the inner psyches of patient and healer. The quarry, in this case, can be disease or the goal of surgical intervention. I will later describe this trancelike state in medical and surgical practice.

# 3  THE EXPLORER

## Himalayan Epiphany

Each step I took was an effort, even though the walking was much easier now. Just beyond the amphitheater I came to a saddle in the ridge, where I collapsed beneath a moru oak. . . . For ten or fifteen minutes I lay there with my eyes closed and if anyone had come upon me they would have thought that I was dead.

When I eventually opened my eyes, I felt sure that I had breathed my last and gone straight to heaven. Two rays of sunlight were streaming through the branches of the oaks and falling away directly on a smaller tree that stood twenty feet away. Though it had no leaves this tree was covered in flowers that seemed to glow in the shafts of light.

Lying there against the roots of the massive oak, my first impression was that I was hallucinating, for the vision of this flowering tree and the sunlit glade were magical. I dared not move for fear of disturbing the perfection of that scene. . . . But in the stillness of the glade I was acutely aware of something greater than myself. Awe is the only word that might describe the experience. I had walked right past the flowering trees but in my exhaustion I hadn't noticed the blossoms and only now was I aware of its transcendent beauty. The catharsis that it evoked was so powerful that I felt weightless, as if the ground had dropped away beneath me. Lying there, I found myself in tears, emotions welling up inside of my chest, as if the roots of the tree had penetrated deep into my soul.[1]

The writer Stephen Alter wrote this after trekking through the foothills of the Himalayas. He was seeking the inner and outer sources of the religious roots and the spiritual sanctuaries of the most sacred sites of Hindu religion. This experience occurred when he was utterly alone on a remote ridge between the Yamuna and Bagirathi rivers. As he related the experience to me, the sacred groves of the headwaters of the Ganges would surely have given the same epiphany to the first pilgrim, centuries ago, as did this grove of moru oaks. Such *loci consecrati* are, as the English geographer Paul Devereux suggests, recognized by a universal instinct, a part of topophilia, the love of place. These dramatic settings of water, earth, and plants are often associated by human beings with a mysterious power that evokes a spiritual feeling of connection.[2]

## Inner Exploration

Our primal self is strongly stirred by such an intimate contact with nature. Feelings, often buried under tons of civilization, are wrenched to the surface in a few moments. It is as if an electrical potential between the self and nature is released and a flow of electrical current ignites the momentary ecstasy. The reality of that moment is utterly true; nothing can alter that knowing. Many lovers of nature and the outdoors know this feeling. It comes often with the motion and exertion of the body that seems to condition the mind to be receptive to that magic flash of current that signifies mystical experience.

Indeed, a degree of physical stress is often associated with the unifying feeling brought on by total immersion in nature. As we will see, there is often a neurochemical component to these mystical encounters. The nature writer and Zen disciple Peter Matthiessen, for example, was once caught in a terrifying storm. He became physically and emotionally overwhelmed with utter exhaustion and loss of sense of self.

Finally, after the storm passed, "In the clearness of the Himalayan air, mountains draw near, and in such splendor, tears come quietly to my eyes and cool on my sunburned cheeks. . . . [T]his feeling is astonishing: not so long ago I could say truthfully that I had not shed a tear in twenty years."[3] The power of nature can break through our emotional barriers.

Sitting by the ocean and feeling the powerful, repetitive rhythm of the breaking waves, the physicist Fritjof Capra experienced an ecstasy so overwhelming that he burst into tears. That moment was a catharsis leading to a creative vision, *The Tao of Physics.*

Tears may often surprise the most rugged voyager, as they did Nietzsche when trekking the hills of Italy: "A rapture whose tremendous tension occasionally discharges itself in a flood of tears."[4]

Who has not experienced something similar? Possibly a lump in the throat or a sob when hearing beautiful music, seeing a dramatic painting or sunset, or reading a poem. In psychological terms, the unleashing of such emotions follows the retreat of the ego from its usual domination of our so-called civilized and social behavior. A wall (the persona?) is breached that allows the psyche a more free and uninhibited range of emotional expression.

Yet a quiet walk through a forest can also evoke deep emotion. The nineteenth-century Russian writer Turgenev wrote, "The heart at one time throbs and beats, plunging passionately forward; at another it is drowned beyond recall in memories. Your whole life, as it were, unrolls lightly and rapidly before you; a man at such times possesses all his past, all his feelings and his powers—all his soul."[5] Turgenev had entered an inner dimension, a spiritual continuum with the natural world.

Childhood, as we will see, is often the time when the passion of spiritual experience seems greatest. Take, for example, what the Nobel laureate Christian de Duve remembered:

> On a clear summer night almost 75 years ago, I was sitting . . . with
> a group of . . . youngsters circling a fire. . . . The flames rose straight

toward an inky sky studded with stars. . . . All of a sudden, for a brief instant, light fused with darkness, song and silence became one, and I felt carried to another world, seized by intense emotion, suffused with a sense of unfathomable mystery, feeling, beyond the infinite depths of space, the awesome majesty of God.[6]

In ancient times and continuing still in aboriginal cultures, there are rituals of solitary pilgrimages into the wilderness, of vision quests supported by communal prayer and fasting, often the rites of passage to adulthood. These traditions are followed by numerous organizations and wilderness guides in bringing the spiritual side of nature to young people.[7] One of the final tests for participants in the international program Outward Bound, as I understand it, is to stay entirely alone in the wild for a night or more. Although, I am sure, the exercise is designed to further equip the participant with skills of surviving in the wilderness, it may also offer the chance to develop nature spirituality.

An ultimate form of Outward Bound occurred when, according to his disciples, Jesus spent forty days alone in the desert. Mystics, religious and other, often practice such a period of solitude and fasting, in generally less extreme form. The ascetic is truly emptied, psychically and physically. Neurophysiologic processes, as we shall see later, interact with the spiritual, to allow the inner self, the "uncluttered Throne room of God," as the American theologian and writer Barbara Brown Taylor calls it, to reverberate in harmony with the cosmos, unhampered by extraneous resistance.[8]

Jesus emerged from that retreat surely a changed man and undoubtedly blessed by extraordinary enlightenment, which is also called satori by some. He went on to deliver the glorious humanitarian teachings that are eternal.

This sort of conditioning is found in a much more modest form through camping, an experience that most of humanity in increasingly urbanized societies lacks. As we stray further away from nature, our lifeblood, as the New England naturalist Henry Beston suggests, thins, and we become spiritual wraiths. At the very least, let everyone gaze up to the unfettered starry sky to renew our connection with nature. Seeing those billions of points of light, even if we can only see them through atmospheric pollution, can transmit that connection deep into our souls.

## Topophilia

Part of our connection to nature is the feeling for a place where one belongs, perhaps where one is born, or had an extraordinary experience. There is a term in Swedish for this, *smultronstället,* "the place of the wild strawberries," a secret site for which one yearns, the sacred place that will nurture and heal the spirit. From the earliest times, it is likely that this affinity for certain sites led prehistoric peoples to erect shrines and temples where they could experience the mystical heartbeat of Earth's connection to life. These were surely the roots of organized religions. Often they were places with particular unions of water, trees, and mountains. Humankind seeks such places even at great distances. Such are the great holy shrines of India at the headwaters of the Ganges that Stephen Alter saw and wrote about.

For many years I returned regularly to a secret "place of the wild strawberries" in northern New Mexico. I will forever remember that day of discovery when wading up a small river high in the Jemez Mountains. My slow exploration of the Rio San Antonio had led up past the gorge to a bend in the river around which I saw a spectacular sight: the towering brick red cliffs of the outer edge of the ancient crater loomed above; beyond, the canyon suddenly widened, bisected by the now peacefully meandering stream bordered by alpine meadows. At the bend, one meadow was encircled by willows, aspens, and firs to form a small natural amphitheater. From this meadow I could look upstream to see the red cliffs now glowing like fire from the light of the setting sun. Above was the translucent dark blue through which pierced the distant cold light of Venus. The beauty and harmony of the setting transmitted equanimity straight into my soul.[9]

That place tugged at me to return again and again to feel a mysterious nurturing of my spirit as I camped for days, alone except for the occasional beaver and bear, and left refreshed.[10] Why do certain places evoke the feelings that I had? Those with a Freudian bent may postulate that it represents a desire to return to the comfort of the womb. Perhaps so, but it is the womb of creation, of our Mother Nature. These deep and primal connections led Paul Devereux to conclude his book *The Sacred Place* with the sentence, "The idea of the holy was inherent in the landscape from all time and it was the landscape that made it stir within our heart and mind."[11]

In his memories of boyhood in Patagonia, W. H. Hudson, too, described returning again and again to a certain place, not knowing why.[12] His state of awareness and suspense recalls the experience of Edward Wilson when he entered the forest glade in Surinam. The practice and principles of feng shui certainly have their origins in this mystical affinity for certain combinations and arrangements of the natural landscape.

Children, their innate spirituality still unhampered by the burdens of materialism, often instinctively seek solitary sites that offer beauty and peace. Secret gardens and murmuring brooks are places of refuge that can give the opportunity for imaginative journeys. These "ecstatic places," according to the child psychologist Louise Chawla, evoke "ecstatic memories [that] shine like jewels within the casing of our lives."[13]

Water is often a special attraction in our search for pleasure and comfort. It is our ultimate original mother, the nurturing medium of the origins of life. I experience a mysterious yearning particularly for salt water. Without the occasional swim, most months of the year, I feel certain emptiness. The joyous splashings in rivers, ponds, waterfalls, and ocean surf form the matrix of fond memories of childhood and youth. Water sports are a large part of recreational activities. It is sad to realize that so many, often raised in urban settings, have scarcely ever splashed freely in natural bodies of water and are so often unable to swim. The natural being, raised near an aquatic setting, takes to water as part of the total environmental experience. Recall Captain Cook's remarks upon the ease and joy of the Tahitian men and women swimming out to greet his ship.

At the very beginning of the American classic *Moby Dick,* Herman Melville, through his protagonist Ishmael, captures the power that attracts us to this element, a part of the immense fabric of nature. Ishmael observes the New Yorkers "pent up in lath and plaster—tied to couches, nailed to benches, cinched to desks," flocking to the water fronts and seashores on Sundays, "fixed in ocean reveries."[14] Ishmael's fellow citizens are attracted like the magnetized needle of a compass to the water. Truly, as he says, meditation and water are wedded together. The sound of the waves, the murmur of the brook, the crash of a waterfall give us connections to what we have been and all that we will be.

The American geographer Yi-Fu Tuan defines *topophilia* as including all of our affective ties with the material environment. These can range from a place as a means of livelihood to one evoking an intense sense of belonging.[15] These intense experiences may come by surprise. The veils of preconceived and acquired notions of beauty and order suddenly drop, revealing a scene, inner or outer, that is breathtaking and nurtures unforgettable memories of the ecstatic places, the places of wild strawberries, and the spirit of place.

For individuals with no knowledge of nature, an intense experience of the wilderness may change forever their relationship to the Earth Mother. Many of our deepest emotions are grounded in transcendent moments that sweep through consciousness, revealing a vast dimension of reality of which we are ordinarily not aware. Such are the possibilities for vast numbers that presently live in the concrete deserts of urban sprawl and that are bereft of memories of nature's solace.

Mountains, too, evoke the awe often encountered in great cathedrals, the reciprocally inverted spaces that also foster the conditions for mystical experience. I recall, with a shiver of awe, a frisson, the sight of the great eighth-century Kailas Temple near Ellora in central India. It is magnificently carved from the solid rock cliffs in a shape evoking the Himalayan peak, Kailas, sacred to all Hindus and itself the physical embodiment of the mythical Mount Meru, the Cosmic Mountain. The temple emits a vibration, an aura of spirit, a *genus loci*, which conveys a sense of timeless mystery. The silence of that place was charged with a profound presence, recalling what E. M. Forster sought to convey in his great novel, *A Passage to India,* the deep and resonant *boum* inside the Marabar cave.

## The Despotic Eye and Goethe's *Phantasie*

*I speak in recollection of a time*
*When the bodily eye, in every stage of life*
*The most despotic of our senses, gained*
*Such strength in "me" as often held my mind*
*In absolute dominion. Gladly here,*
*Entering upon abstruser argument,*
*Could I unfold the means*
*Which Nature studiously employs to thwart*
*This tyranny, summons all the senses each*
*To counteract the other. And themselves,*
*And makes them all, and the objects with which all*
*Are conversant, subservient in their turn*
*To the great ends of Liberty and Power.*[16]

           WORDSWORTH, THE PRELUDE, BOOK TWELFTH

*An object, if it were before*
*My eye, was by Dame Nature's law,*
*Within my soul.*[17]

           THOMAS TRAHERNE, "MY SPIRIT"

In "Method of Nature," Ralph Waldo Emerson says, "Man must look at nature with a super natural eye."[18] Visions of mountains, seas, rivers, and forests can expand perceptions that lead the beholder toward a transcendent communion with nature. Spinoza considered that the universe contained creative forces comprehended only through intuition, not by mathematics. He influenced Goethe's way of looking at nature, who defined *exakte sinnliche Phantasie* as the pathway from the sensation of observation (*Sinne*) to the subconscious imagination (*Phantasie*).[19] The literary critic and Goethe scholar Norman Skillen comments, "What Goethe meant by this is the practical application of imagination as an instrument of scientific observation. As such it represents a slowing down and a conscious cultivation of the 'oceanic feeling' [see chapter 7's section on Freud and the oceanic feeling]. What occurs in the oceanic feeling is a spontaneous expansion of consciousness through which natural phenomena acquire an unaccustomed depth, become charged with meaning, seem to lose their separateness both from each other and their observer, and appear in all their intense relatedness."[20] Another way of appreciating Goethe's vision, according to the German biologist Andreas Suchantke, is to turn imagination outward, after the direct observation and synthesis of that observation in the imagination.[21]

The static and noise of our materialistic world often press in on our deeper thoughts, distracting us from the reality of truths that lie just beyond our ken. Ancient wisdom tells us that there is a vast, unexplored world of the spirit and the door to that world of imagination can be opened a bit further if only we allow it, as when Keats wrote, "Then let the winged Fancy wander / Through the thought still spread beyond her: / Open wide the mind's cage-door, / She'll dart forth, and cloudward soar."[22]

*Deep form* was coined by the ecopsychologists Betty and Theodore Roszak to mean "a correspondence between the formative processes of the mind and the formative processes in nature." The similarity to Goethe's concept is clear: it is the power of our imagination to create a connection of the observed object with something deep in our psyche. Goethe's participatory consciousness represents to me the deep inspiration that can occur in the quiet contemplation of an ocean, a sunset, and a mountain vista.

Examples by artists such as Paul Klee demonstrate the vivid connection with nature, leading through imaginative processes to the unleashing of great creative energy. "The creative imagination returns us to an aesthetic both old and new, to a mode of knowing the natural world which can be the ally of science. The human (being) again becomes an integral part of nature; life and mind become part of a vital matrix as vast and as old as the universe."[23] Deep form as well relates to the Swedenborgian doctrine of correspondences, which will be discussed in a later section.

In some memorable sentences from his first and greatest book, *Nature,* Ralph Waldo Emerson said succinctly, to the admiration of many but also the amusement of unimaginative contemporaries: "Standing on the bare ground,—my head bathed by the blithe air, and uplifted into infinite space,—all mean egotism vanishes. I become a transparent Eye-ball. I am nothing. I see all."[24] (See figure 3.1 on page 56.) Emerson's words breathe a truth that, as will be seen, may expand to encompass the universe.

The physicist John Archibald Wheeler created, apparently entirely independently, a similar image of Emerson's all-seeing eyeball. (See figure 3.2 on page 57.) According to Wheeler, our understanding of the origin of the cosmos, "the building of all that is," is dependent on the revolutionary law of quantum mechanics. That cosmic image can scarcely be grasped through our mundane intellect; it may require a truly mystical disassociation with our everyday perceptions.

Emerson, seeing all, loses himself in the quantum world of Wheeler's eyeball that records its reciprocal connection to a universe without boundary in space or time.[25] Emerson's words from 1830 of his emerging philosophy that later became known as transcendentalism are peculiarly akin to Goethe's participatory imagination. All seem destined to become enfolded into the boundless and incomprehensible vastness of quantum phenomena. As Emerson suggested, the reality of experience may transcend all the values of what we know as the concrete and materialistic world. The individual feels, smells, hears, and sees things that

*Fig. 3.1. The universe through the eye of Ralph Waldo Emerson. "Standing on the bare ground,—my head bathed by the blithe air, and uplifted into infinite space,—all mean egotism vanishes. I become a transparent Eye-ball" (Emerson, Nature, 13). A caricature drawn by his friend and fellow transcendentalist, Christopher Pearce Cranch. Illustrations of the New Philosophy, 1835 (courtesy of the Houghton Library, Harvard University).*

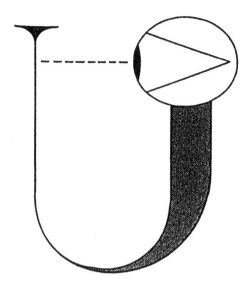

*Fig. 3.2. The universe through the eye of the physicist John Archibald Wheeler. "The universe, symbolized by the letter U, starts small at the big bang (upper left), grows in size, gives rise to life and observers, and observing equipment; and the observing equipment, in turn, through the elementary quantum processes that terminate on it, takes part in giving a tangible 'reality' to events that occurred long before there was any life anywhere" (Wheeler, in Elvee,* Mind in Nature, *18). One could imagine Wheeler's observing equipment to be Emerson's transparent eyeball that is viewing all eternity.*

may exist only through those senses. Wheeler's Participatory Principle argues that the "observer" brings reality to the universe. Without our senses there would be no universe. This corollary of the Anthropic Principle evokes Emerson's words when, as the transparent eyeball, he continues, "I see all; the currents of the Universal Being circulate through me; I am part and particle of God."[26]

When I search or stalk in a wilderness, the "despotic eye" becomes passive. The images go into an inner world where all my other senses merge in quiet harmony. There is an outward communication and, intuitively, I seem to join the object like Emerson's transparent eyeball and all "mean egotism" vanishes. I stalk a trout and somehow become part of it. Its thoughts, reactions, life history, and evolution (of what I may know) flash through my mind. The stream, trees, and sky all seem to crystallize into a small universe of a new understanding of meaning. I am strangely moved—and ecstatic. I feel that my comprehension of that scene is so full that I could write an encyclopedia about it. Camuto also sees another dimension in perceiving nature: "Perhaps the wildness of our most haunting landscapes is just the strange otherness of the universe seen up close."[27]

The direct cognitive vision probes and analyzes. I watch marvels of creation through the microscope, whirling rotifers, probing paramecia, and oozing amoebae. I stop thinking and through associative processes another vision unfolds: a vision of these animalcules in a time warp of evolution, in a creative broth containing my ancestral cell. I see not just *with* the eye, but also *through* the eye.

Helen Keller, blind and deaf, was blessed by a "spiritual vision" that enabled her to perceive, through inner recesses of her creative imagination and extraordinary intellect, the living energy of the living world:

> My mystic world is lovely with trees and clouds and stars and eddying streams I have never "seen." I am often conscious of beautiful flowers and birds and laughing children when to my associates there is nothing. The skeptical declare that I see "light that never was on sea or land," but I know that this mystic sense is dormant and that is why there are so many barren places in their lives.[28]

The poet and writer Annie Dillard's other way of seeing also is "letting go." About watching shiners—tiny fish—she writes, "I saw linear flashes, gleaming silver, like stars being born at random down a rolling scroll of time. . . . When I see this way, I see truly. As Thoreau says, I return to my senses."[29] The need to return to sensation is akin to the principle of gravity. We may wander far afield with our intellects, our cognitive reasoning, and engage in wonderful mental adventures, but we will always tend to return to the true reality provided through our senses that has always been and always will be our ground of being.

There can be two landscapes—one outside the self, the other within. The external landscape comprises the details of topography, the plants and animals, weather, geology, and evolution. The second landscape is an interior projection, the speculations, intuitions, and ideas relating to the exterior with purpose and order.[30] This evocative mindscape that nature writer Barry Lopez experiences is a transcendental correspondence perceived through the all-seeing eyeball of Emerson.

Thoreau coined an apt expression of this perceptive process: "a sauntering of the eye."[31] He derives this term, no doubt, from Wordsworth's "relaxed attention," which he quotes earlier in his journal. The seeing begins when understanding ceases; that is, the cognitive process may hinder the attainment of pure vision.

The keen powers of observation that Thoreau used to write his detailed descriptions developed with years of practice. Eventually this disciplined method evolved into a deeper, less conscious process whereby vision expanded into a new dimension of an "utter, non-controlling openness to the perceptible universe" resembling Annie Dillard's *via negativa* and William James's "involuntary attention."[32, 33] It is reasonable to speculate that the opening of the channels of perception into deeper recesses of consciousness can lead to enhanced interactions with memory and association. The sensations that flow through those channels are not merely passive; they ultimately help to create, somewhere deep in our psyche, our own worldview.

The German philosopher Schopenhauer linked esthetics and scientific knowledge with our understanding of how visual perception affected the imagination.[34] He thus tried to free the observer from "the despotic eye" to attain a transcendental perception, that of Emerson's all-seeing eyeball merging with the cosmos of Wheeler's quantum vision.

This powerful connection between imaginative perception and the spiritual feelings that arise from contact with nature, "Platonic sight," was perhaps the inspiration for Goethe in developing his theories of color and of participatory sensation. Gustav Fechner supported this view when he said that vision had an "emotive and autonomous" content that could be expressed through a mathematical equation relating sensation to stimulus.[35]

Thoreau, too, described the colors of a sunset, but in an extraordinary and wonderful way:

> I witness a beauty in the form or coloring of the clouds which addresses itself to my imagination, for which you account scientifically to my understanding, but do not so account to my imagination. . . . I, standing twenty miles off, see a crimson cloud in the horizon. You tell me it is a mass of vapor which absorbs all other rays and reflects the red, but that is nothing to the purpose, for this red vision excites me, stirs my blood, and I have new and indescribable fancies, and you have not touched the secret of that influence. If there is not something mystical in your explanation, something unexplainable to the understanding, some elements of mystery, it is quite insufficient. If there is nothing in it which speaks to the imagination, what boots it? What sort of science is that which enriches the understanding, but robs the imagination?[36]

That passionate statement and question rings true with my own feelings experienced upon seeing a winter sunset in a similar New England sky. Thoreau wrote that the "least film of thought" from such a sensory experience could lead, through building and comparing different concepts, to developing truths that are practical for everyday life. The power of imaginative association is the essence of Thoreau's statement and a basic tenet of Goethe's science.

Thoreau realized the ineffable, the unexplainable, emotional dimension of his vision of that distant scene. Indeed, we know that color, as we perceive it, does not exist in the material universe. As the Swiss chemist and creator of LSD, Albert Hofmann, reminds us: "The optical range of what we call reality does not exist on the outside; it exists on the psychic screen inside every individual."[37]

Only our five senses provide the conduit of information from the outer world to our consciousness. The opening to the inner perceptions that can lead to the extraordinary mystical feelings that have been described is a "vast expansion," as William James put it, of our ordinary waking consciousness. It is a transmission into the recesses of the spirit, of a noetic reality. Swedenborg asserted that a person has two sights, one from cognitive faith, and the other from love. Cognitive vision has a correspondence with this internal sight, "the light above that of the world."[38]

Many who have described mystical experiences, particularly in nature, repeatedly remark upon "seeing things more clearly than ever seen before," or "When I see this way, I see truly," or of "seeing something as it truly was." But visual sensation is not the only pathway to the inner spirit. The other senses, such as hearing, can catalyze a deep emotion, such as when the musician heard a note that was "the essence that we all seek." Our own reality is by perception through our sense organs of the existence of the material world.

The Native American Lakotas believe that the physical world is a spirit seen from without and that the spiritual world is the physical viewed from another dimension. The vision quest is a journey, according to the anthropologist Elaine Jahner, to an inner spiritual landscape that shows the direction to follow in travels through the physical landscape. The quester may experience a moment when sensations intensify and something sacred is revealed, leading him to another realm of reality.

> The vision (generally a dream) gave its seeker the courage to face the mysterious dimensions of life with the calm foreknowledge that comes from a personal sense of mystery and an inner departure for the continuing journey of exploration that is life itself. The light of the vision illumines some of the night of uncertainty for both the individual and the group. Or, to use another set of images, the vision is a way of climbing a hill so high that the visionary has a perspective from which to view the many lower hills stretching toward the horizon of death.[39]

This way of "seeing" is shared by other Native Americans, by Native Australians, and very likely by many "aboriginal" peoples and others throughout the world. It can, however, form a barrier of communication between peoples, notably with those raised in Western cultures who are not aware of such differences. I recall, for example, conversing with an elderly man in the Taos Pueblo. There was no difficulty in understanding each other's speech; however, there was a gap in communication. It seemed as if this man were seeing me in another dimension as he addressed my questions in a way that seemed oblique and obscure. I am sure my conversation was equally so to him. I asked him, "Have you hunted in those beautiful mountains above the pueblo?" He answered, "My ancestors live up there. I see the snow, and the rivers coming down to give us water. The water is good." But communication may come more easily without words.

I had the following experience while fishing in Patagonia. The Rio Petrohué was swift and the wading treacherous. René, my guide, carefully led me across, hand in hand. He pointed to where a large trout lurked under a bank. I did not see it. I tried to cast the big fly to that spot clear across the stream. The fly failed to reach its target. I had tried too hard. Finally he took my rod, cast rapidly and accurately to the far shore, and retrieved the line in short jerks. A dark shadow seemed to follow, the water surface convulsed, and René shouted, *"¡Hola, trucha!"* Rene's natural and fluid movements spoke volumes about our differences.

After releasing the big rainbow we shook hands and lay down to rest on the grassy bank. René smiled and said, "Next time." Our verbal communication was in a few words of English or Spanish but much more was nonverbal: gestures, looks, what is now often called "body language." René was Mapuché, native to this part of Chilean Patagonia. Spanish was his second language and English a very distant third. He was, perhaps, five feet four inches tall, with a powerful stocky body, broad face, and warm, sparkling, grave Mongolian eyes. We had been together three days now. I had observed him closely. His senses were superbly acute, fine-tuned to the surroundings. He saw a hawk, a rare plant, and a deep dwelling fish far earlier than I, oblivious to so much that he saw, smelled, or simply, inexplicably, sensed.

He radiated a feeling of peacefulness that seemed to vibrate harmonically with the outer world. Perhaps that inner peace was inherited. His ancestors resisted the Spanish invasion of Patagonia. They were never conquered, never subdued. This land was still theirs. No reservations, no government agencies had corrupted their souls and bodies.

We waded together back across the river, steadying each other against the thrust of the cold current. Although we came from very different worlds of perception, we were brother hunters.

## Solitude

Solitude is a nearly universal precondition for mystical experience in nature. No human distraction should disturb the intimate connection that somehow leads a person into a new dimension. "To go into solitude, a man needs to retire as much from his chamber as from society. I am not solitary whilst I read and write, though nobody is with me. But if a man would be alone, let him look at the stars. The rays that come from those heavenly worlds will separate between him and what he touches. One might think the atmosphere was made transparent with this design, to give man, in the heavenly bodies, the perpetual presence of the sublime."[40]

One's deepest thoughts and feelings are nurtured when alone. They can occur anywhere—in a study, a monk's cell, or a crowded airport—but the space that nature provides is an unsurpassed vessel of generosity and receptivity. My memories of nights at sea or camping in the mountains are filled with the brilliance of the universe, the stars and galaxies throbbing in luminous energy, a direct beacon for the unitive experience that is termed *mystical*. My ego is humbled and the magic moment tempers my thoughts and questions about the purpose of life.

The capacity to be alone is a form of self-reliance. Solitude provides the quiet space that is needed for contemplation, prayer, and originality of thought. It gives the opportunity to get in touch with one's deepest feelings and to reassess them in respect to the ever-changing conditions of the outer world. Most of the mystical experiences described in this book occurred in occasions of solitude. In *Solitude: A Return to the Self,* the English psychiatrist Anthony Storr writes, "some development of the capacity to be alone is necessary if the brain is to function at its best, and if the individual is to fulfill his highest potential. Human beings easily become alienated from their deepest needs and feelings. Learning, thinking, innovation, and maintaining contact with one's own inner world are all facilitated by solitude."[41]

Storr equates many experiences of solitude, voluntary or involuntary (such as when imprisoned), with moments of ecstasy. Among solitary vigils in nature, Richard Byrd described the winter of 1934 in the Antarctic, and came away humbled with the beauty and the miracle of aloneness.[42]

With solitude comes simplicity. Anne Morrow Lindbergh ponders on the simple bare beauty of a channeled whelk shell found on the beach. She compares it to the shape of her life: "how untidy it has become! Blurred with moss, knobby with barnacles, it's hardly recognizable anymore." She seeks "a singleness of eye, a purity of intention, a central core of my life" in order to live in inner harmony, "in grace." To do this, a simplification of life is needed. And this she does, living alone on the beach, shedding belongings, furniture, and the chattel that accumulates like moss around our lives. "How little one (can) get along with, and what extraordinary freedom and peace such simplification can bring."[43]

Those words resonate as I contemplate the crazy pace of urban life, increasing throughout the world as the impact of IT (information technology) grabs and directs our easily manipulated minds. Viewing the London scene of over two hundred years ago, Wordsworth deplored the craving for "extraordinary moment" and for "outrageous stimulation." Our modern culture, too, tends to replace the spaces of those inner resources with psychic noise: sensational entertainment, gadgets, toys, and other basically unnecessary paraphernalia. Certainly we seek and need interaction with fellow human beings, but it seems that the self-reliance of which Emerson spoke so eloquently is a quality that is shrinking in many evolving materialistic cultures, East and West. Solitude for many with few inner resources, according to one psychologist, may lead to depression, passivity, and other "negative states."[44]

### Spirit in Nature

*Several of nature's people*
*I know, and they know me;*
*I feel for them a transport*
*Of cordiality.*[45]

EMILY DICKINSON, *COLLECTED POEMS*

It is in the outdoors of our world to where my thoughts continuously return. They come also to the words of the nature mystic Henry David Thoreau. The essay on walking expresses, close to my heart, the kernel of his philosophy: "I believe that there is a subtle magnetism in Nature, which, if we subconsciously yield to it, will direct us aright."[46] Thoreau's words soar as he recalls the joys of walking in New England: "So we saunter toward the Holy Land, till one day the sun shall shine more brightly than ever he has done, shall perchance shine into our minds and hearts, and light up our lives with a great awakening light, as warm and serene and golden as on a bankside in autumn."*[47]

Thoreau saw Walden Pond in a creative dimension that unified him with the object of his vision and daily sensibility. His perception of the

---

*Thoreau's essay on walking epitomizes the nearly obsessive love of nature that Thoreau experienced in those early days of the American expansion and "taming" of the environment. At that time more than three-fourths of the primeval forest in Massachusetts had been felled. Walden Pond was surrounded by a relatively barren landscape. Today the forest has regained a toehold and over three-fourths of Massachusetts is again wooded. If he were alive today, Thoreau might not recognize his haunts along the shores of Walden Pond.

wind moving over water recalls images we now have of the dynamic whorls of clouds seen from space. He surely felt the living unity now called Gaia when he wrote:

> A field of water betrays the spirit that is in the air. It is continually receiving new life and motion from above. It is intermediate in its nature between land and sky. On land only the grass and trees wave, but the water itself is rippled by the wind. I see where the breeze dashes across it by the streaks or flakes of light. It is remarkable that we can look down on its surface. We shall, perhaps, look down thus on the surface of air at length, and mark where a subtler spirit sweeps over it.[48]

This harmonic resonance with the elemental natural forces persists in me even into old age, unlike the mystical transports, no longer experienced, that remain fond and unforgettable memories. Those forces have been described sometimes as moody, unforgiving, or vengeful. But nature's "terror" is alien to the Taoist who considers the natural world to be a spiritual home. Nature is impassive: it just—is. No anthropocentrism is called for. I feel at home in the face of storms as well as sunsets.

The correspondence between the outer world, nature, and our inner world, spirit, brought Emerson to wonder about "the secret sympathy that connects man to all animals and all the inanimate beings around him."[49] As he wandered through the woods near Concord, Massachusetts, the plants "nodding their heads" as he passed, Emerson surely felt the emotional contact that Edward Wilson considers an inherent quality of humanity, and to which he attached the term *biophilia*.

This interpretation of the human relationship to nature seems to manifest itself in the Swedenborgian concept of correspondence when Emerson said, "The whole of nature is a metaphor of the human mind."[50] This cornerstone of New England transcendentalism furthered the belief in the common origins of all life and, indeed, all reality. Thus the individual self merged in a harmonious unity with "the whole of nature." Emerson's essay "The Over-Soul" explored the spiritual roots of what was later called biophilia when he defined the "Supreme Critic" to be "That great nature in which we rest, that Unity, that Over-Soul, within which every man's particular being is contained."[51]

As I walk in the woodlands around Walden Pond, a shiver of revelation often comes as I feel the shades of Emerson, Alcott, Thoreau, and other Concord friends wandering the same paths, feeling the same emotions of the glorious conjunction with fellow life. The feeling of the immanence of God could have been the purest joy of those quiet walks from Concord.

This affinity or vibration evokes the doctrine of *correspondences* that Emmanuel Swedenborg, the Swedish mystic and theologian, developed: "The intercourse of the soul with the body is such as is the influx of the spiritual world with the natural . . . this is according to correspondences."[52]

Thoreau, too, asks, "Is it not as language that all natural objects affect the poet? He sees a flower or other object, and it is beautiful or affecting to him because it is a symbol of his thought. . . . The objects I behold correspond to my mood."[53]

The correspondences of Swedenborg lie at the roots of New England transcendentalism and pervade what I try to express in the mystical connections with nature. Eugene Taylor goes further to suggest that the psychological significance of correspondences is to express the symbolism of nature whereby spiritual truths are found in the observed objects: "Each leaf . . . rich in poetic memory; each twig a light toward self-knowledge."[54]

Our present knowledge of evolution and the biosphere enhances the appreciation of Thoreau's vision, so limited in its sentience by his parochial New England, yet limitless in its spirit and his message to the modern world. Thoreau inhaled the enchantment of that time beside Walden Pond and expressed his feelings in ecstatic passages:

Sometimes we are clarified and calmed healthily as we were never before in our lives—not by an opiate—but by some subconscious obedience to the all-just laws—so that we become like a still lake of purest crystal and without effort our depths are revealed to ourselves.[55]

I often visit a farm in Sweden. It is an area of exceptional wildness, of lakes and forests, with few signs of human ingress. My host, my cousin's husband, is bluff and hearty, coming from a long lineage of local peasants, and knows the land and all thereon through centuries of transmitted and inherited wisdom. Tourists, refugees from overdeveloped and overcrowded parts of continental Europe, have found this Nordic oasis of the spirit. The farmer appreciates why they hunger for nature and proposes to develop a "healing resort," not by building stark new cabins but renovating some old abandoned cottages, widening a few paths through the dense forest, and providing boats on a few of the many lakes. The impact of his entrepreneurial ambitions upon the nature he loves will be small; perhaps the impact upon tense, harried inhabitants from concrete warrens will be great.

We see the magnetic pull of nature upon human instincts in everyday life when people flock to the seashore, mountains, and woods for what they call relaxation—but what is fundamentally healing is the replenishment of the emptiness most of us experience in urban and semiurban existence. The nature writer W. H. Hudson, who was reared on the pampas of southern Argentina, expressed the impact of the natural environment in our primal psyche when he brought up "a subject not yet mentioned in my narrative: this is animism, or that sense of something in nature which to the enlightened or civilized man is . . . but a faint survival of a phase of the primitive mind." Hudson's animism was a projection of himself into nature. He felt that there existed an intelligence more powerful than his own, inhabiting "all visible things" and that lived also in many, like himself, "born and bred amidst rural surroundings, where there are hills and woods and rocks and streams and waterfalls, these being the conditions which are most favorable to it—the scenes that have 'inherited associations' for us."[56]

Hudson's animism corresponds closely to Wilson's biophilia. The evolution of our genome and consciousness in parallel with all life through billions of years gives credence to our affinity with all our fellow creatures, plant and animal. This is expressed in the myriad activities of human beings in nurturing (and also devouring) life. They include gardening, camping, hunting and fishing, flower arranging, snorkeling, bird watching, outdoor photography, and landscape painting. The popularity of rugged programs such as Outward Bound, often designed for inner-city children, are examples of our innate need to connect with nature.

That yearning for a closer relationship with nature is echoed by Henry Beston in *Outermost House,* the account of a sojourn in a small cabin on Cape Cod. "The world today is sick to its thin blood for lack of elemental things, for fire before the hands, for water welling from the earth, for air, for the dear earth underfoot. In my world of beach and dune these elemental presences lived and had their being, and under their arch there moved an incomparable pageant of nature and the year."[57]

Those feelings represent a superabundance of joy and enthusiasm, the knowing that we are truly connected. They are deeply etched into our memories and often bring a fresh upwelling of fond emotions years and decades later. Nearing my ninth decade of life there is comfort, balance, and perspective as I recall those unforgettable moments of my past. They leaven the burden and struggle that is inevitable in human existence.

The essence of mystic experience in nature may indeed be the apprehension that we are not apart from the world, the unitive dimension, which is the basis, as I urge, of biophilia. The cosmic consciousness of Bucke, perhaps long considered not just mystical but also vague and dreamy, comes ever closer to concepts of the new physics. The worlds of biological, psychic, and quantum evolution are merging into a unifying dimension that is difficult for me to grasp yet appears firmly rooted in experimental science. Eddington, long ago, saw what was developing and felt that "the harmony and beauty of the face of Nature is at root one with the gladness that transfigures the face of man."[58]

But Newtonian mathematics did not anticipate the emerging concept of a pervasive continuum of cosmic energy predicted by quantum mechanics. We seem now to be in a transitional epoch where, as in the Chinese proverb quoted by Capra, mystics understand the roots of Tao but not the branches, while scientists understand the branches but not the roots. These separate worldviews may be merging.

As I watch the night sky, high up in the Rockies, the dazzling impact of the heavens stirs a primal feeling. I wonder what the impact of that cosmic power was on the minds of our early ancestors. It seemed to guide them toward observation and measurement, as seen in the ancient megaliths that many believed to be astronomical observatories. But it may have given them the feeling of the connection of their destiny with the forces of nature, a mystic and unitive impact of that ancient sky vision.

The exhilaration of being in nature was felt frequently by Emerson and recalled the feelings of other nature mystics such as John Muir and William Wordsworth.

Compare, for example, Muir's words following his stormy ride high in a tree, words such as "wild exuberance of light and motion," "an invincible gladness as remote from exultation as from fear," and "wild ecstasy."[59] From Wordsworth's "Tintern Abbey," "I bounded o'er the mountains," "dizzy raptures," "a sense sublime," "wild ecstasies," and "a Worshipper of nature."[60] Those treasured moments of transcendence and self-affirmation can bring the spirit to a crystalline level of awareness of cosmic unity.

These meditative, exaltational, and trancelike states are none other than intense moments of nearly total awareness. They are the complete opposite of the ecstatic drug scene where "dropping out" of the world appears to be the goal. This antithesis is at the heart of opposing worldviews of our moral commitment to preserving the biosphere. I believe that the world of "recreational" drugs reflects the sickness that has infested a generation or more with cynicism and pessimism about our future.

Far from dropping out, the expansion of consciousness binds the mystic to his surroundings in a way that so often is said to be unitive. That unitive feeling can lead to creative effort, composing a work of art, performing a surgical operation, or making love. It lies at the heart of our evolutionary bond with nature and supports our efforts to save the biosphere and ourselves.

Beauty is nature—plants, animals, minerals, landscapes evoke emotions that are part of our evolutionary heritage. The structure of the universe has very likely imprinted itself on our thoughts and our sense of beauty. Perhaps as that winter sunset evoked the contemplative and harmonious feelings of cosmic unity, so too can there be a relationship between evolutionary engrams and the human appreciation of color, order, movement, and sound in nature. These perceptions of our environment may have evolved as adaptations for survival but now largely evoke the emotions of distant and forgotten encounters from the past.

The aesthetic appeal of nature is an important part of biophilia, which Stephen Kellert suggested was an advantage in human evolution leading to the increased likelihood of acquiring nourishment and protection.[61] Perhaps so, but I feel that it goes even deeper, that our aesthetic affinity with nature resonates despite our mundane needs. Robinson Jeffers wrote, "It would be better for men to be a few and live apart . . . then slowly the sanity of field and moorland and the cold ocean and glittering stars might enter their minds."[62] Behold the starry sky and the rosy sunset!

Wordsworth, too, recollecting his memories of pastoral scenes along the Wye, wrote in "Tintern Abbey":

> *But oft, in lonely rooms, and mid the din*
> *Of towns and cities, I have owed to them,*
> *In hours of weariness, sensations sweet,*

> *Felt in the blood, and felt along the heart,*
> *And passing ever into my purer mind*
> *With tranquil restoration. . . .*[63]

Such memories of pastoral scenes, of fields, moorlands, oceans, and stars provide psychic nourishment that is an antidote to our frantic and aggressive lives.

What primitive instincts do we retain to help us cope with utter wilderness or with circumstances that detract us from orientation even in the midst of civilization? Erik Jonsson shows what can go wrong when our sense of inner navigation goes astray. He believes that people do retain an inner compass but that the confusion of being hemmed in by artificial distractions deters our natural orientation. Given that several primitive species, such as mollusks, crustaceans, insects, frogs, newts, and fishes, have a magnetic sense, then it is likely, Jonsson reasons, to find a primitive ancestor of ours that also had a magnetic sense. This ability would not have disappeared as we evolved, unless there was a very long period when we did not use it. Thus it is probable that we still have a magnetic sense to fall back on when there are no outer cues for direction.[64]

I can argue, however, that there are always clues for direction in nature. The senses, if they are acute enough, will detect the very slightest cue: the waft of a breeze, the change of temperature, of light, of terrain, sky, or stars. However, our ability to cope in the warrens of "civilization" clearly requires an enormous amount of learning. This may deny us the innate, instinctive, and genetically programmed resources of consciousness that Erik Jonsson claims exist in us through hundreds of millennia.[65]

The awareness of this vast dimension of evolutionary time and space linking humankind to her natural roots may sometimes be startling. On a journey through East Africa, Carl Jung watched vast herds of wild animals grazing in "soundless stillness," as they had done from time immemorial. "I felt then as if I were the first man, the first creature to know that it is. The whole world around me was still in the primitive silence and knew not that it was. In this very moment in which I knew it the world came into existence and without this moment it would never have been."[66]

The greater Mother is nature and its loss or absence can produce deep lacunae in our souls. The naturalist Sigurd Olson canoed through the vast and remote waterways of the Quetico-Superior Wilderness and felt that power when he wrote in his *The Singing Wilderness:* "Uncounted centuries of the primitive have left their mark upon us, and civilization has not changed emotional needs that were ours before the dawn of history."*[67]

That state of mind can lead to an equanimity that offers us a perspective over our frantic race for power and materialism. How easy it is to simplify life and see into the heart of things that which is really of value.

---

*Sigurd Olson spent a lifetime exploring the wild lake country of the Quetico-Superior and beyond. His invocation of music as a metaphor for the primeval roots of our search for attachment with nature is echoed in Bruce Chatwin's *Song Lines* about the Australian Aborigines.

# 4 THE WARRIOR AND THE ATHLETE

*Strife is the source and master of all things.*

HERACLITUS

*You will recall, if you saw the film* Patton, *the scene in which the American general, who commanded the Third Army in the 1944–45 drive across France into Germany, walks across the field after a battle: churned earth, burnt tanks, dead men. The general takes up a dying officer, kisses him, surveys the havoc, and says: "I love it. God help me I do so love it. I love it more than my life."*

JAMES HILLMAN, A BLUE FIRE

## War as a Mystical Experience

Strife and danger exist in nature. Human nature is competitive and *Homo sapiens*'s heritage as a hunter connects to his role as warrior, defending family and territory or seeking his own. Our genes have not changed significantly in the past fifty thousand years. Human history and mythology is full of war. The *Mahabharata* and its Bhagavad Gita, the *Iliad,* the *Aenead,* the Celtic *Lebor Gabála Érenn,* and the Norse *Edda* are to a large degree "war books," according to the Jungian psychologist James Hillman. Even our Bible contains many accounts of battles, wars, and captains of wars.[1] In the midst of war there can come mystical experiences that hark back to our primeval past—where nothing obstructed the stark realities of strife and the visions of imminent death. Similarly to the cinematic but also real-life Patton, the Jesuit priest, mystic, and philosopher Teilhard de Chardin, who served as a medical orderly in the First World War, described his "Nostalgia for the Front" when "for a moment they [his comrades] knew real emotions, they were united, they were raised above themselves." He was profoundly affected by his service during the violence, suffering, and death of war and recalls moments at time of war that gave a sense of "rising to a higher level of human existence."[2]

The duty to do battle lies near the deep heart of our origins; the struggle to survive is inescapable. In the Bhagavad Gita, Lord Krishna spoke of a perpetual and eternal energy that demanded action, the compelling call to duty that was a summons to the warrior prince Arjuna to gird himself in battle against a foe that included family and friends. Krishna tells Arjuna, "Perform every action with your heart fixed on the Supreme Lord. . . . Renounce attachment to the fruits."[3] The Gita remains a profound statement of the universality of strife and of the call for transcendental resolutions of human fears and conflicts.

Joan of Arc and Florence Nightingale, T. E. Lawrence, and Generals Orde Wingate, "Chinese" Gordon, and Patton were among many mystics of war, suffering, battle, and death. There is a "true and virile" mysticism that emerges in time of war. "We, horrified by the external circumstances, the devastation, the misery and evil, know little of the spiritual drama which is brought so far into being by the present war [1914–1918]. But in so far as we accept the mystic belief: and where there is suffering, difficulty and effort, and this is met by loyalty and courage, there is always hope. This war, thus regarded, is a crucible for souls."[4]

A crucible, indeed, but one we wish were never needed. But deadly conflict brings the warrior face to face with the stark reality of life and the specter of death. Primitive neurophysiological mechanisms mobilize the individual for "fight or flight." The surge of enkephalins and other neurotransmitters in the limbic system, as we will see, undoubtedly induces a tranquillity and hyperawareness in the face of extreme danger that are also important evolutionary coping mechanisms for survival.

The memories of such encounters, as described by those surviving close battle, match the feelings of explorers, mountaineers, and others facing the looming tensions of danger and those of athletes in the stresses of competition. These feelings are frequently colloquially labeled as "highs" and often include all the criteria that William James listed for mystical experience.

## Transcendental Athletics

"I was playing out of my mind!" One hears this often from athletes. It is awareness that the thinking mind was not the controlling force in the intricate coordination of muscular power and neurological signals needed in athletic achievement.

From the practices of war and hunting there developed competitive sports as exercises and ultimately athletics (from the Greek *athlein,* "to contend for a prize"). Today the pursuit of amateur and professional sports occupies a significant portion of leisure time throughout the world. It is little wonder that our competitive traits stem from the genes associated with hunting instincts that evolved with increasing brain size. As with the hunt, a psychic connection developed with the quarry, the opponent, the target, the goal, through extreme concentration and effort. Athletics and competitive games are simply a substitute for war and hunt.

The words *flow, groove, zone,* and *high* are associated with athletics and are ecstatic experiences associated with expressions such as "something totally pure," "profound joy," "action seemed in slow motion," and "strange calmness." Many of these experiences relate to extreme physical stress, a known trigger for the increased activity of enkephalins in the brain, but other mechanisms, some still not understood, are significant. For example, as with Herrigel's archery, repetitious practice in order to hone the muscular strength and coordination, coupled with the seemingly paradoxical combination of concentration and detachment of the mind, can enable the athlete, just like the hunter, to experience an expansion of his awareness that permits him to perform extraordinary feats.

In the heat of play there come feelings of effortlessness and acute intuition. The senses of altered time, "everything was in slow motion," and enhanced luminosity (photism) are frequently experienced.[5]

One of my own experiences strikingly supports the existence of those magical moments. I participated once in a sailing race near San Diego. The day was windy with a driving fog. We dodged in and out of several banks of opaque mist and emerged suddenly into bright sunlight. There, a few boat lengths ahead, we were startled to see several competitors charging on a collision course with us. The situation demanded lightning decisions. Throughout the race I had been anxious about skippering the thirty-five-foot sloop that belonged to a friend. At that moment of crisis, suddenly and somehow miraculously, I experienced a unique calmness and clarity of vision. The entire scene took on an enhanced brightness of light, time seemed to slow down, and the commotion of shouting sailors, surging waves, and slatting sails faded. A rush of confidence replaced anxiety. The crew looked back anxiously, awaiting orders. I gave them; we maneuvered with a few feet of safety to spare. We finished the race and the sensation was forgotten until much later when I pondered over this strange experience.

I do not consider myself a person who copes quickly in crisis. I usually take valuable time to think out the possible course of action. In this incident it seemed as if some greater power inside me had suddenly appeared to cope with the crisis and then, just as suddenly, had disappeared.

This "self-transcendence" (the most profound characteristic of playing "in the zone") cannot be produced by force of will. "If the Self tries to go beyond itself it just creates more Self."[6] In fact a self-conscious attempt to go beyond these limits may result in the paralytic disaster of "choking," a condition well known to most athletes and also public speakers.

Perceptive observers often appreciate these transcendent moments in athletes. In the Wimbledon tennis matches on July 4, 2001, the sports commentator described that the player Roger Federer was "in the zone." His appearance was calm, remote, untouched by the crowd's or opponent's emotions, and he was creating "amazing shots." This remarkable player continues to display an inner calm and strength of demeanor in his matches. Another tennis player once described "the zone" as "so complete and intense that it evoked a state of almost semiconscious euphoria—one that many believe bears a resemblance to hypnosis, and enables a top player to achieve his or her peak performance."[7]

The winner of the first four-minute mile, Roger Bannister, wrote, "The earth seemed almost to move with me. I was running—and a fresh rhythm entered my body. No longer conscious of my movement I discovered a new unity of nature. I had found a new source of power and beauty, a source I never dreamt existed."*[8]

The Russian weightlifter Yuri Vlasov wrote, "While the blood is pounding in your head, all suddenly becomes quiet within you. At that moment you have the conviction that you contain all the power in the world, that you are capable of everything, that you have wings. There is no more precious moment in life than this . . . and you will work very hard for years just to taste it again."[9]

Long-distance running, whether alone or in competition, is associated with many accounts of ecstatic experience. *Runner's high* is now a well-known term, connoting a euphoric feeling that occurs well into a run. Valerie Andrews, a long-distance runner, describes the

---

*Roger Bannister, later Sir Roger, then a medical student at Oxford, broke the four-minute barrier in the English mile run on May 6, 1954.

stages of mental change when after thirty minutes of running there comes a renewed energy and relaxing of the brain's censoring device. "Thoughts and feelings pour out uninhibited by the usual veneer of self-consciousness." After an hour of running there comes an altered state of consciousness similar to meditation, prayer, some drug experiences, and dreaming. Emotions may well up from some untapped source and tears may come unexpectedly.*[10]

Running can be part of religious rituals. In Hopi and Navajo ceremonies, young men engage in long and exhausting traditional runs. Buddhist novice monks in some monasteries in Japan also practice long-distance running. These ritual exercises may produce a deep transformation, a mystical participation with the forces of surrounding nature.

Simple labor can also bring similar spiritual encounters. Take, for example, Tolstoy's description of the ecstatic experience of his alter ego, Count Levin, in *Anna Karenina*. Levin joins his serfs in mowing the estate's fields with scythes. It seems that Tolstoy himself had the mystical encounters he described in the novel. He vividly shows the influence of the freedom Levin feels in the wide expanses of the land, the sun beating down, the peasants joining him in an unaccustomed camaraderie. The flow of the repetitious, strenuous mowing leads to an exaltation, blocked only as "he began thinking what he was doing and trying to do it better, he was at once conscious how hard the task was, and would mow badly."[11]

Tolstoy continues, in Levin's skin, to mow, "and more and more often now came those moments of oblivion, when it was possible not

---

*Valerie Andrews often quotes the psychiatrist Thaddeus Kostrubala (*The Joy of Running*), himself an avid runner who developed a clinic and psychotherapeutic program based on running. His concept of Paleoanalytic psychology is based on the idea that man's unique capacity and superiority in long-distance running is the principal evolutionary step toward our present status and is recapitulated in embryogenesis. According to Kostrubala, our consciousness is a direct result of these evolutionary stages of running capacity. Perhaps paleoanthroplogists and evolutionary biologists will disagree that this represents a "principal" step, but concede that running plays a role in our evolutionary history.

to think of what one was doing." Tolstoy cannot leave that scene of happy memories: "the scythe seemed to mow of itself, a body full of life and consciousness of its own, and as though by magic, without a thought being given to it, the work did itself regularly and carefully— These were the most blessed moments."[12] In no other part of the novel, it seems, do Levin's feelings rise to this pitch.

## Mountains and the Ecstasy of Danger

Mountaineering must now be ranked among competitive sports, particularly in the drive for first ascents of great peaks around the world. Extreme exertion, hypoxia (oxygen deficiency), and danger are combined with spectacular mountain panoramas in a chemistry of often-addictive proportions. Lucien Devies, the French mountain climber, describes the first ascent of Annapurna: "In the extreme tension of the struggle, in the frontier of death, the universe disappears and drops way beneath us. Space, time, fear, suffering no longer exist. Everything then becomes quite simple. As on the crest of a wave or in the heart of a cyclone, we are strangely calm—not the calm of emptiness but the heart of action itself."*[13] Mountains, as already noted, evoke spirits that burrow into the emotional guts of climbers. Danger itself is a psychic tonic and much of mountaineering is about danger and seeking out this ultimate excitement.

John Muir, the great naturalist, conservationist, and founder of the Sierra Club, described a difficult moment while climbing: "After gaining a point halfway to the top, I was suddenly brought to a dead stop, unable to move hand or foot either up or down. My doom appeared fixed. I must fall. There would be a moment of bewilderment, and then a lifeless rumble down the one general precipice to the glacier below."

Muir describes the inner conflict and resolution, "When this final danger flashed on me, I became nerve-shaken for the first time since

---

*Annapurna was the first peak over eight thousand meters to be climbed.

setting foot on the mountain, and my mind seemed to fill with stifling smoke. But this terrible eclipse lasted only a moment, when life blazed forth again with preternatural clearness. I seemed suddenly to become possessed by a new sense. The other self—the ghost of by-gone experiences, Instinct, or Guardian Angel—call it what you will—came forward and assumed control. Then my trembling muscles became firm again, every rift and flaw in the rock was seen as through a microscope, and my limbs moved with a positivism with which I seemed to have nothing to do. Had I been borne aloft upon wings, my deliverance could not have been more complete."*[14]

The sharp jabs of ecstatic moments of danger lying beyond "civilization's safety net" could give meaning to what it is to be alive. There is, in fact, an exquisite edge to facing danger. Primitive engrams in the brain are triggered to prepare us for "fight or flight." Physiological reactions stir up the body. It is often claimed that the "adrenaline rush" is the attraction of deliberately courting danger. Adrenaline (norepinephrine) is a hormone generated by various tissues, particularly the adrenal glands, which stimulate the sympathetic nervous system. Its effects are to increase the rate of heartbeat, constrict the pupils, and increase intestinal motility, perspiration, and blood pressure. It is likely that the adrenaline rush includes an outpouring of endorphins in the brain, relieving anxiety and the fear of death.

For example, the climber Laura Waterman found herself in a life-threatening situation. "Oddly enough I wasn't scared but beyond fear. Our precarious situation was so patently obvious that I felt an immense calmness and clear-headedness that comes only when you are on the thin edge between living and dying."[15] Remarkable experiences such as this have often been described in the heat of battle and in other moments of extreme danger. These experiences frequently include the stigmata of ecstatic experience, including an altered perception of time, time "standing still," of light, "a brilliant light shone," of incredible

---

*Muir made the first ascent of Mount Ritter in the Sierra Nevada in 1872. As usual, he climbed alone and without any climbing paraphernalia.

calmness, confidence, and exceptional physical achievement. The four Jamesian criteria of ineffability, noetic quality, transiency, and passivity are invariably obeyed. A mysterious "power" appears and "takes charge," enabling the individual to cope with and, if she survives to tell the tale, as Laura Waterman did, overcome the predicament.

Numbers of people today seem to be attracted to danger—from the current spate of violent horror films to riding roller coasters.[16] In today's world, among affluent societies, there have also appeared extreme sports, which include ice climbing, bungee jumping, skydiving, sea kayaking in storms, and other bizarre challenges to death. It seems a perversion when, "like the kendo practitioner who lays aside his wooden sword to duel with live blades, the climber—in freeing him or herself of the rope on routes where falling is synonymous with extinction—becomes a kind of mystic."[17] It may reflect on the secure, affluent, boring society from which such participants come. They search for the "ultimate" but possibly also for that primeval hunter inside.

Then there are explorers, adventurous in every sense, who face risks for the reward of the thrill of discovery. Their cognitive functions control, through—hopefully—prudent action, the consequences of failure: falling down a mountain, drowning, or being attacked by aggressive predators. These reactions are not limited to wilderness adventurers, to soldiers and policemen and others faced with human violence, but also healers such as doctors when confronted with devastating human carnage. In every emergency room there arise situations that must be addressed immediately with a coping response triggered by the above reactions.

Ernest Hemingway obsessively captured the ritual confrontation with death of the Spanish torero. In the ultimate human drama of giving and receiving mortality, "the faena [the final act of the bullfight] . . . takes a man out of himself . . . gives him an ecstasy that is, while momentary, as profound as any religious ecstasy."[18] In his short story, Francis Macomber, too, shone with transcendent light after overcoming cowardice and looking death in the face, the face of a charging, wounded lion. His "short, happy life" was ecstatic after that coping response, which, inborn but rarely used, was unleashed.

Similar to Hemingway's character, the protagonist of Stephen Crane's *The Red Badge of Courage* experienced a transformative epiphany following the violent emotions of fear and cowardice in the face of danger. As "the youth" was buffeted by the shock and awe of pitched battle, he experienced a remarkable sensory phenomenon often described in this book: "Each blade of grass was bold and clear. He [the youth] thought that he was aware of every change in the thin, transparent vapor [gun smoke] that floated idly in sheets."[19] He achieved a fleeting but "sublime absence of selfishness." In modern terms it would seem that the transitory loss of ego, of the subsidence of the overlay of conflicting mental conflicts, contributed to his mystical experience.

A unitive transformation came to the youth after the battle, "a large sympathy for the machine of the universe," where "in the space-wide whirl of events no grain like him would be lost."[20] The stream of consciousness that these brilliant writers conveyed was the transition of psychic states at times of high drama from primitive fear to epiphany, undoubtedly part of our innate coping mechanisms developed through long evolution. This spiritual dimension, a part of natural mystical experience, seems to ring true in these fictional narratives that were created by remarkably intuitive authors. As in all literature, truth emerges from experiential reality.

The confrontation of danger described by Maurice Herzog and John Muir are undoubtedly mystical experiences from a totally different source of action, yet may be the same phenomenon that illuminates the Zen meditator or the nature tracker.

From all the encounters of this wide spectrum of individuals, engaged in nearly every conceivable activity—from the peaceful contemplation of wild nature, a Zen garden, or a work of art or music, to the most strenuous or violent challenges, on dangerous mountains, or in deadly battle against fellow creatures, human or otherwise—there may come similar transcendent feelings. The metaphoric mountain, up which these spiritual journeys ascend, through its ravines and over its ridges, culminates perhaps in a single peak. Many may well not reach that peak, which can represent satori, individuation, bliss, nirvana, ecstasy, or all the other expressions that describe the transformation created by a profound mystical experience. There is a lasting memory of that state of transformation. It is often the unitive feeling with nature that, for me, is the key element to the true love that can lead to the active efforts to preserve it.

The mechanisms, as will be discussed, appear connected to our limbic system and to the autonomic nervous system where the release of enkephalins and corticosteroids, including adrenaline, are triggered by the various physical and psychic forces acting upon us in such moments of exhaustion, pain, danger, and beauty.

Whatever the neurophysiological details are, the end result is an ineffable and noetic mystical experience that tempers our psyche and leaves permanent memories that expand the spirit and draw us close to the unitive connection with nature.

# 5  THE POET AND
# THE ARTIST

*But what is it that sits in my heart,*
*That breathes so quietly, and without lungs—*
*That is here, here in this world, and yet not here?*

MARY OLIVER, *RIPRAP*

*In the world's audience hall, the simple blade of grass sits on*
*The same carpet with the sunbeam and the stars of midnight.*
*Thus my songs share their seats in the heart of the world with*
*The music of the clouds and forests.*

RABINDRANATH TAGORE, *THE GARDENER*

## Poetry and Nature

In a way, poets are mystics: they attempt to put into words feelings that are difficult or impossible to express in everyday prose. These feelings extend beyond the bounds of the spoken or written word, beyond the range of the "discursive intellect." It may be poetic metaphor that approaches most clearly the expression of transcendent states of consciousness. In essence, the syntax of poetry seeks to express the inexplicit, as do music and visual art.

The poetic response to nature is intertwined with the human response, just as on that ecstatic night experienced by William James on Mount Marcy: "I now know what a poet is. He is a person who can feel the immense complexity of influences that I felt, and make some partial tracks in them for verbal statement."

The poet tries to strip the outer foliage of everyday life to reveal the bare structure of what nourishes our inner selves, without which, as without food or water, we spiritually die. To increase the understanding of ourselves in this tiny biosphere shared with every cell of every microorganism, plant, or animal in the vast incomprehensible space of the universe—that is the task of the nature poet. Their poetry imparts the spirit of nature with a liberating symbolism of metaphor, rhyme, and rhythm, bringing us closer to the true reality of being. "A thought so passionate and alive, that, like the spirit of a plant or an animal, it has an architecture of its own, and adorns nature with a new thing."[1]

Nature's various moods can evoke profound stirrings in the acute observer, who then becomes a spiritual participant in the dialogue. The nature poet, in an "endless dialectic of inner experience," seeks not outer knowledge, but knowledge of being, through a dialogue between the outer and the inner, the explicit and the tacit.[2]

There may be comfort in accepting the divinity of nature alongside the divinity of a theological power. A deep sense of social meaning comes from belonging to a particular organized religion. Western theologies, in particular, focus on individual duty toward self and humanity and the importance of love, selflessness, and ethical behavior, and they see the image of God or his prophet as being generally a male human figure.

Therefore someone raised within such traditions may not recognize or appreciate the beneficence of a spirit that pervades all being. Wallace Stevens did, and he beautifully expressed and reconciled the distinction for the poet between theocratic and natural or pantheistic religion:

> An old argument with me is that the true religious force in the world
> is not in the church but the world itself: the mysterious callings of

Nature and our responses. What incessant murmurs fill that ever-laboring, tireless church! But today in my walk I thought that after all there is no conflict of forces but rather a contrast. In the cathedral I felt one presence; on the highway I felt another. Two different deities presented themselves; and, though I have only cloudy visions of either, yet I feel the distinction between them. The priest in me worshipped one God at one shrine; the poet another God at another shrine. . . . As I sat dreaming with the Congregation I felt how the glittering altar worked on my senses stimulating and consoling them; and as I went tramping through the fields and woods I beheld every leaf and blade of grass revealing or betokening the Invisible.[3]

## Sublimity and Delightful Horror

In eighteenth-century Europe there emerged a new appreciation of nature as a source of beauty and emotion. The essayist Edmund Burke, using terminology that strikes many today as quaint and awkward, wrote, "The passion caused by the great and sublime in nature . . . is Astonishment; and astonishment is that state of the soul, in which all its motions are suspended, with some degree of horror." He added, "The sublime . . . anticipates our reasonings, and hurries us on by an irresistible force."[4]

In his philosophical inquiry into the origin of our ideas of the sublime and beautiful, he commented, "Infinity has a tendency to fill the mind with the sort of delightful horror, which is the most genuine effect, and truest test of the sublime."[5]

The interpretation of these statements must be made with knowledge of the contemporary meanings and usages of certain words such as *astonishment, the sublime,* and *horror.* New expressions such as these came from Latin or Greek roots, with which all literati of that era were conversant.

*Astonishment, surprise,* meant a little more for the classicist. The Latin root *tonare,* "to thunder," connotes surprise from a natural event of large impact. It is a pliant word suggesting the passivity that William James associated with mystical experience.

*Sublime,* from the Latin *sublimes,* derived from *sub,* "under," and *limen,* "threshold" or "lintel," has a less clear derivation. *The Oxford English Dictionary* considers *sub-* in this instance to mean "up to," not "under." Yet nowhere is this supported in the various definitions of the prefix. *Sublime* is generally defined as "the highest regions of thought, affecting the mind with a sense of overwhelming grandeur or irresistible power, deep reverence, or lofty emotion." Certainly the current term *subliminal* means under the threshold (of consciousness). Burke used the term *sublime* more in the context of a feeling, something inward, rather than as a descriptive term.

Finally, the word *horror* and its derivatives are today readily associated with terror, loathsomeness, and shock. But its Latin root, *horrere,* means "to bristle or shudder," and in the eighteenth century it could mean ruggedness, as in nature, that caused a shudder or a thrill. Indeed, the phrase "delightful horror" immediately suggests the idea of a frisson, the emotional thrill of a beautiful and transcending experience.

The Romantic Era brought back the feeling of the connection of human beings with their natural roots. Where the scurrying forces of urbanization and industrialization tended to see nature as an alien and often threatening power, the naturalists, poets, and scientists assimilated the spirit of the biosphere into their thinking and emotions. That love and understanding of nature lives on today, but it is being displaced by the overwhelming forces of industrialization and global consumer economies that threaten our biosphere and our survival.

## Wordsworth as a Nature Mystic

*How oft, in spirit, have I returned to thee,*
*O sylvan Wye! Thou wanderer thro' the woods,*
*How often has my spirit returned to thee!*[6]

I read and reread his "Lines Composed a Few Miles above Tintern Abbey" and others, soaring and lyrical, resonating within my deep emotional recesses, and I marvel at the power of these words that flood over me when they are put together as only poets can do.

Wordsworth recalls memories "Of the deep rivers, and the lonely streams" and returns often to the "banks of this delightful stream" flowing to the ocean, reminiscent of life flowing into eternity:

> *For I have learned*
> *To look on nature, not as in the hour*
> *Of thoughtless youth; but hearing oftentimes*
> *The still sad music of humanity,*
> *Nor harsh nor grating, though of ample power*
> *To chasten and subdue. And I have felt a presence*
> *That disturbs me with joy of elevated thoughts; a sense*
>    *sublime*
> *Of something more deeply interfused,*
> *Whose dwelling is the light of setting suns,*
> *And the round ocean and living air,*
> *And the blue sky, and the mind of man:*
> *A motion and a spirit, that impels*
> *All thinking things, all objects of thought,*
> *And rolls through all things. Therefore am I still*
> *A lover of meadows and woods,*
> *And mountains; and of all the mighty world*
> *Of eye, and ear, —both what they half create,*
> *And what perceive; well pleased to recognize*
> *In nature and the language of the sense,*
> *The anchor of purest thoughts, the nurse,*
> *The guide, the guardian of my heart, and soul*
> *Of all my moral being.*[7]

Wordsworth revived, in simple language often strange to the ears of eighteenth-century English literati, the reverence for nature that had lain largely dormant during centuries of Christian theology. In his way, he helped to turn the contemporary dogmatic theology back toward a more spiritual religion.

It is likely only in our supposedly enlightened era, through the rationality of knowledge and scientific thought, that Wordsworth's poetic insights could portray nature as it is, free of anthropocentric and ignorant fears and superstitions. Thus the spirit could merge directly and freely with the life and matter that compose our cosmos, with the divinity of nature.

There may be a fork ahead in the path of history where a fundamental and fateful collective decision will be needed to choose the right direction. Wordsworth foresaw that dilemma, perhaps, when he heard "the still sad music of humanity" as a distant drumbeat of ominous danger to the sanctity of the natural world.

His prescience about what we now know from cosmology and evolutionary biology enhances the impact of his timeless ode to nature. Quantum energy is deeply interfused in the light of setting suns. The round ocean and living air are truly living. The motion and spirit of all thinking things suggest all of life, not only the minds of men.

The dynamic homeostatic changes in these media, part of our biosphere, were certainly not known in Wordsworth's day. After he formulated his concept of evolutionary humanism, Julian Huxley connected the truths of Wordsworth's words with contemporary scientific thought.[8]

Early in his youth, Wordsworth embraced and was transformed by a vision of the life force of nature. He devoted much, in his earlier works, to the detailed analysis of the processes of his own feelings. Every relevant experience, no matter how trivial, was included in his goal to share these deep feelings with others.[9]

Wordsworth's prose and poetry are pervaded by the theme of connection to his environment, including childhood memories such as the following from *The Prelude* (book 1):

*Was it for this*
*That one, the fairest of all rivers, loved*
*To blend his murmurs with my nurse's song,*
*And from his alder shades and rocky falls,*
*And from his fords and shallows, sent a voice*
*That flowed along my dreams? For this, didst thou,*
*O Derwent! Winding among grassy holms*
*Where I was looking on, a babe in arms,*
*Make ceaseless music that composed my thoughts*
*To more than infant softness, giving me*
*Amid the fretful buildings of mankind*
*A foretaste. A dim earnest, of the calm*
*That Nature breathes among the hills and groves.*[10]

The river has nourished the poet as his nurse of nature. The "fretful build-ings of mankind" become chastened by the power of his connection through the River Derwent to the primal sources of his, and our, ultimate birth.

His feelings become more ecstatic and primitive as the image of the river continues, and a truly erotic union with Mother Nature ensues:

*Oh, many a time have I, a five years' child,*
*In a small mill-race severed from the stream,*
*Made one long bathing of a summer's day;*
*Basked in the sun, and plunged and basked again*
*Alternate, all a summer's day, or scoured*
*The sandy fields, leaping through flowery groves*
*Of yellow ragwort; or, when rock and hill,*
*The woods, and distant Skiddaw's lofty height,*
*Were bronzed with deep radiance, stood alone*
*Beneath the sky, as if I were born*
*On Indian plains, and from my mother's hut*
*Had run abroad in wantonness, to sport*
*A naked savage, in the thunder shower.*[11]

Ancient pagan rituals, particularly among Northern European tribes, involved wild dances of naked ecstasy in the sun-warmed forests of midsummer. To this day, many "civilized" individuals feel the need to divest their clothes in attempting to more closely connect with nature—which in Scandinavia at least is a socially accepted midsummer behavior. Wordsworth was among the first to be called a "nature poet," and the "mystical germ" was surely in him. He is, however, not without critics. The outspoken Aldous Huxley asserted that

> the Wordsworthian adoration of Nature has two principal defects. The first is that it is only possible where Nature has been nearly or quite enslaved by man. The second is that it is only possible for those who are prepared to falsify their immediate intuitions of Nature.... Our direct intuitions of Nature tell us that the world is bottomlessly strange: alien, even when it is kind and beautiful, sometimes even unimaginably, because inhumanly, evil.[12]

There is much to criticize in that statement. It is almost incomprehensible in this postmodern time to accept the anthropocentric idea of nature, in any manifestation, as being evil or even alien. Our scientific understanding of the forces that operate in this universe permits us to accept the impassivity of destiny. Consequently love is possible for even an unenslaved nature. The "Wordsworthian adoration" was his true intuition of nature, be it slave or wild.

Huxley continues to lambaste the poet: "A voyage through the tropics would have cured him [Wordsworth] of his too easy and comfortable pantheism."[13] Poor Wordsworth! He had only his bucolic, rural, eighteenth-century England as inspiration (beside the obligatory tours to the Continent). Perhaps he, as most other Europeans of that era were, would have been overcome by tropical heat and lushness. We are all, however, more or less, captives of our native environment, accustomed to our own climate and geography. Perhaps there are or have been Asian, African, or Siberian poets equivalent to Wordsworth who would be dismayed by the rainy and foggy English countryside!

In addition to Huxley, there are others who have criticized or satirized the sometimes overblown and laudatory paeans to nature that became popular in the Romantic era, particularly the nineteenth century. It is well perhaps to balance excessive feelings that may arise from strong emotions evoked by any object. The writer Joyce Carol Oates, in amusement, writes, "IT [nature] inspires a painfully limited set of responses from 'nature-writers'—REVERENCE, AWE, PIETY, MYSTICAL ONENESS [capitalization in original]." She goes on to take issue with the anthropocentricism, the "Nature-adoration," the "Nature-as-(moral)-instruction for mankind" of some of the genres of nature writing.[14]

The dilettantism of some nature writing, it seems to me, is a valid criticism by Oates. It is easy to bask in the glory of a sunset, in the majesty of snow-clad peaks, and the splendor of whatever-you-will. But I believe nature writing has now gone well beyond romanticism and is addressing the heart of the question of humanity's relationship with the environment, the need for respect of "nature-as-it-is," not as an experience but as a living, breathing presence, a being to which we owe our existence.

It appears that throughout Oates's essay, an inner voice is speaking, one that is remarkably united with that dimension that envelops us, even in the throes of her frightening bout of cardiac arrhythmia, perforce lying down on the ground and looking at the sky, "near-bodiless," seeing the infinity of that blueness and of one's own life.*[15]

In more serious criticisms of Wordsworth, the Asian scholar Robert Zaehner and the psychiatrist Richard Bucke questioned his mystical antecedents. Zaehner stated that it is likely that, "to judge from his writings, he does not seem to have had a 'unitive' experience."[16] There is, however, an incident that was recorded by his friend, Thomas De Quincey, in which Wordsworth experienced and described such a phenomenon. In Wordsworth's words:

---

*The popular writer seemed to admire only Thoreau's nature writing, although she called *Walden* "the most artfully composed of prose fictions" (241).

I have remarked, from my earliest days, that if, under any circumstances, the attention is energetically braced up to an act of steady observation, or of steady expectation, then, if this intense condition of vigilance should suddenly relax, at that moment any beautiful, any impressively visual object, or collection of objects, falling upon the eye, is carried to the heart with a power not known under other circumstances.

Just now, my ear was placed upon the stretch, in order to catch any sound of wheels that might come down upon the Lake of Wythburn from the Keswick road; at the very instant when I raised my head from the ground, in final abandonment of hope for this night, at the very instant when the organs of attention were all once relaxing from their tension, the bright star hanging in the air above those outlines of massy blackness fell suddenly upon my eye, and penetrated my capacity of apprehension with a pathos and a sense of the Infinite, that would not have arrested me under other circumstances.[17]

The poet had spontaneously found a mystical moment and had recognized the experience. The circumstances are strikingly similar to Zen techniques of receptive meditation and to the transcendental experience of the hunter's trance. The glittering, bright star appeared to then trigger the full ecstatic moment, like the piercing cold light of Venus over the New Mexico Mountains.

The relationship of his poetry to the writings of the eighteenth-century German mystic Jacob Boehm further demonstrates Wordsworth's mystical view of nature.[18] The interpretation of aesthetic values by this worldview shows that the poet sees beauty as created by our natural world—that there is no other basis for aesthetic creation. Wordsworth's "wise passiveness" is a "peaceful and detached reverie" that freed him from mundane concerns and enabled the fringes and depths of consciousness to become manifest.[19]

The task of this poet to convey his muse to an audience in a comprehensible way was addressed by the English poet and philosopher

Frederic William Henry Myers (1842–1901), the same who introduced the term "subliminal consciousness" and strongly influenced William James's thinking in this area. Myers put the following conditions to poetic understanding:

> The communion with Nature, which is capable of being at times sublimed to an incommunicable ecstasy, must be capable also of explaining Nature to us so far as she can be explained; there must be *axiomata media* (middle truth) of natural religion; there must be something in the poetic truths standing midway between mystic intuition and delicate observation.[20]

Indeed, the task is to bridge the tacit and the explicit, and this I believe Wordsworth did.

Wordsworth is a poet of solitude. The intuitions he experienced on his walks along the rivers and into the hills evolved eventually to moral convictions. His reflections about nature are not as much for their sentient aspects as for their mystic significance. He perceived and expressed that the spirit of nature (for he undoubtedly believed that nature, animate and inanimate, was living) communicated with man, thus enabling humanity to grasp the certainty of an absolute union with nature.

"The meanest flower that blooms contains thoughts too deep for tears."[21] Wordsworth's panpsychism (the feeling that all matter is living, thus conscious) arose surely from his childhood memories. His feelings were that humanity's interest was to receive nature's blessings and not to impose its own caprices, as evocatively expressed in *The Prelude:* "I know that Nature never did betray the heart that loved her."[22]

The practices of Taoism and Zen would have suited this English poet. That space of distance spanned an understanding of discovery, as with so many over the centuries, of the calm and centering that comes from the spiritual union with nature.

# Henry David Thoreau

In his journal, Henry David Thoreau says:

> If with closed ears and eyes I consult consciousness for a moment—
> Immediately are all walls and barriers dissipated—earth rolls from
> under me, and I float, by the impetus derived from the earth and
> the system—a subjective heavily-laden thought, in the midst of an
> unknown and infinite sea, or else and swell like a vast ocean of
> thought—without rock or headland. Where are all riddles solved,
> all straight lines making their two ends to meet—eternity and space
> gamboling familiarly through my depths? I am a restful kernel in
> the magazine of the universe.[23]

Thoreau is little recognized as a poet, yet much that he wrote about nature is poetic. In addition to the lines that are deliberately conceived as verse, often, to our ears now stilted in the conventions of his time, his prose in *Walden* and other books, and particularly in his journals, is laced throughout with the free and spontaneous qualities of poetic expression.

This strange, solitary, yet all-too-human man broke through the constraints of nineteenth-century conventions to become among the first to awaken the American spirit to honor its deep connection with its natural roots. Whereas much of American society was focused on "conquering" the land (and its original inhabitants), voices such as Thoreau's rang out, louder with each succeeding generation—to reach, hopefully, the numbers now needed to make a significant turn away from ecological disaster.

The New England transcendentalists, indeed, were rebels, questioning the precepts of both their contemporary church and society. At the heart of their philosophy lay the lessons learned from intuition, from direct experience. One's destiny came largely from individual choice. Emerson's "great nature" was the vessel of all being, the source of a universal soul, apprehended by the subconscious state. And the evolution of humanity demonstrated the fall from grace; "Man is a dwarf of himself," according to Emerson, "for he was once filled with the spirit of nature but shrank from what he was and could be."[24] The mystical and Swedenborgian mirroring of nature and spirit may have influenced Emerson when he wrote, "Every natural fact is a symbol of some spiritual fact. Every appearance in nature corresponds to some state of mind, and that state of mind can only be described by presenting that natural appearance as its picture."[25]

Thoreau responded to Emerson's words with his feelings in defining the perfect correspondence of nature to man to be "that he is home in her!"[26] Nature mysticism was surely close to the ideals of the transcendentalist movement.

I recall in nostalgic memory a near perfect correspondence with nature on a Connecticut river. Many years ago I often waded and fished the Hammonasset and came to know, like a well-worn and comfortable chair, all its nooks and crannies. The river taught me much about fish and fishing, and about nature. Its beauty, moods, and colors became etched deep inside and are relived in my dreams, both waking and sleeping. The seasons governed the moods of the river. My favorite was autumn. The brilliant hues of the changing leaves were reflected in quiet, cold pools. The air was crisp and occasionally a whiff of fermenting and rotting apples would drift from a nearby abandoned orchard. I will always associate that apple scent with the Hammonasset.[27] Who has not drawn comfort from such memories?

Thoreau embraced "wildness" and drew it into his self. He perceived the world as a means and a symbol, and became, to the admiration of Emerson, a transcendentalist of simplicity and roughness.[28] His spiritual unity with nature went beyond physical proximity. It was when nature presented a mystical mirror of himself that Thoreau created, particularly in his early years, the poetic writings that are recorded in his private journal. Those words were unfettered by the need to publish in the accepted style of the time. In one entry he described the function of the (nature) poet:

He must be more than natural—even supernatural. Nature will not speak through but along with him. His voice will not proceed from her midst, but, breathing on her, will make her the expression of his thought. He then poeticizes when he takes a fact out of nature into spirit. He speaks without reference to time or place. His thought is one world, hers another. He is another Nature,—Nature's brother. Kindly offices do they perform for one another. Each publishes the other's truth.[29]

But Thoreau the poet could voice the elegiac song, which he briefly reveals in the often lyrical *A Week on the Concord and Merrimack Rivers.*

> *But now there comes unsought, unseen,*
> *Some clear, divine electuary,*
> *And I who had but sensual been,*
> *Grow sensible, and as God is, am wary.*
>
> *I hearing get who had but ears,*
> *And sight, who had but eyes before,*
> *I moments lived who lived but years,*
> *And truth discern who knew but learning's lore.*
>
> *I hear beyond the range of sound,*
> *I see beyond the range of sight,*
> *New earths and skies and seas around,*
> *And in my day the sun doth pale his light.*
>
> *A clear and ancient harmony*
> *Pierces my soul through all its din,*
> *As through its utmost melody,—*
> *Farther behind than they—farther within.*

*More swift its bolt than lightning is,*
*Its voice than thunder is more loud,*
*It doth expand my privacies*
*To all, and leave me single in the crowd.*

*It speaks with such authority,*
*With so serene and lofty tone,*
*That idle Time runs gadding by,*
*And leaves me with eternity alone.*

*Then chiefly is my natal hour,*
*And only then my prime of life,*
*Of manhood's strength it is the flower,*
*'Tis peace's end and war's beginning strife.*[30]

Following Thoreau and the other transcendental poets of New England—with whom I also include Emily Dickinson, Walt Whitman, and Herman Melville—there have come generations of American poets who have carried on the traditions that extol the human connections with nature. The mystical connection, too, is part of this poetry. In *Imagining the Earth: Poetry and the Vision of Nature,* John Elder selects the writings of Robinson Jeffers, Gary Snyder, Annie Dillard, Peter Matthiessen, A. R. Ammons, and Robert Bly, and comments, "Through their attentiveness, expansiveness, and strategies for reaching beyond what they have learned to say, America's poets of nature, too [referring also to Wordsworth] surprise us into imagining the earth."[31]

Among modern American poets, perhaps Annie Dillard best exemplifies to me the appellation of "nature mystic." Like Thoreau, much of her poetry is found in her prose, notably *Pilgrim at Tinker Creek.* She stalks her prey so that she can see herself, through brilliant imagination, inverted, as in the astonishing scene of the giant water bug and the frog. Much of *Pilgrim* is prose poetry, where the writer puts down words that, together, express thoughts that fly beyond our immediate grasp but settle slowly into our psyche, evoking in turn a unique emotional connection to some part of nature.

Her two kinds of "seeing"—one meticulous, detailed, obsessive observation; the other "letting go," the "despotic eye" of Wordsworth versus the "sauntering eye" of Thoreau—is amply illustrated in Dillard's concise prose. She acknowledges her debt to Thoreau in keeping a "meteorological" journal of the mind.

These shifting perceptive processes create waves of different heights impinging in her consciousness, some that lap on the shores of James's vast sea of subconsciousness (see chapter 8). Through her observational process, Dillard achieves the immediacy of self to object in a creative and dynamic correspondence to the *exakte sinnliche Phantasie* that Goethe urged as a basis for scientific observation. The Jamesian criteria of what constitutes mystical experience can be found in much of what Dillard writes.[32]

## Ted Hughes

When I read Ted Hughes, I feel the raw guts of nature that stir ancient memories of the primeval past.

The late Poet Laureate grew up, as did Wordsworth, in rural England, but in a wilder area, West Yorkshire. Hughes, strongly influenced by the local traditions of bards and druids, wrote often about Brigit, Celtic Goddess of Poetry and a nature deity. He created, two centuries after Wordsworth, nature poetry of even more mystical expression. Many consider him to be among the greatest of contemporary poets and the first among modern nature poets.

The poems in *River* (1983) reveal this mystical connection to ancient Celtic lore, to creatures of myth and legend, to fish and fishing (the "hydraulic hunting" of the American naturalist and writer, Paul Shepard), and to the savagery of animal, including human, instincts. Hughes expresses a shamanic reverence for the Salmon of Wisdom and other creatures of Celtic myth.

A passionate angler, Hughes faced the accusations of ecopoets as a betrayer of his social obligations toward nature conservation ("You bastard!"—when he described the death throes of a captured salmon).*[33] Hughes addresses this savage part of our nature without yielding one iota to a passion for an unblemished natural world.

The maternal reflection of the river, also heard in Wordsworth's lines, resonates in "September": "In this river / Whose grandmotherly, earth-guarded, sweetened hands / Welcome me with tremblings, give me the old feel / Of realities reassurance—". And again from "River":

"Fallen from heaven, lies across / The lap of his mother, broken by world."[34]

The connection to earth and water of "Go Fishing" is heard in Hughes's abrupt, unromantic verses contrasting with the often "pastoral" Wordsworthian poetry:

> *Join water, wade in underbeing*
> *Let brain mist into moist earth*
> *Ghost loosen away downstream*
> *Gulp river and gravity.*
> *Lose words*
> *Cease*
> *Be assumed into the womb of lymph*
> *As if creation were a wound*
> *As if this flow were all plasm healing.*[35]

He joins his quarry, the salmon, wading into the river as spent spawners gulp from hypoxia (caused by the necrosing gills), and die, ghosting downstream, rejoining the womb of water and earth that renews the life cycle.

---

*"Green poetry" or "ecopoetry" goes a step further than nature poetry: the poet is not just an observer but is directly engaged in environmental issues. The poetry of Ted Hughes is considered a bold attempt to explore the processes that involve the natural world.

Hughes's explanatory notes to his poetry reveal his meticulous absorption in the subject matter of each poem. For example, his notes for the poem "Rain-Charm for the Duchy" record the topography and hydrography of the salmon rivers in Devon as only a keen and passionate observer and participant can. The spawning habits of the salmon that ascend these rivers are vividly described. And, as is so characteristic of his mystic naturalism, he writes, "One of the rewards of . . . an obsessive salmon fisher is that salmon remain installed in some depth of your awareness, like a great network of private meteorological stations, one in every pool you know, in every river you ever fished, in that primitive underworld, inside this one, where memory carries on 'as if real'. You can receive a report from any of these stations at any moment, usually unexpectedly. The motion of a cloud noticed through a window, the sudden stirring of a flower in a mid-city border, can be enough."[36]

That awareness in the depths of the "primitive underworld" of memory emerges into consciousness, "unexpectedly," as do similar mystical encounters in nature. The poet appears at times sublimely in touch with his environment. His homage to the lowly eel also shows his deep nature mysticism:

> *Her life is a cell*
> *Sealed from event, her patience*
> *Global and furthered with love*
> *By the bending stars as if she*
> *Was earth's sole initiate. Alone*
> *In her millions, the moon's pilgrim,*
> *The nun of water.*[37]

The spawning migrations of eels, traveling thousands of miles, are guided by the stars. The pilgrimage ends when the moon's signals dictate the primeval union in the remote sea. Hughes's knowledge of science and biology enhances his mystic appreciation of nature's rites of passage.

The circle of life and death expresses Hughes's exuberant vitalism, which burns into the reader's feelings. From the orgiastic turmoil of living that fascinates him comes, ultimately, the celebration of the life process in an ethereal plane—so different from Wordsworth, yet strangely akin.

There can be differences between what is now called ecopoetry and nature poetry. Hughes admitted that his poetry tended to suffer when he tried to address ecological issues directly. For him, "Semi-protest pieces of verse" did not work.[38]

## Paleolithic Legacy

Humanity's drive to achieve a higher consciousness is seen in Paleolithic art. The graceful paint strokes on the bare stone of deep and dark caves tell us that our ancestors had already transcended their daily needs by creating imagery expressing their inner and outer visions.

In the caves of Spain and France we come face to face with the handprints and painting strokes of those forbears from the Upper Paleolithic era. *Homo sapiens,* by that time, thirty-five thousand years ago, appeared very much like what we are today in brain size and stature. The hunter was in his prime, and his cave art offers a window into that time.

To behold the abode of that remarkable and beautiful work evokes the mystery and presence of our human heritage. Anyone who has entered deep caves experiences an aura of mystery, perhaps fear. Our Paleolithic ancestors explored far into these caves. Most of the art that has been found is located in remarkably remote parts of these caves, as distant as a kilometer or more from the ancient entrance.

Entering such a cave system once, in the northern Spanish cordillera flanking the Bay of Biscay, we were guided through vast caverns, now beautifully illuminated, to ever narrower passages, and finally, a long distance from the entrance, to the wall paintings. The outline of a human hand, traced by ocherous pigment, struck the visitors with awe.

No natural light or sound reaches these remote spaces. Imagine the ancient people hesitatingly exploring this *mysterium tremendum*, threatened by cave bears, yet finally, with the feeble light of tallow lamps, beginning to inscribe symbols and representational drawings, etchings, and paintings on the rock walls and ceilings. Graham Dunstan Martin points out that "by descending into the cave, primitive man reached the void of his own consciousness—the 'ground' of the world—which is found in silence and darkness."[39] That "ground" is the plenum of space conceived by the physicist David Bohm, the ground for the existence of everything.[40]

What was the motivation leading to this creativity? The trance of the hunter in stalking his quarry may have led to its expression in those incredibly distant subterranean spaces. Others have claimed that the Paleolithic hunter created these works from a source of spiritual energy, an expression of mystic connection, not just with fellow life but also with the physical world and the heavens of his nightly wonder.[41]

Many who enter deep caves remark on the absolute sensory deprivation, as did Barbara Hurd, who described her intense personal experience upon entering the uncanny dimension of total darkness and silence. With extended time in such surroundings, some have experiences that verge on the hallucinatory. Extraordinary sensitivity to any stimulus occurs. These deep psychic feelings may correspond with what our Paleolithic ancestors experienced.[42]

Shamanism may have its origins from the Paleolithic and possibly earlier eras. The act of representation, of pictures, symbols, eventually language, which are continuous steps of layering of consciousness, probably evolved through at least tens of thousands of years of humanity's history. The roots of this consciousness, however, may go back to the earliest organized life, Sinnot's source of consciousness (see chapter 1). If conscious thinking can be traced through the animal world to the level of insects, as the animal psychologist Donald Griffin maintains,[43] and in the plant world, as supported by Tompkins and Bird, then a continuous pathway of the evolution of consciousness from the earliest life appears plausible. From what we see today in those caves where Paleolithic peoples ventured, we might speculate, as does the writer Graham Dunstan Martin, "the mystical was with us from the beginning."[44]

## Homage to the Rock

From the mysterious art of Paleolithic peoples we come to a contrasting form of human creativity. Natural formations in the landscape such as rocks probably have been venerated and worshipped from earliest times. These rocks can be seen today in the form of megaliths (giant stones) scattered around the world, rearranged sometimes, such as at Stonehenge, other times as single, often spectacular objects. This practice appears to date back at least to the beginnings of the agricultural era ten thousand years ago. We can appreciate the enormous efforts that were made to move and place them. In some cases the location and arrangement of rocks were designed with relationship to predicted celestial events such as the winter solstice.

The simplest and most enigmatic of these structures are called menhir, being large, solitary rocks, sometimes rising vertically to several dozens of feet.[45] Others such as dolmen have been arranged in formations that surely presage churches and temples.

Upon seeing Stonehenge, I feel perhaps a bit of the awe that the Celtic population experienced, coming from great distances to gaze upon that architectural wonder. The looming majesty of the silent megaliths stirs up numinous feelings, much as in the dark echoing silence in the depths of a Paleolithic cave site. Nature is often a mysterious place for us to inhabit. But the magic celestial mantle, the limitless vistas across deserts and plains, the soaring mountains, and the boundless oceans also give us nurture. But we are not content to leave things alone. We evolved as tool-using creatures and have acquired talents and compulsions to assemble, build, and erect. Perhaps that is why these megaliths were dug out and mounted as sources of veneration. Later came the pyramids of Egypt and Mexico, giant stone heads of Easter Island, cathedrals, temples, and much more. We seem compelled to erect substitutes for nature.

In China, the veneration of natural rocks has been woven into its history up to the present and is part of Taoism, Confucianism, and Buddhism. What are the roots of this art form?

The feeling for a harmony with nature was vital to the Tao, the road leading to spiritual integration and creative fulfillment. Taoism considers that there is a spirit in all things, living and nonliving. Indeed, a spirit pervades the cosmos. I can readily understand this philosophy as I, too, see a rock in a different light. Viewing such a simple and inanimate object reveals far more than immediately strikes the eye. The rock has a history. It has been created out of ancient forces with powers beyond immediate comprehension. Certain rocks are even closer to me, such as limestones and marbles, being laid down by my ancestral cells. In addition to its composition the stone's history is further shown by the furrows, fissures, crenulations, holes, and spurs created by the weathering from thousands or millions of years of wind, rain, frost, and sun.

Emerson felt such omnipresence in natural things when he wrote of "the all in each particle, that Nature reappears in every leaf and moss." His belief that the "genius and creative principle" of all eras was found in some part of his mind that manifested itself in the "all-in-each" credo of Anaxagoras.[46]

This rock, then, is a macroform of Blake's grain of sand. It has a correspondence, as Emerson suggested, where "Each particle is a microcosm, and faithfully renders the likeness of the world."[47] The rock may reveal what existed before the creation of the universe and every event thereafter to the present moment of its contemplation. It is, to the receptive observer, a spiritual being emanating the power, *qi,* which joins the subject to the object, resulting in a cosmic union. This object of nature is not a deity, a thing to be worshipped. The intensity of feeling for its symbolism is rather veneration, a deeply cultural characteristic in the traditional ways of China and Japan. The art scholar George

Rowley wrote, "We must never forget that a culture which is sustained on faith in a personal God cannot seek reality in nature, and that the Chinese, without that faith, could find reality in nature beyond our understanding."[48]

Given the right conditions, the observer of the rock enters that dimension of creative energy, a form of meditation that can be transforming. The process can be like Goethe's *sinnliche Phantasie* and connects the observer through the visualized rock to all nature and beyond. This step in the Way, Tao, is that of *te,* which can bring the participant closer to self-realization. The Tao of an individual incorporates the inner and outer worlds, a nature mysticism that appears close to Swedenborg's correspondences.

Humanity's destiny appears directed toward increasing urbanization. This can lead us also, if we are not aware, to the loss of environmental memory. Nature programs on PBS and the Discovery Channel, the parkway, the zoo, and the botanical garden may not suffice. The meditative contemplation of natural art provides a rich and deep resource for the spirit.

Thus an admiration of natural forms, living and static, is a predominant form of Chinese art. The human figure appears to be secondary in much of this art, in sharp contrast to Greek art of the same era.

There are unusual and dramatic rocks that came to be called scholars' rocks because they were most prized by the literati and intellectuals.[49] These are often dramatic rock formations, placed in gardens or parks when large, or, when smaller, mounted on beautifully carved stands and set in places of honor in a scholar's study. Scholars, often in crowded cities, tried to bring in a feeling of nature in the form of gardens and natural rock formations. As seen also in the bonsai of Japanese homes, these arts reached great heights. For the Chinese, the simplicity of a rock could stimulate the imagination to perceive a microcosm of the natural world. Rocks can represent to such petrophiles a condensation of nature's potent power, a concentration of the natural forces implied in the Tao.

These fractal patterns of nature connect with our psychic and organic heritage. We instinctively understand the chaotic geometry that is everywhere. It is appreciated at intellectual levels, as by Chinese scholars, but, in the past, it was perhaps simply valued by our native sense of beauty. A small piece of limestone, like Blake's grain of sand, can enter, like Goethe's *exakte sinnliche Phantasie,* into the imagination to become a soaring mountain range.

Scholars' rocks have not just aesthetic appeal but also a mystical one, in accordance with Taoism, as being alive, imbued with energy and power (qi). The late American sculptor Richard Rosenblum gathered what is considered to be the finest collection of these rocks in the West. He explains the essence of this art in one telling paragraph:

> Our twentieth-century notions of art tell us that the act of seeing is a form of making. The conceptual process of creating the many and varied forms of Chinese nature art begins with the initial action of seeing or identifying a particularly evocative natural object; but then the process goes one step further, by extracting the object from its original environment. The intention, however, is never to denature that object or to alienate it as a part of nature that is at once complete in itself and representative of a greater whole in both a formal and an organic sense. A scholars' rock, for example, is a little piece of a wrinkle from which you can imagine the whole wrinkle; it's a little piece of rock from which you can imagine the whole rock; it's a little piece of a mountain from which you can imagine the whole mountain.[50]

Thus Blake's grain of sand. The Chinese scholars' rocks, like bonsai, *suiseki* (the Japanese term for scholars' rocks) and the Zen stone garden, are, consequently, mere substitutes for and representations of wild nature, our true and ultimate nourishing source. They serve well, however, to uplift our spirit and renew our mystical connection to nature. Sitting in a room, in a city, blocked from our natural environment, we

*Fig. 5.1. Mi Fu bowing to the rock. This classical Chinese scene is known and loved to this day. From the author's collection.*

can experience transcendence, as if on a magic carpet, to the wild.

A traditional story is told about the great calligrapher and connoisseur Mi Fu (1051–1107). Upon receiving a government appointment at a provincial capital, he shocked the local officials when presenting himself and his credentials by bowing instead before a nearby famous and revered rock.*[51] This event has become part of legend and the scene depicted in paintings and sculptures to this day.

---

*The garden and rock were objects of Chinese art connoisseurs' admiration of nature as a thing in itself.

# 6 THE HEALER

## A Universal Art of Nature

The art of healing is rooted in nature. Humankind has treated illness and injury for thousands of centuries with plants and minerals that have often yielded remarkable remedies. These substances continue to play a major role in medical therapy. Take, for example, digitalis, quinine, belladonna, and aspirin—just a few in the kaleidoscopic array of substances that have very specific effects on certain human diseases and more general benefits for the symptoms of suffering from disease or injury. Nowadays most of the essential ingredients of these substances are synthesized and chemically modified, but pharmaceutical research continues to explore the benefits of new and rare plants. Teams of investigators travel throughout the forests and jungles of the world to find and test promising new plant derivatives.

Of course, not all contact with the plant world is benign. Plants have developed their own defense mechanisms to ward off predators that may threaten the ultimate goals (shared with all other life) of propagation and dissemination. There are both internal and external toxic substances. Some of these substances are effective in destroying disease-causing predators of human beings. Many antibiotics and anti-cancer drugs from the plant world have been identified and put into use. Undoubtedly many more remain to be discovered.

Plants have become our allies, protecting us from the scourges of malaria and other infestations, relieving pain and suffering through plant-derived narcotics, and yielding tonics for failing organs, such as digitalis. The modern healer needs to recall this connection.

In any city, one finds stores full of "natural" remedies and nutritional supplements, not always as natural as expected. There are newsletters, circulars, and directories for naturopaths, ayurvedic practitioners, spiritualists, practitioners of reiki, and so forth. There is a widespread distrust of so-called academic or organized medicine. This distrust may drive patients to the care of natural healers who may provide psychological comfort but not effective treatment of the disease. This seems particularly true when people get cancer, which strikes fear into most minds.

During my years of practice in San Diego, there came a steady stream of patients from Mexico—Americans and others who had sought the care of practitioners who touted effective treatments for often advanced cancers. Finding the treatments ineffective and with their conditions worsening, they desperately sought the nearest help. By this time, for many, it was far too late to give effective treatment.

The credo of the great Canadian physician Sir William Osler has always guided me in my practice: "To cure sometimes, to relieve often, to comfort always." In cancer practice it is the last phrase of this aphorism that demands the most skill and spiritual energy.

The physician's craft is both art and science. It bridges a broad spectrum of what we deem normal or abnormal. The basic understanding of the psyche, however, has in Western medicine traditionally taken second place to our often urgent need to deal with the soma. This is now changing with the pioneering advances in psychosomatic medicine and psychiatry, and the rediscovery of the advantages of traditional healing arts. It is not surprising that the experiences of many healers, ancient and modern, in their search for the relief of pain and illness have led them to transcendent mental states. This is a part of shamanism (from *saman,* "to know," of the Siberian Tungas language, or "to practice austerity" from ancient Amerindian roots), an ancient tradition of mankind wherein the shaman reaches into his or her deeply hidden psyche to convey to others the inner vision of enlightenment and the very practical powers of healing.[1] The shaman is rooted in the natural world, which brings a mystical strength derived from this primeval connection. In today's Western society such an individual may be a teacher, priest, or physician.

The spiritual transcendence from an encounter in nature, like other mystical experiences, is healing both to the psyche and the body. Ample evidence exists from the studies of the Harvard physician Herbert Benson and others of the quieting of the autonomic nervous system and of the release of endorphins, both processes leading to lowered blood pressure, reduced heart beat, and a feeling of calmness and tranquillity.[2] The emotional catharsis, even including tears, from a profound encounter is yet another physiological manifestation of our own limbic system. We will discuss this further in chapter 8.

## Encounter with a Traditional Healer

The ancient and modern healer and shaman both need to know the beneficial effects of plants. But modern physicians are losing contact with their roots because of the demands of scientific learning and advanced technology that go under the guise of "modern medicine." This has led to the large countermovement of "alternative" medicine, caused in part by the frustration of instinctive needs to come closer to the mystical healing powers provided by nature and transmitted by healers and shamans.

I recall a patient that I was treating. She was a village woman, poor, barefoot, but erect and proud, dressed in her best sari and bearing wrist, arm, and ankle bracelets. Her problem was a difficult one, an advanced inoperable sarcoma invading the pelvis. She was in great pain. I was initially unsure and indecisive about how to help her. But she emanated an aura of deep calm, great awareness, and profound inner strength. Somehow a magical transfer of energy occurred, this time from patient to healer, which enabled me to formulate an effective treatment program that eventually gave her needed pain relief and comfort. I later came to know that she was the healer of her small village, a shaman with great visionary power. The power that she often transmitted to her patients she had transmitted to me, a healer that was in a sense healed through a mystic process.

Many years ago a friend in Madras, a flutist, broke a bone in his hand. He was a famous virtuoso of Carnatic music and this injury represented a potential disaster for him and for the musical community of South India. Although medical specialists skilled in orthopedic surgery were available in and near the city, my friend chose to go to a traditional healer. The healer, renowned for his work with bone fractures, lived in a remote and small village. I could do little to argue the merits of Western medicine and finally agreed to drive my friend and a supporting retinue to the village.

Once there he was received in a small hut where the healer, clad only in a dhoti and with the marks of the healer's caste drawn on his forehead, examined my friend. He disdained to glance at the accompanying X-ray, and forthwith he set the break without benefit of anesthesia or premedication. My friend winced from the pain but received support and sympathy from his entourage that had crowded into the hut. There followed a fascinating scene where the healer and his assistants, in the flickering light of oil lamps, assembled a variety of herbal pastes, plant fibers, and leaves to immobilize the fracture site. The scene evoked for me images of possibly similar scenes going back eons, of early humankind, skilled with tools, slowly learning the powers of his natural ally, the plant world, in healing disease and injury.*

The path of the healer, from the realm of nature to the care of fellow humanity, persists in an ever-diminishing number of societies. Many of the traditions are worth upholding and reviving in the technologically advanced bastions of modern medicine. There is an evolution-

---

*The traditional healer, like his modern counterpart, is not always successful. My friend eventually had to have his misaligned fracture reset by an orthopedist.

ary continuity that should not be broken, where the modern physician and surgeon should honor those roots of the healing tradition and allow himself and herself to feel the mystical connection between practitioner and patient that is the psychic core of the healing process.

There is ample evidence for the importance of psychological well-being, positive attitude, and confidence in the healing process. The placebo effect (from the Latin *piacere,* "to please") is a beneficial treatment, although it is not directly therapeutic. Benson has introduced the term *nocebo effect,* which means the opposite of the placebo effect. Nocebo effects may result from the destructive influences of society or individuals, such as the preaching of hate, suspicion, race superiority, and so forth. Benson's caveat is that the open, receptive mind can fall prey to negative influences.[3] As we will see later, "false mysticism," a term coined by French-American Trappist monk Thomas Merton, has been abundantly documented throughout human history to bring destructive tendencies in society.

## Wisdom and Healing

I have known medical students and colleagues who seem to have inherited the mantle of spiritual wisdom early in life. The calling of medicine seems to be entirely natural to them as they flower as sages and wise healers. I look upon them with respect and some envy. The calling as a healer is not easy to achieve and for most of us in the helping professions, I am sure, it demands a long and strenuous education and practical experience. However, after years of struggle to master facts, concepts, and techniques, the moment does come, I believe, to most physicians when they can communicate directly with their patients past all the chattel of technology, through their own emotional cobwebs and the anxieties of the patients. That moment, if and when it comes, signals the shamanistic moment of truth. It is an ecstasy: one stands "beside oneself." A connection has been established, be it a face-to-face confrontation about a serious diagnosis or a surgical or other procedure, to an altered consciousness during the process of healing. It is, in fact, a form of flow, according to the psychologist Mihaly Csikszentmihalyi, as well as a mystical experience where the healer loses the sense of self and becomes unified with his patient and with the process of extirpating or correcting the illness.

Csikszentmihalyi cites interviews with surgeons who described this phenomenon in their practice. In many respects these experiences resemble those that have been called mystical. There was a feeling of "transcendence," a loss of awareness of self, and a distorted sense of time where the clock no longer served as an "analog" of experience. Like the boulderer, the surgeon loses ego feeling and becomes united with his manipulation. Surgeons share the "beauty and power of a harmonious transpersonal system."[4]

I, too, recall similar occasions in the operating theater, itself resembling a temple of silence and devotion, where I lost the awareness of time, of extraneous stimuli other than those pertinent to the procedure, and I became strangely connected to the generally unconscious patient. This was particularly the case during my service in a hospital in South India, where it was the custom for the surgical team to utter a short prayer before beginning the operation. The hallowed atmosphere was a powerful influence to attaining a mystical state. It has often been observed how conscious patients will endure painful surgery with equanimity when induced into possibly transcendent states. For example, surgery under acupuncture in China appears to resemble an induced mystical state in the patient.

Much human illness nowadays involves psychic damage. The psychologist or psychiatrist may have benefited from the ancient lore of native healers and employ their methods in what is now called holistic healing. Others, including physicians and surgeons bogged down in the morass of scientific knowledge and technology, are also rediscovering that healing of disease and wounds also involves the psyche. Modern psychosomatic medicine such as exemplified by Herbert Benson and his clinic brings holistic concepts to current teaching and practice.*

---

*Benson's book *Timeless Healing* discusses many of the remarkable psychic influences upon physiological responses as well as what may happen when psyches go awry.

Shamanism offers the holistic worldview that bridges the vast transition between our inheritance of the intuitive wisdom of nature and modern science. That intuitive wisdom, as we will see, is a part of E. O. Wilson's concept of biophilia and lies at the root of the direction humanity needs to take to avoid human and ecological meltdown. As the psychiatrist Roger Walsh states: "we are engaged in a race between consciousness and catastrophe, and the outcome is uncertain."[5] The shaman, "the wounded healer," is an example to others in the helping professions. Being wounded, suffering along with the patient, often evokes optimum treatment. In a global sense, the healing of the world may be accomplished when we, humanity, are willing to see "the human diminish so that other life forms might flourish."[6]

## The Healer's Trance

In a similar way to each other, the shaman and the modern healer enter a trancelike meditation in the process of healing. As a physician, this state of mind is familiar to me, as I am sure it is to many colleagues if they stop to think about it. It represents a mind-set that focuses—or should I say "defocuses"—upon a given problem, say, the diagnosis of an illness.

When I am with a patient, the clinical history, physical examination, and laboratory data are entered into my psyche. I look again at the patient and slip into a sort of reverie—yes, trance. This helps block out extraneous "noise," the next staff meeting, the location of my car keys, the plans for the week.

The residents look askance at me. Am I "with it"? But with time they, too, enter into the mood, and a vibrant creative communication, unspoken at first, can develop between us and, often, the patient. Fringes of my consciousness appear and the magic process of thinking, feeling, and intuiting ferment to reach a hopefully beneficial solution.

This process is not unique to me: I have seen it in mentors and have learned much from the almost sacred ritual of patient rounds and bedside teaching. It is repeated, too, in the operating room, where the ritual is experienced, often silently, through the deft coordination of surgical movements, akin to the mystic dimension of coordination in bouldering (see chapter 2). I have never seen a shaman at work, but I surmise that as far as healing is concerned, we are not all that different. And the analogy can be expanded widely to a multitude of occupations, trades, and other activities. It is quite simple, in fact, to mobilize one's consciousness to reach a plenitude of goals. But one must be careful not to try too hard, for then some rational intruder seems to appear and block the process.

This healer's trance or shamanic meditation must come from deep psychic roots whereby the direct perception of the patient's illness or injury is transmitted through engrams, the established neural circuits, of association in the memory. This process, whether it is called parallelism or creative imagination, associates that experience of perception with intuitive processes. From this comes, hopefully, a solution, mental or manipulative, to the patient's problem. As in other meditative states, apophasis, the emptying out of the mind, may facilitate the creative process of the healer.

In part 1, I focused on our origins and the phenomenology, the actual experience, of the spiritual encounters occurring to different individuals, primarily in natural settings. Let us now see how these experiences fit more theoretical percepts and how some at least can be interpreted on the basis of scientific knowledge.

PART TWO

*Theory and Perspective*

# 7 THE MYSTIC LADDER

## Climbing the Mountain

William James once climbed a mountain and experienced a moment that changed his life. It came after a strenuous hike to the peak of Mount Marcy, the highest in New York State at 5,344 feet. James wrote later to his wife:

> The moon rose and hung above the scene before midnight, leaving only a few of the larger stars visible, and I got into a state of spiritual alertness of the most vital description. The influences of Nature . . . all fermented within me till it became a regular Walpurgis Night. I spent a good deal of it in the woods, where the streaming moonlight lit up things in a magical checkered play, and it seemed as if the Gods of all the nature-mythologies were holding an indescribable meeting in my breast with the moral Gods of the inner life. . . . It was one of the happiest lonesome nights of my existence, and I understand now what a poet is. He is a person who can feel the immense complexity of influences that I felt, and make some partial tracks in them for verbal statement. In point of fact I can't make a single word for all that significance, and don't know what it was significant of, so there it remains, a mere boulder of impression. Doubtless in more ways than one, things in the Edinburgh lectures will be traceable to it.[1]

From that ecstasy on Mount Marcy, William James predicted its creative outcome in the monumental *Varieties of Religious Experience.*

In the sixteenth lecture that he delivered in Edinburgh, James described four properties of mystical experience. Let us look at them again to better understand this widespread phenomenon, which we illustrated by several examples in part 1.

## Ineffability

Ineffability is characteristic of that dimension of our consciousness that cannot be expressed in words. In his *Tractatus,* the philosopher Ludwig Wittgenstein wrote, "There are indeed things that cannot be put into words. They make themselves manifest. They are what is mystical."[2] We search for words to describe mystic experience, yet fail. It is Plato's tacitness of higher truths. Ansel Adams had "no words to convey the moods" of the ecstasy that came over him while climbing in the Sierras. Only our intuition grasps the attempts to describe the indescribable. Thus words do have a role, like the shadows that suggest the shapes of objects that themselves can be delineated only in distorted outline. Intuition is the bridge that connects that shadow of the spoken word to the reality of its subject. For some, that intuition is less developed than in others. Freud struggled but failed to grasp Romain Rolland's words. The wordlessness of the unfocused mystic and the alertness of the hunter in nature are not inarticulate. Their consciousness is fully engaged and connected. It is rather a state of mind beyond language.

The *Nei-yeh* [inner training of Taoism] embraces the paradox of ineffability:

> *As for the Way:*
> *It is what the mouth cannot speak of,*
> *The eyes cannot see,*
> *And the ears cannot hear.*

The Way (Tao) of Inward Training declares that within the mind there can be an "awareness that precedes words." These teachings clarify the paradoxes that may befuddle the casual observer when confronted with the natural world, at once a concrete reality, and from a mystical viewpoint, an abstraction.[3] A Buddhist expression is *sunyata* (emptiness or the void), which also expresses the Ultimate. It is, however, not an empty word; rather, it represents a reality beyond thought. The doctrine of emptiness, *sunyavada,* applies as well to language, which is inadequate to describe the reality of experience, thus, ineffability.[4]

It corresponds perhaps to the metaphor of a mental gearshift when experiencing something. The reality of that experience may lie in a different level of consciousness until I try to express it in words. I then must put my thinking mind into gear. Experience is like being in neutral gear, without friction. That tacit understanding is processed by the somewhat inefficient gearshift into explicit expression with a certain loss of the original tacit knowing, just as there is an energy loss through frictional heat in mechanical gears. It is like a person with a speech impediment who tries, painfully and with great difficulty, to physically express a thought. But other symbolic representation such as parables and other metaphors can become paths of expression to illuminate the noetic ferment surging inside.

Clearing out the mind is known beyond Zen and mysticism as a necessary prelude to "getting in touch" and with creative moments. Psychologists, too, realize the unusual creative abilities of autistic patients and the type of brain damage that can lead to those skills. One group has gone so far as to try to block certain areas of the brain, assuming that "savantlike" abilities may emerge when incoming cerebral signals are interrupted. An article published in *New Scientist* in 2004 reported that a method called transcranial magnetic stimulation temporarily enhanced creative abilities in a small number of volunteer subjects.[5] Perhaps the verb *to grasp* comes close to expressing the tacit experience that we seek to know, to feel, to sense. Thus I may grasp with emotion and certainty the reality of climbing a mountain and gazing over the snowy landscape, my heart pounding, filled with awe and wonder at this beautiful world, my world. That experience is, however, ineffable. I try but cannot truly describe it. The reality of experience is often obscured by the "film of familiarity" that Coleridge described when "we have eyes that see not, ears that hear not, and hearts that neither feel nor understand."*[6] As he struggled to express his feelings for nature, Richard Jeffries wrote: "Clumsy indeed are all words the moment the wooden stage of life is left."[7]

*Qi* (also spelled *chi*) is a word from the ancient Chinese that may express the bridging of the reality of tacit knowing and the abstraction of explicit expression. It is vitality, giving the breath of life to all matter, an animistic principle. It evokes through poetry the ineffable state of mind that lies at the heart of mystical experience.[8] It is the "endless dialectic of inner experience" that Wordsworth among many sought to express.

Qi is a way toward the core of Chinese aesthetics. For example, a peculiarly shaped rock or oddly twisted tree trunk can evoke, through qi, a transcendent feeling, not directly pleasure, but something deeper in the heart of things, at the heart of the universe perhaps. From that aesthetic experience may come much of the art of Zen.

Simplicity, after all, is the ground for transcendence. When I see a particular silhouette of a mountain framed by a sunset, or that cold light of Venus above the fire red cliffs, or simply a certain pattern of leaves on the water, a feeling enters me that I know. That is an approximation in words of what qi represents. Those feelings are the essence

---

*Coleridge and Wordsworth spent days discussing the "cardinal points of poetry." Coleridge agreed to choose "incidents and agents to be . . . supernatural, with dramatic truths of such emotions," while "Mr. Wordsworth, on the other hand, was to propose to himself as his subject to give the charm of novelty to things of every day, and to excite a feeling analogous to the supernatural, by awakening the mind's attention from the lethargy of custom, and directing it to the loveliness and the wonders of the world before us; an inexhaustible treasure, but for which, in consequence of the film of familiarity and selfish solicitude, we have eyes yet see not, ears that hear not, and hearts that neither feel nor understand" (*Biographia Literaria*, 247).

of reality, the conduit to our connection with the universe. William James, perceptive and articulate, in discussing individuality, wrote, "the recesses of feeling, the darker, blinder strata of character, are the only places in the world in which we catch real fact in the making."[9] Hidden deep in each of us, these "strata" are near to what some may speculate is the soul. They are reachable when we clear the way by sweeping aside the bits of information, the "noise" that blocks the inner journey to the plenum of our ground state. While the philosopher Paul Tillich may say that God is the ground of all being and the Hindus state that Brahman is the ground of all being, many physicists claim that the quantum is the ground of all being.

The "transparent eyeball" of Emerson, Goethe's *exakte sinnliche Phantasie,* the *via negativa* of Annie Dillard, the hunter's trance—all serve to connect the ineffable process of mystical experience to explicit understanding.

## Noetic Quality

Noetic quality (*noeo* comes from the Greek and means "apprehend") is claimed by James to be "states of insight into depths of truth unplumbed by the discursive intellect" that carry with them "a curious sense of authority for after-time."[10] It is unshakable truth, intuitively apprehended, ineffable and lasting to the one experiencing it.

Yet that experience is not verifiable by others. How can another person know? It would seem that mystics draw cocoons around themselves and nurture their souls with their "ineffable" experiences. But there are ways of communicating. We are not isolated islands; "Conanicut and Newport hear each other's foghorns,"[11] and even islands connect to each other through the ocean bottom. So many words have been written about what are called ineffable experiences, yet like the poet's effort, we can see a glimmer through the forest of words, from the rustle of leaves, the formation of metaphors, and shimmering of light that can illuminate the innermost reaches of our understanding.

The Canadian psychiatrist Richard Bucke expressed the noetic dimension as "cosmic consciousness." Although difficult to grasp intellectually, my intuition is attuned to the message of the New Physics and its open-ended world as interpreted by quantum theory. It may be that James, Fechner, Bucke, and other early visionaries are smiling in their graves as a radical new vision gradually unfolds a dimension where our consciousness is not alone but at one with a consciousness of all life, indeed, a cosmic consciousness.

Swedenborg, in his *Secrets of Heaven,* considered that the certainty of reality, which I consider an equivalent to James's noetic quality, came from an inner voice from the Lord, flowing into the deeper parts of our thought, which could be our subconscious.[12] Revelations from perception (the input from our senses) represented the "good and true" (intuitive, noetic, or tacit knowing), whereas verbal revelation (discursive or explicit knowing) lacked true meaning.

I believe noetic knowing is in a part of the psyche that houses intuition. But the "discursive intellect" refuses to accept it unless proved by the scientific method to which my limited intelligence has been trained.

Stephen Alter's epiphany in the Himalayan hills was a noetic experience, a certainty of a reality that lay in another dimension of being. Associated, it seems likely, with noetic certainty is its memory, lasting and immutable. It can be so clearly etched into our minds that the smallest details of the circumstances that triggered the mystical moment remain forever stored and retrievable. That memory, burned into our soul, can transform one's life, perhaps only in a small way, such as an increased understanding of one's place in the world, or, to a greater degree, a total change of one's life.

Intuition, like a ray of light, can pierce the darkness not comprehended by the intellect and reveal the unity of the spirit with the universe. It is "the immediate apprehension of the mind without reasoning," analogous to *yin,* the transcendental realm of tacit knowing.

"In the humanity of which we are a part, intuition is, in fact, almost completely sacrificed to intellect."[13] Henri Bergson postulated that a supraconsciousness was the origin of life and that choice rather than passive and random steps in evolutionary change lay at the heart of all. That supraconsciousness, according to the French philosopher, lay in a dimension beyond our rational comprehension, yet our intuition, like a ray of light, could pierce that darkness not comprehended by our intellect and reveal the unity of spirit with the universe.

Bergson included in this unity the simultaneous evolution of all life when he said, "All organized beings, from the humblest to the highest, from the first origins of life to the time in which we are, and in all places as in all times, do but evidence a single impulse, the inverse of the movement of matter, and in itself indivisible."[14]

## Transiency

The apprehension of mystical experience is swift and sure. Somehow it also passes swiftly and is stored, as I have noted, forever in the memory and surely changes the individual who has experienced it. This transience may be just as well given that most of us need to get on with mundane matters. There are neurochemical mechanisms leading to this transiency that may come from evolutionary patterns of survival. Humanity and all other life would scarcely survive if caught up in a beatific mystical moment forever.

## Passivity

Passivity has two components: one is the sudden and often surprising act of mystical revelation, catching the subject unawares. Ansel Adams was "suddenly arrested" by the awareness of light. The other is that the mind is made receptive for intuition, either deliberately as in meditation or other exercise, or through the *via negativa* of the unmediated mind; the hunter, for example, expands the inner vision that allows the magical feeling to enter.

Thus mystical exaltation can enter one's being spontaneously. There is no recipe for this phenomenon, since, according to James, "Being a secret and a mystery, it often comes in mysteriously unexpected ways."[15] This was Alter's experience, the mysterious power that saved John Muir from falling to his death, and William James's own magic night on Mount Marcy. It happened, for example, when a mysterious power took over the tiller when I was steering into possible disaster. It cannot be ascribed simply to fight-or-flight reflexes or other neurological pathways that are certainly involved in these situations.

Many more components can be added to the definition of mystical experience than these classical four that William James presented in Edinburgh.

As I indicated earlier, a transformation in a person as a consequence of a mystical experience is never forgotten; its memory somehow changes one forever. The feeling of cosmic or worldly unity is often expressed. The loss of sense of ego is part of the unitive experience, the sense of becoming one with the universe, with the One, with godhead, with nature. It is an immanence that reveals to us the reality of being. A sense of timelessness, or a slowing of time, is frequent. Athletes have particularly noted this, where the factor of time is important in the activity. "Time stood quietly" for Ansel Adams as it did for many, some recounted in this book. The extraordinary sensation of light, of photism (described in the chapter on psychobiology), seems to be fairly common and is often dramatic. Such moments have come to me and, I am sure, to many of you. It is not an "intellectual" experience, it is emotional. But, somehow, it sets mental wheels in motion that may have been little used, perhaps rusty, which can address a remarkable spectrum of human activity, ranging from intellectual to sheer physical.

In what way can we distinguish, if we must, the differences between religious and nonreligious or nature mysticism, a nebulous and slippery area? Many have tried.

The American psychologist W. T. Stace created a distinction between "extravertive" and "introvertive" mystical experience. "Introvertive" is inward looking, as in meditation or experiencing a supernatural figure or power, in comparison to outward looking, looking into nature or the cosmos, which he called extravertive and equated with nature mysticism. Robert Zaehner, the Oxford orientalist, begins by simply dividing mysticism into two categories, "sacred" and "profane." But "profane" nature mysticism, too, can lead to organized religious activity. Even Buddhism, which comes as close as any religion toward extolling nature mysticism, has to a certain extent become a theocracy.

Yet mystical experience is considered the root of religion and the perception of a power beyond knowing, that is, God. What if an atheist has a mystical experience? Does he perceive God? Perhaps that is why so many other terms have been introduced to describe the same experience and still avoid the charged word *mysticism*. Nevertheless, whatever the superimposed connotation may be, we are all seeking, one way or another, this universal spiritual voyage to the edges of our consciousness—and perhaps beyond.

The deep feelings may be the same. A landscape or a sense of God triggers an inner transcendence that unites me lovingly with a limitless cosmos or force. Whether the process is extravertive or introvertive seems to be more oriented toward the initial step of the spiritual journey rather than the ultimate internal experience. Thus transcendence seems to arise spontaneously or through deliberate meditation without apparent contact with an image, either of nature, from an icon of religion, or an abstract power or being.

## Modern Concepts

Psychologists and neuroscientists continue in attempts to classify this nebulous area of human consciousness. What follows are several examples of modern concepts that mesh or overlap with what William James defined as mystical experience.

One modern explorer of the mind, the late American psychologist

Abraham Maslow, was inspired by William James's Gifford lectures to focus on a more "humanistic" approach to spirituality. Maslow's "peak experience" represented the occurrence of a sudden and intense feeling of inner power, bringing a consolidation of body and feelings that can lead to a heightened sense of awareness, of wonder and awe. Ansel Adams's description of the encounter on Mount Clark closely resembles that of Maslow's definition.

Like James, Maslow tried to grade the quality and intensity of such experiences on a scale from "relative" to "absolute." He considered this to range from "quasi mystical," where the individual is in a state of self-awareness, conscious that it is one's own experience, to a fully mystical event, where a unitive feeling with the object (the loved one, the world, the cosmos) is accompanied by a sense of timelessness and spacelessness. It is natural to attempt to classify, to grade phenomena such as these, yet even Maslow objects to "either-or" classifications such as those of mystical versus religious feelings. He believed that "each person [who has a peak experience] has his own private religion, which he develops out of his own private revelations."[16]

"Flow" is a metaphor and a title for a mental state that the psychologist Mihaly Csikszentmihalyi studied in a wide variety of persons. He describes it as a process of "total involvement with life," a source of psychic energy that focuses attention and motivates action. The potential for flow, according to Csikszentmihalyi, is innate in most of us, but it is expressed most visibly by those who tend to excel in mental and motor skills. These include, for example, musicians, athletes, artists, and rock climbers. The conditions that lead to that expression include several components: immersion in a challenging activity, merger into the action of the activity (becoming one with it), clear goals, feedback, concentration, control, loss of self-consciousness, and transformation of time. He distinguishes between flow as a controlled and cultivated experience, and mystical experience or ecstasy, which he calls "fortuitous epiphany," that is, completely spontaneous.[17]

Yet such a distinction sounds a little arbitrary. Csikszentmihalyi's concept of flow is an engagement in a mental and/or physical activity that may reach a state of euphoria by means of concentration upon the task. That feeling stems from the satisfaction of successfully achieving the goals of the task. The mental and physical concentration involved, as I will point out again in this book, may serve to block or divert psychic "noise," irrelevant information that could subvert the smooth flow of mental and physical energy.

Several elements of the concept of flow seem to be present, therefore, in many of the manifestations of nature mysticism and other mystical experiences. For example, the unitive feeling, of becoming one with the activity, and, ultimately, with the cosmos, follows the concentration and solitude that is involved in the achievement of many ecstasies and that is described in the phenomenon of the hunter's trance. This applies also to the loss of self-consciousness (or ego) and the sense of time. Thus complete absorption in an activity, be it meditating, stalking an elk, or performing surgery, can lead to similar mental states that one might call flow, but another may call mystical.

This nebulous region of the mind engages our tacit intellect, what William James called "pure consciousness," where words are inadequate, yet we know the experience is "true" (noetic), at least to ourselves. Whether the experience is the result of controlled activity, such as meditation or rock climbing, or spontaneous, such as after viewing a sunset or a stone, may not be critical in defining what is flow and what is mystical experience.

"Deep play," according to the writer Diane Ackerman, includes unselfconscious engagement with our surroundings, an exalted feeling of transcendence, and a state of optimal creative capacity. "We spend our lives in pursuit of moments that will allow these altered states to happen."[18] The concept of "deep play" may be related to the title sometimes given to humanity as *Homo ludens,* from the Latin *ludere,* "to play." Play, of course, is a close companion of competition and combat. For example, think of cubs at play, a prelude to life beyond the nurturing comfort of maternal indulgence, an embarkation on the creative journey.

The remarkable affinity of children for wild nature can be seen as they play in the woods and meadows, the streams and ponds. Many of us have known and seen this supreme delight of youth. The memories of such moments stay with us, for they are truly ecstatic moments. Wordsworth's lines ring with similar joyous memories.

The "Break-out Principle" is a method created by the Harvard physician Herbert Benson "to activate the natural trigger that maximizes creativity, athletic performance, productivity, and personal well-being." Benson believes that the physiological, biochemical, and neurological changes that he has observed are, in fact, similar throughout the spectrum that he classifies into six "peaks": self-awareness, creativity, productivity, athleticism, rejuvenation, and finally transcendence.*[19] Much stems from his "relaxation response," a spectrum of physiological changes that Benson and others have shown to occur during meditation or immersion into the quiet of nature. These changes, mediated through the autonomic nervous system from centers in the area of the limbic system, include lowered blood pressure and bradycardia (slowing of the heart), just as E. O. Wilson experienced during his "naturalist's trance" while searching the jungle floor in Surinam. Benson, as well as Ackerman, Maslow, and Csikszentmihalyi, avoid the terms *mysticism* and *ecstasy,* perhaps for the reasons I stated earlier, namely the pejorative connotations of vagueness, spiritualism, and occultism. (There is an important distinction between spirituality, which is concerned with the spirit and the sacred, and spiritualism, the belief that the spirits of the dead can communicate with the living.)

"Magical consciousness" is defined by the English theologian Susan Greenwood to be an "expanded awareness" that develops the power of imagination in its connection to nature spirituality. She writes, "Magical consciousness concerns the awareness of the interrelationship of all things in the world." But she cautions that this state of mind is "primarily natural rather than supernatural or mystical." She uses the

---

*Herbert Benson has applied his studies to the counseling and treatment of patients at his clinic in Boston.

word *magic* to imply the ability to mobilize the imagination and thus, through emotion and concentration, to change or alter consciousness.[20]

As I interpret her philosophy, I see much in it of the experiences that I have described that could be considered nature mysticism. I find no conflict in using the word *mysticism* interchangeably with *magic consciousness,* the sense of mystery of what lies within our mind, not one of supernatural beings and forces.

"Exuberance" spans spiritual, creative, and religious passions that can reach the extreme forms of mental and psychic activity that have been called manic.[21] The psychiatrist Kay Redfield Jamison describes experiences that seem in nearly every way similar to ecstasy. Indeed, the partition between what is called normal and abnormal, or physiological and pathological, between healthy and unhealthy, cannot be closely delineated. We can only wonder about the peaks and valleys of the human instinct to search for a greater meaning in life, for the amazing complexity that is our mind, yet is deeply rooted in the primeval tendrils of our psychic evolution.

When James attempted to construct the "mystic ladder," he termed the lower rungs "mundane." He thus implied that there is no sharp distinction between ordinary experience and mystical. In his discussions of "flow," Csikszentmihalyi ranges over a broad spectrum of human activity, from intellectual to physical. As the word *flow* itself suggests, at a certain point any activity begins to run smoothly with the diminution or elimination of mental inhibitions and obstacles. This "background noise" is a hindrance, in fact, to all creative activity and to mystic experience.

The continuity of flow, from the simplest functions through the range of transcendental experience toward the enlightenment of intense ecstasy, has more than one dimension. It is not just a ladder, but also a mountain up which one can climb from various ridges, glaciers, and cols (passes in a mountain chain), of varying degrees of difficulty, with one point, the apex, at the very top. Thus the slopes of this mountain represent a vast area of human creative activity that borders on the surrounding plains of everyday life and thought, where just the slightest effort to climb the mountain leads to the beginnings of mystical and creative experience. (Climbing a mountain seems to me an apt metaphor. In real-life mountain climbing, I, and I'm sure many of you, have become lost, exhausted, and may have never reached or even seen the top. The sublime moments multiply when the difficulties have been surmounted and the peak comes into view or is even reached.)

For example, when I focus on some task, be it repairing a motor, preparing a meal, creating a work of art, writing a treatise, or performing a surgical operation, extraneous cerebral noise becomes gradually suppressed. The focus becomes sharper and the task easier and smoother, often, as has been said, "without thinking," which in fact is true. The inner self, our interior mind, takes over and guides us to achieve the task. A sublime feeling may accompany this creative achievement. That feeling can reach such intensity as to be experienced as mystical.

Thus I paint with a broad brush and freely use the term *mystical* to describe experiences that are to many ordinary. There is no sharp edge to that border. I walk along a beach, pondering prosaic matters, and glance at the sunset, or a seashell or a bird. An indescribable feeling suddenly sweeps over me. It seems to come from a vast reservoir of transformative energy waiting somewhere inside me. How can I describe the indescribable? Yet its outer margins can perhaps be framed in words about feelings: a sob of joy, a stab of light into some inner space, a sudden clarity of mind; and the prosaic matters tumble out of their hold on my consciousness for a moment.

The moment passes, yet I am forever changed, perhaps in a very small way, as I return to the mundane thoughts, possibly with a fresh perspective. Every human being may experience that type of mystical moment at times, perhaps without further thoughts on its import. It is the first rung in the Jamesian ladder.

The neurologist and Zen disciple James Austin attempted to do this by staging the "ordinary and extraordinary alternate states of consciousness" into nine ascending levels, each level characterized by type and intensity of awareness, sensate perceptions, duration, sequelae, and other properties.[22] The ladder climbed from "ordinary waking states" to "advanced extraordinary alternate states of consciousness."

Stage I defines an ordinary waking state of mundane life with no special meditative states other than occasional daydreams. Stages II and III are levels of dream sleep—"slow wave" and "desynchronized" sleep. In the latter stage, vivid and imaginative dreams can arise during REM (rapid eye movement) episodes. Austin believes that the dream material can give, although rarely, a comprehensive resolving insight after awaking.

Stage IV consists of awareness of the "suchness of things," a selfless compassion of ongoing duration. In Stage V "epiphanies" occur in natural outdoor settings. Stage VI includes a "vacant, blank interval of no consciousness"; Stage VII, a sudden enlightenment also known as *satori* or *kensho*. Stage VIII is Ultimate Being, a state of grace reserved "for the very few," and finally Stage IX, the rarest of all, is where consciousness leads to "true equanimity, simplicity, and stability," presumably the province of the rare saint, guru, or prophet.

The numerous mystical encounters in nature that I have described— for example, the hunter's trance, the epiphany of Steven Alter, and the transcendental moment of Ansel Adams—could lie between Stage V and VII. The countless experiences that are at the lower rungs of Austin's ladder may often occur in persons who fail to register their impact, or relate such events to others.

What is striking, when viewing some of the world literature, is the similarity of the mystical experience through all lands and cultures. No creed or sect can alter the innate human phenomenon; the criteria appear to be universal. Thus it has been called *philosophia perennis.*

Mystical union, as E. O. Wilson writes, is truly part of the human spirit, and it is a vital subject for investigation and understanding by mystics and scientists alike.[23] But I may add that mystics and scientists are often one and the same. I sense that Wilson belongs to that category.

This superficially perceived dichotomy between science and spirituality is rapidly disappearing in the postmodern era. The Sufi philosopher Khan emphasizes the experiential nature that unites science and mysticism. The English philosopher Bertrand Russell wrote, "Even the cautious and patient investigation of truth by science . . . may be fostered and nourished by the very spirit of reverence in which mysticism lives and moves."[24]

## Freud and the Oceanic Feeling

A theme often repeated in Hindu scriptures is the merging of the soul or the self in that bastion of nature, the ocean. The expression "oceanic feeling" comes from a biography about the nineteenth-century Bengali philosopher Ramakrishna by Romain Rolland, the French poet, writer, and philosopher. As he describes it, Ramakrishna once entered into a deeply disturbed psychic state, and was prepared to kill himself, when suddenly:

> The whole scene, doors, windows, the temple itself vanished. . . . It seemed as if nothing existed anymore. Instead I saw an ocean . . . boundless and dazzling. In whatever direction I looked great luminous waves were rising. They bore down on me with a great roar, as if to swallow me, they broke over me, they engulfed me. I lost all natural consciousness and I fell. How I passed that day and the next I know not. Round me rolled an ocean of ineffable joy. And in the depths of my being I was conscious of the presence of the Divine Mother.[25]

Rolland conveyed his thoughts about this "oceanic feeling" in his correspondence with Sigmund Freud.[26] Freud responded with a description about the chaos that this idea had stirred in his concepts of the mind.

> I had sent him [Rolland] my little book, which treats religion as an illusion, and he answered that he agreed entirely with my views on

religion as an illusion and he answered that he was sorry I had not properly appreciated the ultimate source of religious sentiments. This consists of a peculiar feeling, which never leaves him personally, which he finds shared by many others, and which he may suppose millions more also experience. It is a feeling which he would like to call a sensation of eternity, a feeling as of something limitless, unbounded, something "oceanic". It is, he says, a purely subjective experience, not an article of belief; it implies no assurance of personal immortality, but it is the source of the religious spirit. . . . These views, expressed by my friend whom I so greatly honour and who himself once in poetry described the magic of illusion, put me in a difficult position. I cannot discover this "oceanic" feeling in myself. [27]

It is interesting to note, however, that Freud described an experience many years earlier (1895) that fits the criteria of ecstasy, certainly a feeling close to that which may be called oceanic. Freud had labored nearly continuously on an attempt to describe psychoanalysis in scientific terms, every night for weeks, with all the frustrations and inner turmoil experienced when the solution evades the writer. His exhaustion from this effort seriously affected his daily clinical practice. Then, one night, "tormented with just that amount of pain that seems to be the best state to make my brain function, the barriers were suddenly raised, the veils fell away, and it was possible to see through from the details of the neuroses to the determinants of consciousness. Everything seemed to fit together. The gears were in mesh."[28]

Although we do not see Freud's face as he expressed this experience, it may well have recalled the ecstatic expression of Andrew Wiles. These episodes seem far removed from nature, but they illustrate examples of the mind's exploration into the unknown and of the ecstasy of revelation, an example of flow and transcendence.

## Einstein's Ambivalence

One of Albert Einstein's widely quoted aphorisms begins with the sentences, "The most beautiful and most profound emotion we can experience is the sensation of the mystical. It is the source of all true science." This statement by one of our greatest physicists and thinkers reverberates sympathetically with what I try to describe: a rational mysticism, largely rooted in our evolutionary origins in nature and that underlies our deepest creative instincts. It is interesting, however, that Einstein's original statement does not mention "the mystical," but rather "the mysterious." In his youth, it seems that he vigorously bristled at the term *mysticism,* due possibly to the positivist and materialistic outlook prevalent among scientists in the late nineteenth century.[29]

This reflects the widely held pejorative perception that I discussed in the introduction, of mysticism as a vague and cloudy quasi religion associated with occultism, telekinesis, and the supernatural. In later life, it appears that Einstein acknowledged that the term *mysticism* correctly defined what he was trying to convey as the "most beautiful and most profound emotion" that we could feel. Beginning in the 1930s, this highly creative man spoke and wrote about his belief in "cosmic religious experience" as "the strongest and noblest mainspring of scientific research." Ultimately, he equated his personal belief, his "cosmic religion," with mystical experience.[30]

The human mind's ability to grasp this transcendent, tacit understanding may often be diminished by the pervasive forces of scientific materialism. The Harvard biologist Richard Lewontin, a close colleague of the late Stephen Jay Gould, swung down a verbal cleaver between science and mysticism when he criticized such ideas as sociobiology, evolutionary psychology, and cultural evolution by stating that they "disarm us in our struggle to maintain science against mysticism."[31] Scientists such as David Bohm, Brian Josephson, Fritjof Capra, and John Eccles are questioning this mind-set, which denies a window into ultimate reality.

Like Einstein, the Danish theoretical physicist Niels Bohr rejected the usual understanding of mysticism as a form of fuzzy religious belief. In his correspondence with Werner Heisenberg in 1925, he wrote, "I am at the present, with all my power, pushing myself to enter into the mysticism of nature."[32] From this and other statements, we can believe that Bohr, as many others in theoretical physics particularly, did believe that a rational mysticism could be a pathway toward the apprehension of reality. Heisenberg himself, at the moment of creating and confirming the mathematical proofs for the astonishing theory of quantum mechanics, in the middle of the night on the island of Helgoland, experienced an epiphany sitting on a high rock looking out upon the ocean as dawn came. He described the giddy sensation of looking down into the heart of nature in an interview with the physicists Paul Buckley and David Peat.[33]

## Proust and the Petite Madeleine

The evocation of the senses through distant memories may also lead to transcendental experience. In a classical example, the French writer Marcel Proust, through his protagonist, felt "an exquisite pleasure" upon tasting a Petite Madeleine, an "all-powerful joy" that gave a feeling of detachment and of no longer feeling mediocre (a Proustian neurotic obsession) or mortal. That ecstasy erupted from remote, dormant memories of childhood pleasure and comfort and ranged beyond pleasure into a new dimension, an ineffable feeling that Proust eagerly sought to retrieve.

The evocation, too, of distant memories of place, of the wild; the sound of a waterfall or the ocean beach; the smell of the pine forest; the sight of the billowing colors of a sunset—all can trigger similar ecstasies. Are these memories of one's own experience of the senses or are they from ancient origins? Proust hinted at deeper sources:

> But when from a long distant past nothing subsists, after the people
> are dead, after the things are broken and scattered, taste and smell

alone, more fragile but more enduring, more immaterial, more persistent, more faithful, remain poised a long time, like souls, remembering, awaiting, hoping, amid the ruins of all the rest; and bear unflinchingly, in the tiny drop of their essence, the vast structure of recollection.[34]

That long distant past may include deeply hidden evolutionary roots of our inherent attachment to nature, concealed particularly from many in modern "civilized" societies.

## Spiritual Experience in Childhood

There is a powerful spirituality in children that is not always recognized. Memories of childhood ecstasies can be profound and everlasting. Near-death experiences and the spiritual revelations of dying children have been documented by Elisabeth Kübler-Ross in remarkable and touching accounts. A revealing study of childhood spirituality by the psychologist Edward Hoffman was made in interviews with adults, remembering their early experiences. As we have seen elsewhere, a significant number occurred while in the out of doors, in wilderness, the countryside, farms, seashore, and forest.

Many of these experiences resemble the mystical encounters I recorded in part 1. For example, the phenomenon of photism was frequent. A teenager walking through the Nova Scotia countryside suddenly felt "tremendously elated, and then euphoric. Simultaneously the entire world seemed to be suffused with a tremendous light."[35] Another experience included a unitive feeling. At age four a girl was standing on the seashore, watching breaking waves, when, suddenly, "a door opened, and I became the sun, the wind, and the sea. . . . Sound, smell, taste, touch, shape—all melted into a brilliant light."[36]

An eleven-year-old Little Leaguer experienced the sense of slowing of time: "On the next pitch, something happened. As the pitcher began his regular windup, the illumination on the field seemed to become brighter, and everything became silent and luminous. Everything went into slow motion. The pitch came, and the ball floated in as big as a basketball. I hit it squarely . . . ran to first, tumbled into the grass, and laughed until I cried."[37] That experience resonates wonderfully with my own epiphany in the sailing race, the narrow escape of John Muir, and several episodes of the hunter's trance. I will explore the psychobiological bases of these and other phenomena in the next chapter.

Far more people than we suspect may have undergone peak or mystical experiences in their early years, according to Hoffman. Many of the criteria of mystical experience were met in the 250 episodes that he analyzed. The noetic feeling, leading to a clear and unforgettable memory, is characteristic. It seems, too, that these ecstasies led to or were part of profound changes in the interviewee's lifestyle or worldview.

As the writer E. L. Doctorow wrote in his short story "Willi," the protagonist, recalling his youth, walks in the fields and imagines Earth's soul enveloping him in a divine embrace: "I fell at once into a trance and yet remained incredibly aware. . . . Such states come readily to children. I was resonant with the hum of the universe."[38] That episode, demonstrating all the Jamesian criteria for mystical experience, could surely (and perhaps did in Doctorow's case) lead to a lifelong memory and a continuing respect and love of nature.

My own childhood memories are strongly imprinted by experiences in nature: splashing up streams and finding mysterious creatures under rocks, wading tidal pools and being astonished by brilliantly colored anemones, walking through quiet, cool forests of gigantic redwoods, and hunting oddly shaped fungi. Later a children's microscope brought a whole new world into my senses. Such memories last forever.

But the increasing alienation from nature experienced by children in the urbanizing world society has led, at least in America, to what the social thinker and journalist Richard Louv calls Nature Deficit Disorder.[39] Childhood experiences of playful romps and explorations through meadow and forest are replaced by competitive games on paved playgrounds and, increasingly in this technological age, television viewing (the figures for children are staggering), computer games, and other electronic pastimes that can lead to "social autism."

Louv speculates about a relationship between the epidemic of ADHD (Attention Deficit Hyperactivity Disorder) and alienation from nature. He presents evidence to show that reconnecting children with nature will dramatically improve their behavioral symptoms. The delights of growing up in our small planet with its diversity of life would surely be heightened by more close encounters with the natural world. These ecstatic environmental memories from childhood lead, according to Louise Chawla, through the imagination to the foundation for a firm footing in life and to a mature philosophy of nature.[40]

Childhood experiences in nature can also include moments of fear, of being lost or threatened by strange beasts, by terrifying gales or blizzards. These varying aspects of natural experience lead toward spiritual maturation, toward a worldview where an individual realizes that the values of good and evil are human ideas, and that the natural world is neutral with respect to anthropocentric morality.

Wordsworth and William Blake, the great visionary poets, vividly portrayed their childhoods as part of their spiritual evolution. As many others, Wordsworth saw the ultimate source of truth in the innocence of childhood, uncorrupted by the mundane and ever increasing pollution of materialistic positivism. I, too, plead for the realization that humanity's heritage, the "hope for the future," our children, will increasingly feel, hear, see, and touch what constitutes our natural world. That is the only way they can nurture the innate instincts to cherish and love our world with all its diversity.

## Creativity

Artistic creativity as a daily activity among an entire cultural milieu is unusual nowadays. My wife, the Jungian psychoanalyst Manisha Roy, and I once spent some time in Bali, near the village of Mas, the center for traditional woodcarving. Nearby we observed the carvers gather every workday morning under an open pavilion. After prayers of dedication to their particular deity in the Hindu pantheon, they proceeded with their work. The men worked silently and with serious demeanor. It was as if they had fallen into a trance. They seemed to be in another dimension as they slowly shaped beautiful figures with sureness and skill.

Bali is nearly unique, despite the heavily tourist-laden pressures, in manifesting the creativity of its inhabitants, blessed as they are by natural beauty and abundant crops. Dance and music performances, and the artisan crafts, reflect the deep spiritual dedication to art. The onlooker clearly senses the meditative and ecstatic feelings of the performers and artisans. The poise and calm demeanor of the people, at least in the cultural heart of Bali, clearly connected to religious and cultural tradition and their beautiful nature, demonstrated to me that mysticism is part of their daily life.

This creative union of humanity with nature through occupation survives in a few other cultures around the world. Although often related to religious traditions, ultimately the mystical process of creativity is a personal and individual feeling. It can exalt the dignity of artisanship, and, indeed, of any activity that can transcend the mundane, grinding, and frantic pace that besets so much of the world in its struggle to break through poverty.

There is probably a hidden treasure of memories, concepts, and associations in everyone that can provide the material for the creation of a work of art, a solution to a problem, or simply a better way of washing dishes. This may be why highly creative people often state that "someone else" is guiding their creativity. The musician plays in a sort of trance, the tennis player is "in the zone," the artist's hands are guided by some outer (but yet inner) force. In such instances the experience can reach levels of intensity that could be called "mystical."

Perhaps the ecstatic enjoyment of music, deeply imbedded from eons of the hearing of natural sounds, of birds, waterfalls, thunder, and wind, is part of our natural heritage. Even a single note of musical vibration can lead to an ecstatic experience. I once heard David Harrington, a member of the Kronos String Quartet, express his feelings of a particular note that he played: "That note—what I feel is the essence— I have experienced maybe three or four times in my career. It is that essence that we all seek."[41] Music surely evokes incredibly deep feelings, ranging from the primitive ecstatic emotions generated by jungle drums or rap and rock to sublime harmonies that seem to lift us to a celestial dimension.

Great works of music bring us closer to that transcendental plane. As I listen to Beethoven's Quartet in C-sharp minor, op. 131, for example, the andante cantabile movement transmits directly into my soul the sublime feeling of Beethoven's meditative reverie. This—by then (1826) totally deaf—genius created it from his mind in the form of musical notes that will live on throughout human history.

Although my fellow hunters and anglers seem culturally bound not to display their "soft" emotional feelings (it isn't macho!), I sometimes see their eyes glisten as they talk of their "camps" in Maine, of moments they do not, dare not, describe but that I sense in their terse, oblique references are experiences that may be called ecstatic.

In sharp contrast, others, artists and musicians, for example, may openly express the joy of ecstasy without shame. I recall the transports of a late genius, pianist Glenn Gould. Nothing seemed to inhibit him from physical expression, the body language of the profound inner feelings stirred up from creating and hearing beautiful music, often, unfortunately, to the distraction of hearers who were not in the same ecstatic plane as the performer.

Graphic and structural art, too, no matter how abstract, may imitate nature and affect us in ways that are not just emotional—joy or pathos—but exist, like that musical note, in a dimension beyond.

The discovery of a long-sought solution to a problem can lead to mystical revelation. I once saw an extraordinary demonstration of ecstasy in a television interview with the British mathematician Andrew Wiles, who had for many years worked on the problem of the proof for Pierre

Fermat's Last Theorem.[42] As Wiles recounted his efforts, the radiance from his words and expression convinced me that he had achieved a moment of ecstasy in the sudden finding of the apparent solution. He described it as "an incredible revelation," "indescribably beautiful," "so simple and elegant." His face shone with the joy of having found, he thought, the answer.* The exhilaration of discovery, whatever its nature, may be one of the keenest emotions that can be experienced, exceeding, if one can be brash, that following sexual orgasm or epicurean ecstasy.

Walking in the foothills of Portofino, Friedrich Nietzsche experienced a rapture (*Rausch*) of inspiration, which he described in detail. It was one of the creative moments that led to *Thus Spoke Zarathustra*. "One hears, one does not seek; one accepts, one does not ask who gives; like lightning, a thought flashes up, with necessity, without hesitation regarding its form—I never had any choice."[43]

The term *passivity* evoked by James and others in mystical experience is part of the creative experience, as James Leuba, the American psychologist and contemporary of William James, explains: "There are few beliefs more widely entertained than that of the passivity of the artist at the supreme creative moment. It is a common dictum that he must wait for 'inspiration.'" That word, so ready upon the tongue in connection with artistic creation, points to the spontaneity, the unexpectedness, of this kind of mental production. Leuba pointed out that "Here the great joy, rising almost to ecstasy, follows the illumination as a rational consequence of its perceived significance. It is the ecstasy of Archimedes, running naked through the streets of Syracuse after having discovered the principle of specific gravity, shouting '*eureka, eureka!*'"[44]

Creativity and mystical experience are transcendent states of mind that lie in the same dimension of our consciousness, the hidden well of our being, that Goethe recognized when he wrote: "All productivity of the highest kind, every important conception, every discovery, every

---

*Subsequently, after painstaking reevaluation, Wiles concluded that there might be no solution to Fermat's mysterious theorem. The mathematical community, however, now widely accepts Wiles's proof.

great thought which bears fruit, is in no one's control, and is beyond earthly power. Such things are to be regarded as unexpected gifts from above, as pure divine products.'"[45] The achievement of mystic ecstasy, in nature or anywhere, I repeat, is a form of cognition beyond the mundane. The psychologist Andrew Greeley considers it to be a form of spiritual security as he quotes from an epiphany of the writer John Buchan: "It was like a glimpse of the peace of eternity."[46]

Thoreau described in moving detail the origins of his ecstatic feelings in nature. He recognizes the power of those feelings waning with age, that as a youth they were "an indescribable, infinite, all-absorbing, divine, heavenly pleasure"—yet he knew that he had nothing to do with them, that they were given to him "by a superior Power."[47]

The balance and focus achieved by meditation or any other mystical state can lead on to a nearly unhindered flow of creativity. Diane Ackerman, in *Deep Play,* describes the flow, the peak experiences, of all those human states that bring passion to living, that bring us close to the cosmic consciousness that psychiatrist Richard Bucke laboriously detailed so many years ago and that is the root of the creative process.

These processes of inspiration, creativity, and ecstasy are thus closely linked. In *Tradition and the Individual Talent,* T. S. Eliot argues that "the more perfect the artist, the more completely separate in him will be the man who suffers and the mind which creates."[48] The spirit of intuition and creativity, of mystical understanding, can transcend the "trials and tribulations" of everyday life. Who has not experienced such moments? When all seems terribly difficult, the unconscious steps in to show the way to redemption.

The Tao teaches us how moments of creativity can fuse the artist and the work, as if "another power is working." Those moments, for which every artist lives, have none of the struggle, the "blocking," "freezing," or "choking," shared by artists, writers, athletes, and indeed all creative persons when their creative fire is doused by the water of rationality, when the muse is away, when inspiration is subverted. When that happens, one may as well pack up for the day.

Those teachings of the Way encompass the central thesis for the psychology of "flow" and show the importance of subduing the self in attaining a state of mystical awareness.

The self, however, needs to return to help the individual deal with mundane realities of existence. Only a few of us can afford to spend our lives in mystic contemplation and exultant creativity. Those saints, prophets, and geniuses may occupy a special part of society, and some cultures nurture and support such individuals, much as a hive of bees supports the queen bee.

For the rest of us, the existential circumstances require the active presence of the self most of the time. Perhaps that is a factor in the emergence of Confucianism as a counterbalance to Taoism, giving historical Chinese culture a remarkable balance and relative stability. The Taoists may have been in the alternative culture of their day, while the Confucians, the householders and government servants, took responsibility for the stability of society. The philosopher Arthur Danto says, "It is the tension between and ultimately the harmonization of Confucian and Taoist traits that formed the typical character of the Chinese mind."[49]

# 8 WIDER THAN THE SKY
## The Psychobiology of
## Mystical Experience

*The brain is wider than the sky,*
*For, put them side by side,*
*The one the other will include*
*With ease, and you beside.*

EMILY DICKINSON, "LIFE,"
*COLLECTED POEMS OF EMILY DICKINSON*

*With all your science can you tell how it is, and whence it*
*is, that light comes into the soul?*

HENRY DAVID THOREAU, *JOURNAL*

*Reductionism is a way to understand complexity.*

E. O. WILSON, *CONSILIENCE*

## Mystical Models

The roots of those feelings that we consider to be spiritual or mystical appear to grow from the depths of our consciousness. Beginning with models that served as metaphors for mystical experience, thinkers have repeatedly turned to developing scientific disciplines for the tools to dig ever deeper to reach this frontier of our psyche.

William James considered mystical experience to be the "mother sea and fountain-head" of all religions and to inhabit a dimension beyond that of intellect, an "extended subliminal self with a thin partition through which messages make irruption." Beyond the farther margins of that subliminal field (of consciousness), James evoked the existence beyond of an "Absolute mind" or a "distinct deity."[1]

In a letter following the Edinburgh lectures to his close friend Henry Rankin, James wrote:

> I think that the fixed point in me is the conviction that our "rational" consciousness touches but a portion of the real universe and that our life is fed by the "mystical" region as well. I have no mystical experience of my own, but just enough of the germ of mysticism in me to recognize the region from which their voice comes when I hear it.[2]

One voice, however, sprang from that transcendental moment following the climb up Mount Marcy that he later vividly described to his wife.

James's thoughts on the mystical region of consciousness were soon to be strongly influenced by a now obscure German physician and physicist. Gustav Theodore Fechner (1801–1887) received a medical degree at the University of Leipzig but then proceeded to study physics and mathematics. In a wide-ranging career, he became professor of physics, and later philosophy, at the same institution. He is considered a founder of experimental psychology and was a towering presence in the nineteenth century, an inspiration to, among others, Sigmund Freud. A basic law of psychology attached to his name states that the intensity of sensation increases as the logarithm of the stimulus. His mantle was assumed by Wilhelm Wundt (1832–1920), who attracted numerous future leaders in psychology to his laboratory, including William James.

William James earlier had mixed feelings about Fechner. He called much of Fechner's psychophysics "moonshiny" and elsewhere "patent whimsy" of "such a dear old man."[3] Yet he took seriously many of Fechner's panpsychic writing and devoted a good deal to it in *A Pluralistic Universe,* as well as returning again and again to the oceanic metaphors surrounding Fechner's wave theory of consciousness. The polyglot psychologist from Cambridge carefully read Fechner's now largely forgotten (and untranslated) thoughts on cosmic consciousness and saw in his words the glimmerings of the idea of consciousness as an evolutionary phenomenon leading back to an ultimate collective dimension in the universe. Indeed, well before the new concept of Gaia, Fechner viewed the earth as a sentient organism. James agreed with Fechner's "great analogy" of the relationship of the senses to the mind, not only of humanity, but also with every living thing.[4]

James viewed Fechner in a new light after the Gifford lectures. He has this to say in *A Pluralistic Universe* in 1909:

> The original sin, according to Fechner, of both our popular and scientific thinking, is our inveterate habit of regarding the spiritual not as the rule but as an exception in the midst of nature. Instead of believing our life to be fed at the breasts of the greater life, our individuality to be sustained by the greater individuality, which must necessarily have more consciousness and more independence than all that it brings forth, we habitually treat whatever lies outside of our life as so much slag and ashes of life only; or if we believe in the Divine Spirit, we fancy him on the one side as bodiless and nature as soulless on the other. What comfort or peace, asks Fechner, can come from such a doctrine? The flowers wither at its breath, the stars turn

to stone; our own body grows unworthy of our spirit and sinks into a tenement of carnal senses only. The book of nature turns into a volume on mechanics, in which whatever has life is treated as a sort of anomaly; a great chasm of separation yawns between us and all that is higher than ourselves, and God becomes a nest of thin abstractions.[5]

James presented with openness and candor four of his own patently mystical experiences, which were "sudden and incomprehensible enlargements of the conscious field, bring[ing] with them a curious sense of cognition of real fact."[6] It is of interest that William James described them in 1910, eight years following the Gifford Lectures in Edinburgh when he had said: "Whether my treatment of mystical states will shed more light or darkness, I do not know, for my own constitution shuts me out from their enjoyment almost entirely, and I can speak of them only at second hand."[7]

We know more than we know to tell. Our consciousness is a vast dimension, of which we are little aware at any given moment. Knowing is part of consciousness. The philosopher Michael Polanyi postulates that there are two kinds of knowing, the tacit and the explicit. The explicit type of knowledge can be expressed in words and symbols, whereas tacit knowledge cannot.[8]

Both tacit and explicit knowing occupy certain spaces in our waking consciousness. The important functions of learning, recognition, and sensation—in fact, all experience—is primarily tacit, of which only a tiny bit can be made explicit. Although James Joyce tried in his novels, his words represent an iota of the tip of the mountain projecting above the clouds, below which exists a gigantic tacit mass of unknown dimensions.

James considered Fechner's wave theory to be a major step toward the understanding of consciousness.[9] Fechner conceived a diagrammatic representation of consciousness in the shape of a wave, its crest extending above a horizontal limit that he called the threshold. He then postulated a number of "wavelets" that represented various states of consciousness. The moment and amplitude of these wavelets are variable, as shown in his original diagram (fig. 8.1).[10]

They resemble the pattern of the alpha sine wave of "resting" consciousness discovered much later by the technique of electroencephalography. The threshold, according to Fechner's theory, could vary in height, and it separated waking consciousness (above) from subconsciousness (below).

After translating and studying Fechner's concepts,[11] William James developed the metaphor of an oceanic tide, its water surface being the threshold. The tidal ebb uncovers a vast area of shoreline that is, in other words, the usually hidden subconscious area of our psyche.[12]

James suggested that mystical intuition may be a sudden, large extension of "waking" consciousness, so that knowledge that is ordinarily transmarginal (or subliminal) may become perceived, like land exposed "on an unusually flat shore at the ebb of the spring tide," an apt New England metaphor. James then describes his own experience of a sudden widening of the conscious field (as the tide or threshold falls): "The larger panorama perceived fills the mind with exhilaration and sense of mental power."[13]

James distinguished sensation in his field of consciousness, which can be termed effortful consciousness, from the vast reservoir of memories, concepts, and "conative" states that generally lies below the tidal surface. This reservoir, when suddenly brought into view, gives the conditions for "a kind of consciousness in all essential respects like that termed mystical." He invoked his criteria of mystical states

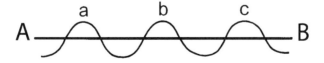

*Fig. 8.1. Fechner's wave-scheme of consciousness. Line AB represents the threshold above which the wave pattern (a, b, c) integrates consciousness, whereas below this threshold lie the fields of unconsciousness* (Unbewusstsein). *From* Elemente der Psychophysik, *530.*

by indicating that these experiences are transient (since the changing level of threshold is transient), and there is a sense of reality (noesis) as well as enlargement, illumination, and unification. The experiences are of intuitive and perceptual quality rather than conceptual, because the field of consciousness exposed to view does not attract attention to individual objects, but rather gives a feeling of "tremendous muchness suddenly revealed."[14] James's "flimsy curtain" that separates waking consciousness from subliminal consciousness has a counterpoint in the "reducing valve" of Aldous Huxley—which allowed a "Mind at large," subliminal consciousness, to flood the waking consciousness in a mystical experience.[15] The dimensions of the region of subliminal consciousness are unknown even to the most advanced students of neurobiology. William James's British contemporary, Frederick W. Myers, and his French colleague Pierre Janet, who described *désagregation,* excited James's interest in the source of the "vast sea" of memory and thought that lies within us in ever deeper layers, perhaps down to ancient inherited engrams that correspond in part to Jung's concept of archetype.

James's colleague and friend, the American philosopher Charles Saunders Peirce, postulated another metaphorical image of consciousness when he said, "I think of consciousness as a bottomless lake, whose waters seem transparent, yet into which we can clearly see but a little way. But in this water there are countless objects at different depths; and certain influences will give certain kinds of these objects an upward influence which may be intense enough and continue long enough to bring them into the upward visible layer. After the impulse ceases they commence to sink downwards."[16]

In these poetic and imaginative metaphors runs a common thread: that consciousness is a continuum through visible layers (waking consciousness) into ever deeper layers (subliminal, subconscious, and unconscious) to an unknown, perhaps infinite ground. The American psychiatrist Allan Hobson visualizes consciousness as a sphere, resembling a balloon, floating in a space with coordinates of apparently scientifically derived parameters. It resembles a Cartesian diver, coming to the surface in waking consciousness and diving deep during sleep. But the models of James, Peirce, Myers, and Janet seem to better express the unfathomable dimensions of consciousness.

These theoretical and metaphorical concepts of Fechner and James can be partially reconciled with modern concepts about consciousness. Neuroscientific research nowadays considers that consciousness is the functional product of different anatomic areas of the brain, often referred to as modules or subsystems, and that there is no single "seat of consciousness."[17] A persistent wave of electrical activity at a periodicity of about forty cycles per second has been discovered that "sweeps regularly from below the forehead to behind the nape of the neck" and appears to orchestrate consciousness from separate centers in the brain.[18] Fechner, decades before modern neurophysiology, anticipated the existence of this wave pattern involved in consciousness.

Quantum theory places consciousness into a "nonphysical dimension" where the signals between brain synapses are connected in a quantum mechanical continuity. With newer techniques of brain function measurement, there may be evidence that neural oscillations at forty cycles per second "are the most likely neural basis for consciousness itself . . . [and] are the neural basis for . . . unitive intelligence [possibly mystic experience]."[19] Theorists of quantum mechanics suggest that "revelatory" experiences may raise brain activity from $10^8$ to some $10^{12}$ bits per second.[20]

In other words, according to this theory, a mystical experience involves (as James suggested) a vast expansion of brain activity (or consciousness), recalling the oceanic metaphor and giving credence to Fechner's wave theory. William James was by no means a disciple of Fechner. When Fechner proposed a "dual perspective theory," where the same thing can be seen in two different ways, James railed at its counterintuitive character. However, Fechner's idea is quite in keeping with current interpretations of quantum theory, which accepts that the material reality depends in part on the position from which it is observed.[21]

Based on Fechner's wave theory of consciousness, William James conceived a model of the stream of thought.[22] He assumed that there was a connection of memory with all conscious moments, the metaphoric "ocean" underlying all awareness vastly larger than any instantaneous conscious state, yet connected. He then constructed a diagrammatic representation of a sentence that demonstrated his concept of the stream of thought:

> If we make a solid wood frame with the sentence written on its front, and the time scale on one of its sides, if we spread flatly a sheet of India rubber over its top, on which rectangular coordinates are painted, and slide a smooth ball under the rubber in the direction of 0 to "yesterday," the bulging of the membrane along this diagonal at successive moments will symbolize the changing of the thought's content in a way plain enough, after what has been said, to call for no more explanation. Or to express it in cerebral terms, it will show the relative intensities, at successive moments, of the several nerve-processes to which the various parts of the thought object correspond.[23]

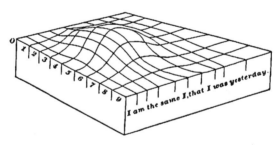

*Fig. 8.2. The stream of thought. William James constructed this topographic model of his concept of the stream of consciousness. One axis (x) represents, according to James, "the objects or contents of (the) thought"; the second axis (y) indicates "relative intensities . . . of the several neural-processes to which the various parts of the thought-object correspond"; and the third axis (z) represents time, "a finite length of thought's stream." From* The Principles of Psychology, *1:180.*

The three axes represent time, intensity, and content. The representation of a stream of thought in this model resembles a Gaussian wave, the statistical normal distribution, rising from a flat substrate that represents subconsciousness. The instantaneous conscious state changes with every moment of time.[24]

The physicist David Bohm similarly visualizes that thought and memory is a ripple upon a stream of consciousness, which itself flows in a vast ocean of the ground state.[25] The attribute common to Fechner's, James's, and Bohm's ideas is movement, the dynamic process of thought that can scarcely be captured in a static image.

How can we go further to define the mystic state in this model? A vast layer of clouds that obscures the subliminal consciousness from "waking" consciousness can also depict Fechner's threshold. The lowering or the dissipation of this threshold of clouds leads to what James considers to be the mystical process of "sudden enhancement of consciousness."[26]

Although utterly simplistic, I have diagrammed a model (fig. 8.3)

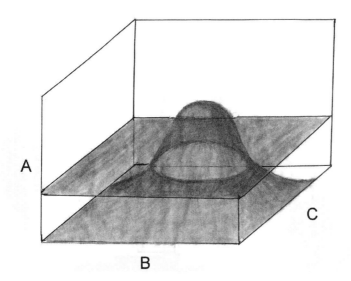

*Fig. 8.3. William James's stream of thought model revised. Axis A represents intensity, Axis B represents content, and Axis C represents time. The horizontal plane is the threshold, separating "waking" consciousness from subconscious states.*

that may also provide an easier understanding of the mystic experience and its connection with creativity. It merges all the possible manifestations of consciousness into a single Gaussian probability function that is defined by intensity, content, and time. A threshold divides "waking" consciousness from subconsciousness. The waking consciousness during sleep, for example, sinks below the threshold. A mystical or "revelatory" experience, on the other hand, vastly raises the intensity of consciousness above the threshold.

We are struggling in a dark cave, like our Paleolithic ancestors, to depict something that we feel more than we know. Models such as these can be looked upon as some sort of tool or handhold encountered in the darkness.

## Chemical or Spiritual?

What happens inside us during the extraordinary moments that have been described as mystical experiences? Can they be explained by the chemical and electrical reactions of neuronal connections? Aldous Huxley, always bold in statement, claimed:

> In one way or another, all our experiences are chemically conditioned, and if we imagine that some are purely "spiritual," purely "intellectual," purely "aesthetic," it is merely because we have never troubled to investigate the internal chemical environment at the moment of their occurrence. Furthermore, it is a matter of historical record that most contemplatives worked systematically to modify their body chemistry, with a view to creating the internal conditions favorable to spiritual insight. When they are not starving themselves into low blood sugar and vitamin deficiency, they were beating themselves into intoxication with histamine, adrenaline, and decomposed protein in uncomfortable positions in order to create the psychophysical symptoms of stress. In the intervals they sang interminable songs, thus increasing the carbon dioxide in the lungs

and the blood stream, or, if they were Orientals, they did breathing exercises to accomplish the same purpose.[27]

This was a preamble to his argument for seeking mystical experience in a much easier way, through drugs. But Huxley anticipated much that we now know scientifically of some of the preconditions for achieving such states. Yet mental and physiological stress is by no means the only path. Dr. Benson's relaxation response follows the tranquil and passive practice of meditation or the immersion into the quietness of nature. The physiological changes include decreased oxygen consumption, heart and respiratory rates, and blood pressure. The decreased sympathetic nervous system activity is associated with activation of certain areas of the limbic system, of which we will hear more. This response is considered by Benson to be an adaptive reaction protecting the body from overstress.[28]

Huxley claimed to have experienced all the transports of ecstasy by ingesting the plant extract mescaline and recommended its use in the everyday services of the Christian church. His chief critic in these extravagant and, to many, outrageous claims was the Oxford orientologist Robert Zaehner, who had this to say:

At the impressionable age of twenty I was in fact the subject of a "mystical" experience, which combined all the principal traits described in the *Doors of Perception*. When Mr. Huxley speaks of being a "Not-self in the Not-self which is a chair", I knew that, as far as the normal, rational consciousness is concerned, he is talking horrid gibberish, but I equally knew that I have myself experienced precisely this and the joy experienced as a result of this uncontrollable and inexplicable expansion of the personality is not to be brushed aside as a mere illusion. On the contrary: beside it the ordinary world of sense experience seems pathetically unreal. This occurred to me when I was an undergraduate and before I became interested in Oriental languages: it came wholly unheralded and no stimulants of any kind were involved.[29]

How do we reconcile these views? First, it is obvious that our inner neurophysiologic environment is affected in both phenomena, one artificially, the other naturally induced. What can our present neurological sciences clarify?

## Altered States of Consciousness

The brash but often perceptive Aldous Huxley may have been right, at least in part. As we have seen, there are physiologically stressful components to many of the mystical encounters described in part 1. Steven Alter had just finished a strenuous trek, Peter Matthiessen bivouacked, exhausted, during a frightening storm, and Leo Tolstoy (in the person of Levin) sweated in the repetitive mowing of wheat. But countless others have experienced similar moments of transcendence in physical states of peace and calm. Is there a common thread joining these two extremes?

Some neurophysiologic insights into these and other spiritual events can be gleaned from a recent comprehensive review by a group of European psychologists of the state of scientific knowledge about altered states of consciousness (ASC).[30] Mystical experience is referred to, often indirectly, in connection with a number of activities, including extreme environmental stress, respiratory maneuvers, sensory deprivation, relaxation, and meditation. This underscores the difficult and limited understanding of the nebulous phenomenon that is mysticism.

Near-Death Experience (NDE) is, of course, an episode generally involving extreme stress that can lead to a number of remembered perceptions including peacefulness, out-of-body experience, dark tunnel experience, photism, hearing of music, slowing of time, and speeding of thought. Naturally NDE cannot be reproduced experimentally, but analogous experiments can reproduce some of the features of NDE.

According to the investigators, cerebral hypoxia (low oxygen levels in the brain) may be a principal consequence of near-terminal life events that can deplete neurotransmitter reserves in the limbic system, thus leading to auditory and visual hallucinations, but also feelings of peace and calm. Some of these perceptions occur in a variety of mystical experiences, stressed or not.[31]

An ASC listed by the authors that does not appear to involve stressful situations is meditation (which is actually a technique, not a state of consciousness). But meditation may involve deliberate breathing exercises that can result in varying blood pH levels (acidity and alkalinity) due to the depletion or increased levels of carbon dioxide. These changes can affect the brain and lead to perceptions of tranquillity, unitive feelings, and so on. The precise neurophysiologic mechanisms are still unknown.[32]

Perhaps closer to a psychobiological explanation of mystical experience are data that come from studies of sensory deprivation. Such experiments have been performed on subjects who volunteer to be in conditions of total absence of sensory input, such as in total darkness and in flotation tanks at body temperature.

As the reader may recall, the mystical drawings of Paleolithic people were created deep inside caves, raising questions whether sensory deprivation was part of a ritual or custom to reach the numinous creativity and spirituality that may have been found serendipitously in earlier cave explorations. Modern cavers have reported similar magical feelings. Indeed, the trancelike states that I have described, and other "quiet" moments of ecstatic revelation, may follow the deliberate or spontaneous cutting off of "psychic noise," the state of apophasis that is also part of meditation techniques.

The results of the sensory deprivation experiments included reduction of blood epinephrine levels (a sympathomimetic hormone) and increase of beta-endorphin levels (an enkephalin mediating certain centers in the limbic system and pretemporal cortex). These, among other changes, may lead to the observed improvements in memory performance, decreased anxiety, and increase in vigor, curiosity, and creativity, as determined by various psychological tests. Of interest, as well, was the appearance of different forms of photism (see section on photism).[33]

The relaxation-response techniques of Herbert Benson show results that often are similar to those following sensory deprivation experiments.

During meditation an increased activity of limbic neurotransmitters may occur, just as was found in the sensory depletion experiments. According to Arnold Mandell, late psychiatry professor at the University of California at San Diego, such activity leads to a decrease of serotonin regulation of the limbic structures, thus releasing effectual and cognitive processes characteristic of mystical ecstasy.[34] It has also been discovered that opioid receptor sites are concentrated in the limbic system and the closely connected frontal lobes of the cerebrum.[35]

The pharmacologist Avram Goldstein studied the "thrill" experienced by students listening to music. He was able to block that thrill in a significant number of participants by administering naloxone, a blocker of opiate action. This suggests that even the ecstasy of hearing music is mediated, at least in part, by the release of endorphin peptides.*[36]

A major effect of these chemical signals may be the process of deafferentation (a cutoff of incoming information). If a neural complex is subjected to deafferentation, it may fire according to its own "inner logic."[37] Through this process a reverberating circuit may occur in the limbic system, essentially closed from cerebral signals, that can lead to a feeling of "absolute unitary being" similar to the feeling of a "greater reality than that of the everyday world" described by William James.[38] Once experienced, that feeling may be sought again and again, as the writer Proust and the weight lifter Vlasov poignantly described. Such natural ecstasies and drug-induced states may surprisingly resemble each other.

Arnold Mandell contends that certain cells in the hippocampus initiate the mental events resulting in ecstasy (fig. 8.4). The hippocampus, among its other functions, integrates two neurological circuits: one is

---

*Goldstein uses the word *thrill* to describe the emotions of hearing music. That word can fit into my broad glossary of synonyms for the mystical experience.

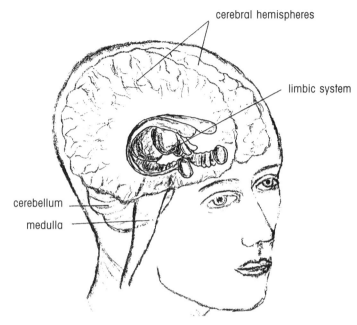

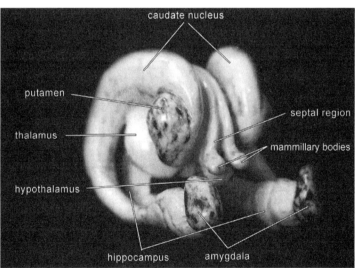

*Fig. 8.4. The human brain and its "limbic" system, flanked by the basal ganglia. The main divisions of the brain are shown. At the base of the forebrain are a number of complex, quaintly named, and oddly shaped structures, which form a sort of coordinated or "limbic" system that has been referred to in the past as the visceral brain. They include the sea-horse (hippocampus), the almonds (amygdala), the lower room (hypothalamus), and other smaller components.*

the external information flow, which may be referred to as the "external circuit"; the other receives relevant subjective information from other parts of the brain and is called the "internal circuit." Following stress or other stimuli, the external circuit may be blocked by enkephalins and the internal circuit is amplified so that it becomes the only source of information. When the external circuit is closed "there arises an experience of peace, calm and even ecstasy."[39]

This feeling of tranquillity following a mystical experience results in a physiological state often manifested by reduced rates of breathing and heartbeat. It originates from autonomic neural activity mediated through the actions of neurotransmitters such as dopamine and the endorphins.

In psychological terms, according to the Jungian psychologist Manisha Roy, this closure of the external and enhancement of the internal circuit may lead in the individual to an overwhelming awareness of the self, following submission of the ego.[40]

## Photism

Enhancements or distortions of light and color are frequent in ecstatic experiences. Typical expressions are: "a flash of light," "there was light everywhere," "luminous." Saul, later the apostle Paul, on his fateful journey to Damascus encountered a "blinding light, stronger than the sun," which led to his conversion to be a disciple of Jesus (Acts 22:6). Extraordinary light was part of my own experience and that of others cited by one of William James's main critics, the psychologist James Leuba: "Few of the lesser trance-phenomena are more striking and incontestably wholly physiological in origin than a peculiar appearance of light or brilliance which may be called photism. The mystics frequently use the word 'light,' but it is not always possible to know whether they use it in a symbolical or in a realistic sense. In a great number of instances, however, the perceptual quality of the experience cannot be doubted." Leuba could not have known, however, of the neurological basis of photism in 1929 when his book was published.[41]

Ansel Adams, too, experienced a "pointed awareness of light," (see page 1) whereas the young Wordsworth was transported when "An auxiliary light / Came to my mind which on the setting sun / Bestowed new splendor . . ."[42] Nietzsche, in a moment of creative ecstasy, described in *Ecce Homo* the perception of "A superabundance of light."[43]

Bill Wilson, the founder of Alcoholics Anonymous, describes a striking example of photism. He had been struggling with depression and alcoholism for years and was at the edge of a spiritual abyss. He was in a state of "complete, absolute surrender" when:

> Suddenly, my room blazed with an indescribably white light. I was seized with an ecstasy beyond description. Every joy I had known was pale by comparison. The light—I was conscious of nothing else for a time. . . . I know not how long I remained in that state, but finally the light and the ecstasy subsided. . . . As I became quieter, a great peace stole over me, and this was accompanied by a sensation difficult to describe. I became acutely conscious of a Presence, which seemed like a veritable sea of living spirit. I lay on the shores of a new world.[44]

Bill Wilson never took another drink and went on to found AA.

The American nature writer Bill McKibben had an extraordinary epiphany after he was attacked by a swarm of wasps while walking through a forest. As possibly dangerous hives developed on his skin, some inner power intervened: "The panic gave way, though, to the most remarkable set of emotions I can recall." The details of his surroundings came into sharp focus. He felt a deep gratitude for all being: "it was as if I were part of all this . . . everything seemed clear and nobler and complete."[45] This luminous state resembled that of Ansel Adams, "I saw more clearly than I have ever seen before or since" (see page 1). McKibben's experience is surely related to the physiological and emotional shock of the wasp attack and the resultant urticaria. Some powerful force triggered the mystical experience, akin to other physiological states of exhaustion such as in the case of Peter Matthiessen.

One of the distinguishing aspects of what the psychiatrist Stanley Dean calls the ultraconscious summit is this extraordinary awareness of light. Dean quotes from Whitman's *Leaves of Grass:* "Light rare, untellable, lighting the very light—beyond all scopes, descriptions, languages." And from Dante's *The Divine Comedy:* "The light I saw was like a blazing river . . . / Fixing my gaze upon the Eternal Light / I saw within its depths, / Bound up with love together in one volume, / The scattered leaves of all the universe."[46]

Photism has also been called "the white light experience" and "light-of-the-void."[47] The psychologist Harry Hunt suggests that meditation may allow the visual field to be more accessible to direct experience. Thus visual perception can be enhanced in meditative and other mystic states, as born out by the experiences already cited.

The association of visual phenomena with ecstatic experiences may relate to a second path of visual perception in the brain that is modulated through the superior colliculus of the thalamus, and which has been called thalamic vision. It is conceivable that as a surge of enkephalins block incoming impulses to the midbrain, the visual cortex signals are thus reduced and the more primitive visual pathway predominates, resulting in the various perceptions of light and color that have been described.[48] This second visual system, according to neurologist James Austin, may have appeared early in evolution.[49] It is more developed in primitive monkeys than in modern primates. The signals from the retina go directly to the superior colliculi through the pulvinar of the thalamus, and finally to the cortex. There may be an evolutionary advantage in that the signals are processed in the midbrain. In other words, no thinking is necessary for a reflexive avoidance of danger. The phenomenon of photism may also be related to that of "blind sight," which is involved in midbrain pathways. Electrical stimulation of the amygdaloid complex, too, has been shown to produce vivid visual hallucinations.[50]

There are other visual manifestations of mystical states that verge on pathological states. Some of these have been associated with creative activities of Neolithic hunters in interpretations by the anthropologists David Lewis-Williams and David Pearce.[51] They assembled a number of experiences by apparently normal individuals that appear to be hallucinatory, that go beyond the visual perception of enhanced or altered light in mystical moments. These images include bright geometric patterns, sensations of floating or flying, passage through a tunnel, and so forth. Many resemble the hallucinations frequently described with Near-Death Experiences and have been termed hypnogogia.

Flying over the Atlantic, fatigued and sleep-deprived, Charles Lindbergh experienced a peculiar sense of vision: "There is no limit to my sight—my skull is one great eye, seeing everywhere at once." The neurologist James Austin calls this "ambient vision," an unbounded sense that "may be a true ground to space." It is, he claims, a result of circuitries connecting to a preconscious space that is brought to awareness through stress or meditative absorption.[52] Perhaps this relates to the all-seeing eyeball of Emerson and to hallucinations such as the délok* of my childhood near drowning, a phenomenon called autoscopy.

Although they can also be reproduced by the intake of hallucinogens, the experiences that the authors describe came spontaneously from normal individuals, but many of whom may have been under extreme mental and/or physical stress.

## Ohm's Law Analogy

Our waking consciousness is normally filled with millions of "bits" of information: what appointments do I have today? Who was that girl I

---

*The Tibetan word *délok* means returned from the dead and often refers to a person who has had a near-death experience.

saw last night? Where are my socks? All these are enough to daily fill a book or more by James Joyce. Wipe out that data by one or another method and you have a sort of cerebral vacuum—in other words, a loss of resistance, which in physical terms can be measured electrically as ohms.

Ohm's Law of electricity states that resistance (R) is inversely proportional to current (A): $R = V/A$ where V is voltage or potential. Experience tells both the hunter and meditator that an enhanced perception comes during moments of the hunter's or meditator's trance: the sky is brighter; the focus is sharper; the thoughts that eventually flood back are remarkably deeper, and energy, fortitude, and endurance seem to be greater. In other words, as our psychic resistance, a product of mental clutter and superfluous information, diminishes, the flow of psychic current increases.

We can stretch this analogy further through the physical phenomenon of superconductivity. Normally a current of electrons flowing through a conducting material such as metal meets a resistance R that, according to Ohm's Law, impedes the current flow. By cooling the conductor sufficiently one can achieve a state where resistance drops to nearly zero and the flow of current is no longer impeded. This is known to be due to the stopping (like freezing) of vibrating atoms in the lattice of the structure of the conducting material. As R nears zero, the possible flow of current approaches infinity.

In the analogy, mental resistance can be "cooled" sufficiently by quenching the neural circuits that impede the internal flow of conscious thought between the hippocampus and cerebrum. In this way mental superconductivity, if it exists, can lead to superconsciousness, an untrammeled flow of internal neural impulses that can lead to extraordinary enlightenment and creativity. Indeed, the core of mystical experience may be pure consciousness, emptied of sensory and cognitive content.

The physicist and writer Alan Lightman gives another analogy. After a great struggle in solving a physics problem he suddenly and spontaneously reached an ecstatic moment of creativity in finding its solution, very similarly to that described by Freud (see page 136) and Andrew Wiles (see page 144). "Something strange was happening to my mind . . . I felt weightless . . . I had absolutely no sense of myself . . . I was simply spirit, in a state of pure exhilaration." He then went on to compare his state of mind to a loss of frictional drag when sailing a boat. At a certain point, when the hull lifts out of the water, the boat is "planing" as the drag approaches near zero.*[53]

Taoistic mystical practice repeatedly invokes apophasis (the emptying out of mundane consciousness)† in order to reach the Way, Tao, the unitive experience leading to wisdom. It is "sweeping out the mind" to reach inner power, te.

Swedenborg, as many other religious mystics, considered that the disciple should empty his soul to become a vessel to receive the divinity of revelation.

This apophasis, the void of being, relates in a curious way to a concept of quantum theory that is called quantum vacuum. As David Peat describes it, the condition for achieving a perfect vacuum is to empty a space completely of energy. This is a ground state of pure cosmic emptiness. Yet, according to quantum mechanics theory, within "incredibly tiny intervals of time" particles can flow in and out of that space, exchange identities, and create a huge amount of energy, to the absolutely incredible point where "the energy within a cubic centimeter of the vacuum state would vastly exceed the energy content of the universe."[54] Consciousness, too, can be considered "empty," with no shape or form, yet containing incredible mental processes. The theologian Robert Forman terms consciousness as "empty plenitude."[55]

---

*Alan Lightman considered that ecstatic moment as a central one in his life. It conforms to a mystic state as defined by the criteria that William James applied.

†*Apophasis* has several meanings, but when used in a philosophical or religious sense, it is a negation or emptying out (from the Greek "to deny" or "to say no") as in so-called negative or apophatic theology, which relates to the *via negativa* of ancient philosophy. A related expression, *exinanition,* often referring to Jesus's crucifixion, means an emptying out of the spirit, desolation, enfeeblement, or exhaustion. The distinction I seek to show is the positive spiritual action of emptying out the mind, at least temporarily, of the cobwebs and dust of the cerebral noise that besets us all in daily life.

Into that vacuum of apophasis can come the energy of love, meaning a union that gives a state of freedom, unshackled from the bonds of hate, prejudice, and ignorance.

## Neurotheology

Beginning with Mandell's pioneering monograph, *Toward a Psychology of Transcendence: God in the Brain,* presented in 1978, a discipline called "neurotheology" has been growing. Other titles, based primarily on discoveries in neurobiology and neuropharmacology, include *Religion in the Minds, Why God Won't Go Away,* and *The Mystical Mind: Probing the Biology of Religious Experience.* In essence they argue that the perception of God arises in our brain.

Modern diagnostic techniques such as PET (photon emission tomography) and SPECT (single photon emission computed tomography) can detect real-time changes in the brain's metabolism during various mental exercises by following the alterations of blood flow in various parts of the brain. These dynamic studies and our new knowledge of neurochemistry have revealed the location of the sites of the brain involved in meditative exercises, and in other conditions that can be termed mystical or religiously ecstatic.

The SPECT studies by the neuroscientists Eugene D'Aquili and Anthony Newberg and others of individuals in active meditation indicate that the prefrontal cortical area has increased blood flow, evidently related to neural activity, while, simultaneously, the portion of parietal cortex known as the orientation association area has decreased blood flow. This suggests to the authors that, while sensory input is blocked, the internal circuit relating the prefrontal cortex to the limbic system operates in the possibly "reverberating" mode suggested by Mandell, which may evoke "ecstatic and blissful" feelings.[56]

Newberg and D'Aquili believe that mystic experience can occur when both the sympathetic and parasympathetic neurohumoral (chemically transmitted) systems are subjected to high levels of prolonged and intense physical activity such as the prolonged concentration or repetitive motion seen in running or mountain climbing.

But these brain scans are still relatively crude ways of measuring the incredibly detailed complexity of the mind. They merely reflect changes in blood flow, an indirect indicator of neural activity, in a limited variety of mental states under laboratory conditions. I wonder what a brain scan of Ansel Adams would show, on that memorable morning climbing Mount Clark, or of Paul on the road to Damascus?

The "pointer readings" (of measuring instruments) of Eddington are now dominating modern neurobiology. The plotting of electrochemical activity in the brain during mystical/religious experiences is providing a vast new array of information. But for what purpose? The Harvard teacher and authority on William James, Eugene Taylor, is concerned about the facile correlation of neurological measurements, including EEG (electroencephalography) and MEG (magneto encephalography), with religious experiences and invokes one of James's caveats regarding interpretation of the "pointer readings." James distinguishes between "existential judgment" and "spiritual judgment." One does not readily translate into the other.[57] Taylor continues, stating that, "Neurology can tell us no more about the reality of religious experience, or any other form of experience, than its mechanics." In other words, Taylor maintains that human experience, particularly religious experience, is beyond scientific interpretation.

This is not necessarily true and is illustrated by Austin's approach to the neurological basis of mystic experience. As a neurologist he painstakingly correlates neurological information with the experiences of Zen practices, particularly meditation. The neurochemical pathways can be traced that transmit and receive the emotional feelings of mystical experience. Even Aldous Huxley predicted this. But in the end reductionism is currently limited in delineating the transcendence of that experience into a dimension that is beyond the powers of our description.

Another question has recently entered the neurotheology arena: Is the perception of God inherited? Is the ability to have a deeply religious or spiritual experience handed down in our genes? Population surveys, some of which have been cited in this book, show that nearly 50 percent of surveyed individuals have recognized such experiences in themselves. If these studies predict that between one-third and one-half of individuals are "spiritual," then why are the others not? Is it because of the presence or absence of an inherited trait or is it because of the presence or absence of cultural conditioning?

Take the topic of this book, nature mysticism. William James, among others, states, "Certain aspects of nature seem to have a peculiar power of awakening . . . mystical moods." Most of the "striking cases" that James collected to illustrate his chapter on mysticism in *Varieties* came from "out of doors."[58] Is it possible, therefore, that as the world population continues its move into urban communities, approaching soon two-thirds of all humanity, we will experience further alienation from our natural world and consequently lose further the opportunities for spiritual experience?

The same question may be raised with organized religion. If suddenly or gradually the places of worship and the religious traditions within families disappeared (as they did in Russia and are doing in many "advanced" cultures), then the religious experience of the affected population and its descendants could wither away. The question remains then: how much is nature and how much is nurture?

One investigator, Dean Hamer, geneticist at the National Institutes of Health, claims to show that it is nature in at least two-thirds of individuals in a particular study. In his book *The God Gene: How Faith Is Hardwired into Our Genes,* Hamer provides a background on the question of the origins of spiritual experience. But there are few facts to support the title. Supposedly there is at least one gene that is associated with spirituality that was determined through a "self-transcendence scale" in a questionnaire to 1,001 college student volunteers.

This "God gene" is one that codes for a monoamine transporter, a protein that controls certain neurotransmitters, "the same brain chemicals that can be triggered by certain drugs that can bring about mystical experience."[59]

Although 47 percent of the subjects were identified to be in a "higher spirituality" group, there are no figures to demonstrate how Hamer associates this group with a higher preponderance of one particular gene. Further, the question of a causal relationship would have to be answered. Much remains to be done.

## Pathological States

There is a state of mind that Thomas Merton refers to as "false mysticism."[60] He cites the example of Hitler and the Nazi philosophy of racial purity, Nordic superiority, and peculiar, primitive nature worship. In addition to other examples by Merton, I can think of numerous ones where false gods blind the minds of human beings by ecstatic promises of eternity, power, and nirvana. It appears that the intellect can be smothered by forms of mob psychology and by hypnotic, charismatic soothsayers. This can lead what appear to be perfectly normal individuals to destroy themselves as a nation, as with Nazi Germany, a cult such as that in Jonestown, and less often as individuals. The entire drug culture fits here. The independence of the mystic is then lost in a mindless collectivization of the masses.

William James had a term for this dark side of our psyche, diabolical mysticism, which he defined as "a sort of religious mysticism turned upside down."[61] According to him this can represent a pathological state of subliminal or transmarginal consciousness. It is associated with paranoid psychoses and what Hunt terms racial occultism, as characterized by the Nazi ideologies, and associated with the more primitive mammalian and reptilian recesses of our brain.[62] This may explain the mindless mass psychoses of hundreds, thousands, and millions of presumably rational human beings being drawn into the self-destructive consequences of succumbing to the charisma of false mystics such as Hitler, Jim Jones, and others throughout history.

The term *mysticism* is used as a pejorative by Reg Morrison to describe the irrationality, inherited delusions of ethnic superiority, religious justification for self-destruction, and anthropocentrism of humanity. His thesis is that mysticism has been the cause of major wars, genocides, and ultimately will bring "a human plague," resulting in the sudden demise of our civilization. He describes "a vital streak of insanity in an increasing rational brain" that has led our race to where it is today through an inherited mystical dimension that is beyond rational comprehension.[63]

Morrison's thesis gives thought, however, to the dark side of mystic experience, the "false mysticism" of Merton. Where does our behavior, mediated through evolutionary changes of our psyche, lead?

## Drugs and Mystical Experience

Thus after a brief review of recent developments in neurochemistry and psychobiology we have come full circle back to the mystical experience of ecstasy. It is presumptuous, perhaps even sacrilegious, to attempt to explain this human experience, the root of religious feeling, by a diagram of electrical and chemical circuits in our brain. However, there is a connection to a disturbing and worldwide problem of immense importance: drug-induced ecstasy. An understanding of the neural mechanisms of mystical experience may someday lead to better ways of coping with the global epidemic of substance abuse.

We know that humankind has used drugs since the earliest times to induce transcendental feeling. Poppies, mushrooms, cacti, cocoa leaves, betel nut, cannabis, tobacco, and other plants, plus alcohol, have all been used in religious rites and as sources for that misused term *recreation*. The road from use to abuse and addiction follows a vision of paradise —an ecstatic experience—after ingesting something that can be grown, extracted, brewed, and bought. It leads, however, down a steepening slope and a point of no return. My main guide, William James, himself experimented with laughing gas, nitrous oxide, and induced in himself a form of ecstasy:

Nitrous oxide and ether, especially nitrous oxide, when sufficiently diluted with air, stimulate the mystical consciousness in an extraordinary degree. Depth beyond depth of truth seems revealed to the inhaler. This truth fades out, however, or escapes, at the moment of coming to; and if any words remain over in which it seemed to clothe itself, they prove to be the veriest nonsense. Nevertheless, the sense of a profound meaning having been there persists; and I know more than one person who is persuaded that in the nitrous oxide trance we have genuine metaphysical revelation.

Some years ago I myself made some observations on this aspect of nitrous oxide intoxication, and reported them in print. One conclusion was forced on my mind at that time, and my impression of its truth has ever since remained unshaken. It is that our waking consciousness, rational consciousness as we call it, is but one special type of consciousness, whilst all about it, parted from it by the filmiest of screens, there lie potential forms of consciousness entirely different. We may go through life without suspecting their existence; but apply the requisite stimulus, and at a touch they are there in all their completeness, definite types of mentality that probably somewhere have their field of application and adaptation. No account of the universe in its totality can be final which leaves these other forms of consciousness quite disregarded.[64]

This remarkable experience, reported by a courageous and honest scientist, psychologist, and philosopher, was followed by the claims of numerous experimenters of psychedelic drugs, in recent years notably by Aldous Huxley and Timothy Leary. The latter, an enthusiastic proselytizer for the benefits of LSD, stirred a whole generation with his slogan of "tune in, turn on, and drop out."[65] Reading him now leaves in me hardly any residue. His words seem to me largely meaningless, and his conclusions, empty. The bold and pioneering experimental approach by William James, however, answers many questions that lie at the heart of our search for meaning and is an example of his genius.[66]

Although Huxley and Leary believed drug experiences could be equated with ecstasy, there are many who disagree. Krishnamurti, a leader of the Theosophical movement, asks: "What is the necessity of taking drugs at all—drugs that promise a psychedelic expansion of the mind, great visions and intensity? Apparently one takes them because one's own perceptions are dull. Clarity is dimmed and one's life is rather shallow, mediocre and meaningless; one takes them to go beyond mediocrity."

The Zen Buddhists, such as Shubuyama, also declare their disapproval: "Recently there have been people who talk about instant enlightenment, or those who take drugs in an attempt to experience satori [enlightenment]. Whatever claims they make, I declare that such approaches are not authentic true Zen at all."[67]

From my own limited experience I would not wish to alter the circumstances, the unforgettable moments, and the feelings of certainty of the few ecstasies most of us are likely to have. The English writer Marghanita Laski estimates that the average number of ecstasies experienced by normal individuals in a lifetime is six. The capacity to experience them diminishes with age, reflecting the diminution of neurotransmitters in the aging process.[68] This naturally induced phenomenon, although not readily attained, often unexpected and thus more precious in its delight, is a revelation of the inner self. As a scientist, however, I seek to explain it in familiar terms, in our language of critical reason. I can visualize the process as one of circuits relating to the inner self, to the managing ego and to incoming signals from the external world. Feedback loops serve to stabilize and equilibrate, yet certain conditions can lead to a dampening of the external circuit, allowing me to know my innermost being momentarily; other signals then automatically quench that moment of self-awareness, as if to say, "that is enough for now." Thus our own natural homeostatic mechanisms that balance us physically and mentally are normally in charge and help to preserve our integrity. This does not occur for drug-induced ecstasy. No enzymatic action appears to effectively terminate the attachment of opiate molecules to limbic neuroreceptors. This consequently leads to conditions of drug dependence and addiction.*[69]

A *New York Times* article from 1998 reported that the National Institute of Drug Abuse estimated that there were four million drug addicts in the United States, two million to three million that were hooked on cocaine. Another 800,000 were heroin addicts. The article said that our government would spend $3.2 billion in 1998 to treat addicts. Other costs, for prevention, drug-related crime, and lost productivity, would total more than $60 billion a year. Dr. Alan Leshner, director of the institute, believed that chemical methods of prevention appeared promising: "We have come to understand how every drug of abuse works in the brain," he stated. "We've identified receptors in the brain and cloned them. We know the circuits that they activate and we know some of the common elements that may relate to addiction."[70]

Dr. George Bigelow, psychiatrist at Johns Hopkins, says that much recent research has focused on the neurotransmitter dopamine. Many drugs of abuse, including cocaine, amphetamine, opiates, marijuana, and nicotine, act on the dopamine system in the midbrain. Bigelow thinks that there is a potential problem with drugs that target the dopamine system. "It might be the final common pathway for all kinds of rewarding things, food, sex, and the joys of music and art," he says. "So it's probably not a pathway we want to eliminate. We need to find a way to block cocaine and let people enjoy other rewards."[71] Even then it may not take care of the cravings that former users feel, often many years after they have quit.

It now appears that a "reward circuitry" operates via a dopamine pathway from the ventral tegmental area just above the hippocampus to the nucleus accumbens, in front of the amygdalae and deep beneath the frontal cortex. The amygdalae are involved in assessing the degree

---

*The Vietnam War resulted in widespread use of heroin or some other form of opium among combat soldiers. Follow-up research showed that less than 10 percent used drugs after returning home. Less than 2 percent persisted in their habit. These data are encouraging in exploring factors of causation and prevention of drug abuse.

of pleasure and sending signals to the hippocampus, which fixes the memories of that experience.[72]

"One thing that makes addiction so difficult is that there is a big learning basis, and we don't have any way of making it go away," Dr. Bigelow says. "People learn to get high by using drugs, and they never forget the experience. It's a burden that addicts carry for life. To me, that's one of the strongest arguments for prevention, and for avoiding even experimental use," he says, "because you risk having experiences that you don't forget and that continue to control and manipulate you in ways you do not want."[73]

Why do people turn to drugs in increasing numbers in America and much of the so-called developed world? Many have argued that every human being is born with an innate drive to experience altered states of consciousness periodically. This drive has been equated with some as the instinct for religious experience. It is possible, therefore, that the attenuation of religious and spiritual feeling in our present era leaves a vacuum for this innate need. Indeed, Andrew Weil, champion of holistic medicine and Harvard Medical School graduate, maintained that, "I and many of my friends would never have thought about meditation, higher levels of consciousness, or spiritual matters if we had not been in contact with the drug subculture and had been through phases of meaningful use of marihuana and hallucinogens."[74] I believe, from hearing him recently, that he regrets that statement now, in his middle and perhaps wiser age.

Michael Ziegler, a rabbi and psychologist, writes about psychedelic religious experiences and urges that humanity today is in need of "powerful medicines" that can reawaken the creative capacity to find new ways to live, with ourselves, with others, and with the planet.[75] Certainly. But Rabbi Ziegler refers to "entheogens" as drugs for "sacred use" in the postmodern era. Is humanity so weak and undeveloped that it must rely on such crutches to achieve the mystical state of mind? Ziegler's statement is cogent, but the "powerful medicine" for me is a big dose of renewal of our sacred bond with nature.

The striking similarities of drug-induced and spontaneous ecstasy have led to other, perhaps less practical solutions to substance abuse. The Hare Krishna movement, for example, appears to substitute chanting for drugs. Other less bizarre solutions must frequently occur. Religious conversion, the learning of meditation, and intense absorption in creative processes have been frequent solutions for reformed addicts.

It seems, however, that the ultimate solution to the drug problems presently can only come from prevention. To accomplish this is seemingly impossible in today's world. Yet I hope that through education, both secular and religious, more people can come to know the incredibly rich resource of ecstatic experience that is available to all, uncovering a new dimension in one's life, and making the need for artificial methods unnecessary.

## PART THREE

# Ecocrisis and Spiritual Necessity

# 9 ECOCRISIS

*For the most part, our society remains embedded in the
Western worldview, which isolates us from the natural
community and leaves us spiritually alienated from
nonhuman life. We have created for ourselves a profound
and imperiling loneliness.*

RICHARD NELSON,
*SEARCHING FOR THE LOST ARROW*

*We cannot win this battle to save species and environments
without forging an emotional bond between ourselves and
nature—for we will not fight to save what we do not love.*

STEPHEN JAY GOULD,
*NATURAL HISTORY*

## The Human Impact

We human beings take up so little space in this world. Calculations
show, according to E. O. Wilson, that our entire present world population of 6.8 billion individuals could be stacked, like cordwood, out
of sight in a corner of the Grand Canyon![1] Yet what we do to our
environment, through all our agriculture, tools, devices, chemicals,

factories, and other paraphernalia, have already affected the world climate and littered or altered the global surface. Scarcely a single view out the window of a jetliner, with the help of binoculars, will not show some souvenir of humanity's presence. This is, indeed, a gigantic footprint.

The loss of natural habitat and the increase of population and industrialization are combining to create a kindling point of global crisis. As the population increases, so will the conditions for disease and war, as surely as those seen in imprisoned primate colonies and with encaged rats. As ecological demise continues, fossil fuel resources will continue for a few hundred more years, an iota of global evolution but a precarious junction for humankind.

See what is happening to our glorious and verdant forests that have bedecked our global terra firma, that were at their maximum dimensions about eight thousand years ago, the beginning of humanity's agricultural era. Now, less than one-half of the world's forests remain, with the rate of destruction particularly severe in the past fifty years. Edward Wilson estimates that the number of species disappears by the fourth root of forest area—which means that when the habitat declines to one-tenth of the original area, there follows an extinction of one half of the species of fauna and flora.[2] The global warming factors continue with increasing levels of methane, carbon dioxide, carbon soot, and sulfates in our atmosphere. The ozone depletion at the polar caps continues although finally atmospheric chlorofluorocarbons are diminishing. How far will anthropogenic interference go in disturbing our climate? A critical point may be near.

Recently a three-kilometer-thick blanket of smog, consisting of aerosols, ash, soot, and other particles that originate from burning forests, crop wastes, and fossil fuels, was detected overlying the Indian Ocean. The darkly ominous smog appears to have originated from heavily populated areas of the Indian subcontinent, among the most polluted areas in the world. Such a cloud, according to the UN Environment Program, can travel halfway around the world in a week. The likely consequences of such a gigantic smog layer include decreased surface temperatures, geographically varied extremes of rainfall and drought, and respiratory illness of all breathing creatures. It has been estimated by Nobel Laureate Paul Crutzen that up to two million people in India alone are dying prematurely per year from atmospheric pollution.[3] Such a "blanket" of smog actually retards global warming through the "parasol" effect. Thus it represents a "coiled spring" which may pop out like a jack-in-the-box if and when the world begins to control atmospheric pollution. The acceleration of global warming can then be rapid and amount to an increased mean global temperature rise of as much as two degrees Centigrade.

The reduction of the ozone layer and the greenhouse effect are also combining and leading to a drastic alteration of our environment. Rising ocean levels will drown out low-lying islands of several Pacific and Indian Ocean cultures within this century. Montana's Glacier National Park will soon be glacierless, all 150 glaciers totally gone within thirty years. It is predicted that by 2030, nearly two-thirds of the world's population will be living in the urban world.[4] At the same time, because of population needs, our natural resources, including available fresh water, are steadily diminishing.

Look at the plight of the Aral Sea in Central Asia, once the world's fourth largest inland body of water. It will totally disappear, all sixty thousand square kilometers, according to current predictions, by 2015. The gradual disappearance has been caused by decades of misguided irrigation and other agricultural schemes. It has been called an unprecedented anthropogenic impact on nature. Similar changes are occurring in the magnificent Lake Chad. Are the Great Lakes in the United States far behind?

Will it all end as it did on Easter Island (Rapa Nui)? Once a thriving creative civilization, it destroyed itself by cutting down every tree, thus terminating its obsessive program of building and transporting the *moai,* the great statues that now stand or lie scattered in silent condemnation of an unthinking society. Without our advantages of hindsight, the human society of Rapa Nui gradually and obliviously committed cultural suicide.

There is an increasing interest in the history and fate of the Easter Islanders, for the simple reason that what happened to them could happen to us. As Jared Diamond wrote in the *New York Review of Books,* "Easter Island is as isolated in the Pacific as the Earth is today in space."[5] The comparison between the fate of Easter Island and our present civilization is "chillingly obvious."

Population pressures are also leading to increased disease and strife. Africa, for example, has several examples of regional devastation by AIDS, malaria, war, and genocide. If this trend continues and expands, there will be a bleak future for humanity—unbelievable suffering from disease, starvation, and war.

Who could imagine that once pristine urban areas such as the San Francisco Bay Region with generally prevailing westerly winds could be overcome at times by smog blankets? The large cities of Asia and South America are seen now from the air covered by immense brown layers extending many miles beyond their borders. Many rivers of Russia and China flow yellow and green with chemical wastes. Lakes and glaciers are disappearing all over the world. The immense solid green expanse of the Amazonian Basin as seen from the air is shorn by great swathes of yellow deforestation. The foothills of northern India and Nepal are, like shorn sheep, denuded of trees. I have seen these changes.

It is simplistic perhaps to call for a "return to nature," yet what alternatives exist? Humanity's connection to our mother, nature, has withered. Whole generations of human beings in this world have scarcely seen a forest, a valley in flower, or a wild animal. But there is a spiritual memory in all of us that, if given the opportunity, can renew the kinship—biophilia—whereby our consciousness and conscience unite again with nature in harmonic balance. That inherited memory cannot be lost in the short era of the industrial and population explosion. But the move toward increased nature consciousness has many conflicting viewpoints and critics. There are a variety of cults and beliefs in the supernatural—beliefs that many consider irrational and unfounded in science. One outspoken critic of the "back to nature movement" is the American Marxist philosopher Murray Bookchin. He writes:

> The new surrogate "reality" that is becoming a widespread feature in our time percolates through the mass media and the publishing industry, which are only too eager to nourish, even celebrate the proliferation of wiccan covens, Goddess-worshipping congregations, assorted pantheistic and animistic cults, "wilderness" devotees and ecofeminist acolytes.[6]

It appears that Bookchin denies any reality but that coming through the rational intellect. He particularly takes to task the "mystical ecologists" for their desire to return to primitivism, the "Noble savage," and the Pleistocene.

As we increasingly realize, the era of the ancient hunting societies was marked with the devastating attenuation and disappearance of wild game. Bookchin calls these ancient hunters "predatory opportunists . . . no less than wolves or coyotes . . . ," and he assails the romantic image of ancient humanity and the desires of some New Age movements to return to "the mystical path of oneness with nature" and to the "timeless, ahistorical misty island of the Lotus Eaters."[7] Indeed, there now is ample evidence for the elimination of large numbers of animal species during the reign of the Paleolithic hunter, the loss of forests in the agricultural era, and the depletion of many other natural resources into modern times.

There are those who seek and sometimes live the primitive life, who practice ancient rites in the effort to merge with the spirit of Gaia. But it seems likely that the majority of nature lovers have developed, in apparent contrast to materialistic thinkers such as Bookchin, an emotional bond that is essential, as Gould states, to catalyze the rational actions needed to preserve our environment.

That emotional bond to nature through spiritual experience can be our salvation when joined by reason, the powerful intellectual tool of *Homo sapiens.* Reason is our resource of rational enlightenment with its tremendous gifts of science, history, hindsight, and common sense.

The spiritual bond with nature that comes through pure experience is a permanent memory, as deeply imprinted as was the recollection of that climb up Mount Clark by Ansel Adams ("Something is changed forever"). This unitary feeling is charged with emotional content, the logic of the heart that we belong to the earth and that it is part of us like the romantic and erotic connection to a lover. We would do anything to protect that person and preserve the relationship.

## Philosophic Reason

To express and elaborate on this connection, the Norwegian philosopher and "deep" ecologist Arne Naess introduced *ecosophy* (Greek *oikos,* "house," and *sophia,* "wisdom") as a term to express the comprehensive understanding about the foundation of life on Earth.[8] The emotional content of these terms comes from the process of identification of human beings with all life. This deep connection with nature is seen, as Wilson claims in *Biophilia,* innate, inherited, and hardwired into our genes. Naess makes a connection between our love of life on this planet to our responsibility to nurture it. The spiritual component of ecosophy is met by the need we all appear to have for self-fulfillment.

Humanity should by now clearly understand that all life is part of the world we share. A rational analysis of the accelerating trend toward a global ecological crisis should arouse feelings of self-preservation, a logical incentive to avert our own demise. But Stephen Jay Gould said that ultimately we will only preserve what we love. This is reflected in the passionate philosophy of Deep Ecology that serves as an "academic and political expression of nature mysticism."[9]

Had human consciousness evolved on the moon, it would be as

barren as the pockmarked lunar desert, according to the ecologist, writer, and poet Thomas Berry.[10] By analogy, as humanity urbanizes and loses contact with its roots in nature, the consequences would be a consciousness barren of the rich diversity of life that is nature. For those city dwellers long divorced from natural contacts, a deep and moving experience in the wild is needed to rekindle the flame of our innate instinct that has been called biophilia. Such spiritual experience can bring back the feeling for the "wilderness ethic," the moral necessity of conserving and preserving nature.

But it may not be enough to go on a bus, car, or train to the countryside and then walk around for a few days. A profound immersion in the wild is needed to stir the senses and light the spirit that so many, living in urban jungles, fruitlessly seek. That experience can hone the senses to a level of acuity that will astonish.

But rationality must coexist with emotion in order to affect a process of transformation. Such ideas were presented by the Finnish philosopher Georg Henrik von Wright, who aroused strong controversy in Scandinavia when he expressed his "provocative pessimism" about humanity's future on planet Earth.[11]

Wright foresees an ultimate and probably irreversible clash between industrialization and world ecology. As energy consumption of fossil fuels increases, so does pollution. The burgeoning world population and vast movements from rural to urban settings are leading to a global growth of industrialization that is nearly exponential.

As the world's population moves into large cities, he suggests, the sacred connection of humanity with nature withers away. Progressively, untold millions will lose the spiritual contact with that from which we have all evolved, the beauty and quiet of the forest, the intimate contact with creatures, small and large, and the evocative smells of multitudinous blooms. It becomes a vicious cycle.

The forces of moral materialism now hold the world's economic direction under their sway. As Arthur Eddington says with irony, "We must not interrupt the 'practical man', these busy molders of history carrying us at ever-increasing pace towards our destiny as an ant-heap of humanity infesting the earth."[12]

What remains for man the hunter in this world? The domestication of animals and the subsequent depletion of territory for wild game are squeezing out the few remaining opportunities to relive and renew our connections with wilderness. Fish, likewise, are disappearing from oceans, rivers, and lakes, depleted usually by our insatiable appetite, with mechanical advances such as gigantic sea-going vacuum cleaners and fish factories, pollution, and the introduction and proliferation of unwanted exotic species.

Nature means space. As Anthony Stevens amply describes, restriction of that space played murderous havoc among a baboon population, and other data support this behavior in other species such as rodents crowded in cages. The philosopher and ethnologist Desmond Morris has compared our (the human) lot to that of animals condemned to languish in a zoo of their own making.[13]

A notorious example of cultural breakdown and degeneration among human beings was reported by the anthropologist C. M. Turnbull. After being forced off their hunting territory and into farming, the Ik tribe of Uganda transformed into an "irrevocably disagreeable collection of unattached, brutish creatures."[14] Among other Swiftian perversions, they defecated on their neighbors' doorsteps. Cities and nations have adopted some Ik-like characteristics. It is perhaps a form of spiritual decompensation demonstrated by a loss of natural habitat and the pollution of streets, water, and atmosphere.

The movement of humanity into urban settings, which furthers the alienation from nature, may lead to other disturbing consequences. Life in nature had dangers and unexpected changes that kept our forebears watchful and humble. The Swiss psychiatrist C. A. Meier views this transition to a more "civilized" society from a Jungian perspective. He believes that as the fears of outer natural dangers turn inward, Western society will approach a crisis from the fears of the inner dangers in the psyche—"for should the outer wilderness disappear altogether, it would inevitably resurrect powerfully from within, whereupon it would immediately be projected."[15] In other words, the beast is within us. There is a resurgence of those inward projections as humanity festers in internecine crises resulting in a global psychosis, as seen in the increasing worldwide incidence of mental illness, particularly depression, that has been reported by the World Health Organization.

But it is the accelerated global warming through the production of vehicular, agricultural, and industrial waste gases that raises the largest specter. The world consumption of fossil fuels today is equivalent to 6.5 billion tons of carbon per year. Although the United States is the largest culprit, it is estimated that China will soon outstrip her.[16] Will India and other great industrializing countries be far behind? The present rate of consumption is calculated to raise the atmospheric carbon dioxide level by three parts per million, not a large figure but significant for the greenhouse effect. Fossil fuels will someday not be available—a dead certainty for the future if society proceeds down this slippery slope. However, in the interim, other world forces are upsetting the homeostatic balance—for example, smog blankets around large areas of industrialized land, ever spreading over the oceans, resulting in unpredictable excesses of rainfall, drought, and surface temperatures.

Fortunately, there are positive effects that must not be ignored. For example, biospheric homeostasis, the "Gaia effect," appears to have adjusted the carbon dioxide levels to less than half of that originally predicted. This is probably due to increased utilization of carbon dioxide by plants as its availability increases. Furthermore, temperate forests are regrowing. Just take New Hampshire: 95 percent of the land was covered by forest in 1680, only 15 percent remained forested in 1880, and now the forest has returned to cover 85 percent.

Humankind is still puny in contrast to the dimensions of the biosphere. Vast dynamic forces have often prevailed to counter the natural destructive activities that this planet has experienced over billions of years. The ominous predictions must be tempered by this realization. However, clearheaded analyses such as *The Limits of Growth: The 30-Year Update* present balanced assessments of our future that should convince even the skeptical that things are going in the wrong direction.[17]

The commercial slaughter of trees continues, particularly in tropical regions, with no end in sight. The glaciers everywhere are rapidly shrinking; the sea level is rising to a predicted level of thirty-five inches or more above present levels. The lack of fresh water will be the next and immediate pressing problem of the burgeoning population.

The future of oil and gas exploitation will bring even further disaster as serious scrabbling for the remaining fossil fuel resources accelerates. One process will include scraping up the tar-bearing shales and sands over thousands of square miles, extracting and refining the tars, then leaving those vast fields filled with sterile sand and shale to devastate the landscape for hundreds of years before life can regrow on them.

In an impressive but disturbing photographic montage of the earth as it appears at night, however, one sees the pattern of electrical lighting seen from space. The wasteful expenditure of energy among many countries is vividly apparent, the United States and Europe leading by far. Because of the reflection of this lighting on our atmosphere, NASA estimates that over one-half of the population of the northern hemisphere cannot see the Milky Way, the galactic nebula to which we belong. Sad as this is, it is only a small part of humankind's blind journey of alienation from nature.

Not only our humanoid ancestors but also that primordial blob of protoplasm emerging from the young earth's hot soup sensed that same bright heaven. As consciousness developed, so surely came the feeling of a cosmic connection.

Now, in a cosmic iota of time, our so-called advanced civilization is burrowing ever deeper into warrens of urban expansion, to emerge blindly, like moles, and, bumping into one another, we pursue meaningless tasks of constructing more hovels and acquiring all the chattel that is associated with an "expanding" society. We are more profoundly perplexed about ourselves than were our ancestors, according to the biologist Edmund Sinnot, who states, "Post modern man . . . is on the verge of spiritual and moral insanity. He does not know who he is."[18]

Georg von Wright, in his thoughtful analysis *Science and Reason*, concludes that there is no reason to expect the present dominating trends to stop or change. Global industrialization will continue, and everyday life, beginning in the most developed countries, will increase its dependence on advanced technology, on mechanized production and roboticized services. In short, the scientific-based industrial technology continues its "giddy dance of bacchanalian frenzy"[19] toward the future. Wright foresees that the environment will be further polluted and ravaged, and artificial products and new forms of energy will replace its disappearing resources. The "explosive rate" of urbanization is accompanied, as the biologist David Suzuki agrees, with "a deterioration of the social fabric that held people together." Consumerism and materialism rather than social goals drive government and corporate policies that make us "strangers in the world."[20]

As humanity becomes ever more subject to nature's "revenge," it will be reminded of its own inability to "control" development. Protesting voices will naturally not go away. Conscientious economists and enlightened statesmen will continue to discuss "a new world economy," the need for "constructive North-South dialogue," "respect for human rights," and other attractive ideals and utopias. But Wright finds it difficult to believe that these will have more than a marginal influence in the immediate future as safety valves for humanity's bad conscience, or as a dreamscape generated by inadequately fulfilled wishes.

What forces can stop or significantly change the trend? Wright foresees one possibility, not unrealistic, "that humanity disappears as a zoological entity." That possibility has often been considered in historical times of unrest and change. But he thinks the threat is greater than ever before, and, to Wright, the thought is not especially disturbing. Someday, without any doubt, "*Homo sapiens* as a species will no longer exist." If it happens after a few hundred thousand years or after a few centuries, its significance as seen from a cosmic perspective, to the philosopher Wright, is not worth "a pinch of snuff." When one considers the number of species of life that humankind has eliminated, then such a nemesis by nature could perhaps be considered just. Many who have looked deeply into the human soul have talked about a death wish equally strong to the will to survive. Wright states that, "There is no reason to believe that they are completely wrong."[21] This point is taken up in the section on pathological states and in Anthony Stevens's observations on war and terrorism. As most readers of history realize, the more complex society becomes, the greater the risk of contagious irrationality and anxiety.

But the extinction of humanity is not the only option. Another is that mankind will adopt lifestyles that many will see as "inhuman." For example, we can colonize space, or eliminate—that is, "rationalize away"—classes of the population that technological development has found superfluous in an industrial society.

But there is still the possibility that there is an instinct strong enough to raise a collective protest to stop the present trend and lead developments in another direction. Wright considers the protests and the activism of the grassroots and green movements. He sympathizes with many of them. They represent our "civilization's bad conscience" that reminds us that our values are at risk of being lost. But they have not, in his opinion, articulated the case well enough to hold the future in their hands. They also tend toward irrational and chaotic behavior, which could be considered jeopardous.[22]

His hope is toward a protest developing from within society's structure, from that power that he considers the strongest, the "rational component of humanity." Reason and common sense have many forms, but the special form that has its role in science has evolved in recent history. For the past four hundred years it has developed into an entity, he believes, that can be an instrument for enormous change for both humanity's outer life duties and for the very structure of society. Simultaneously there have come changes in the new world order that question the rational basis for science's role as an engine for "progress." The comprehension of reality in earlier areas of science has stumbled up against obstacles. To overcome these barriers it has been necessary to change or replace these scientific areas. The new world picture that is slowly emerging appears less willing to support science, as we have known it. According to Wright, those seeking scientific truths may perhaps value again a lifestyle of reason and common sense rather than the power that science gives to control and manipulate life's demands.

Many changes are occurring in the field of science, earlier developing in physics and now continuing in the field of biology. He has come to believe that such a reevaluation is occurring, but cannot predict how these trends will develop or what role that they will play in history. He does not, however, have a strong conviction in the "triumph of reason."

The key words, in my view, of Wright's thoughts are *instinct, reason,* and *common sense.* Instinct is surely the feeling that is deepest. Much that I have written in this book is about the instinct for nature, for our biosphere. It is biophilia and the mystical heritage of our union with all life, seen in the cave paintings of our Paleolithic ancestors, but surely extending back further, to our very origins.

There is also the instinct of self-preservation, which involves the second key word, *reason.* Wright emphasized the connection of reason to science. He decries the power of science in ruling our materialistic lives. Science, however, is neutral. It is the *power* of science that humanity employs in our engine of "progress." Reason and science are the necessary ingredients for a braking and eventual reversal of present trends toward the materialistic complexity that merely adds "noise" to everyday life. Do we need the entire chattel? Science is already being applied, at least in part, to the environmental cleanup, the cleaner sources of energy, and even toward a simplification of lifestyle with reduction of power demands as can be seen in ever-increasing "ecocommunities" in Scandinavia and around the world.

What Wright has neglected or ignored, it seems to me, is the component of emotion, the love that Gould invoked, much of which has been discussed in this book and that stems from deep spiritual encounters in nature. It is common sense, a part of what has been called emotional intelligence. Reason and common sense seem largely buried today under the detritus of material progress.

When Wright mentions a pervasive death wish in humanity, there are many who agree. Anthony Stevens describes how the notion of apocalypse can be attractive to those who are deeply troubled by the present state of existence. Global catastrophe pervades the myths and sagas of numerous cultures. The Nordic Ragnarök, like the blink of Brahma's eye, describes the cyclic end of humanity in fiery chaos, from which a new beginning arises, over and over again. As Stevens asserts, "The cataclysm is inflicted by the gods as punishment for man's transgressions."[23]

Apocalyptic visions of the future that humanity faces are not new. Ancient religions are rife with predictions of fiery disasters or ice-smothered ends of the earth and all that live on it. From a cosmological and scientific understanding these ancient predictions may be true—millions of years hence. But, disturbingly, among sects of at least two great religions, Islam and Christianity, there are evidently millions of believers who await the end of the world within historical time. Such is a fundamentalist Christian doomsday called the Rapture.[24] Those caught in its apocalyptic vision believe that only true followers of Jesus will be saved for eternity. It is apparent to anyone that such individuals, obsessed by the religious hatred of "unbelieving" fellow human beings, can hardly be expected to care "a pinch of snuff" for the problems of our deteriorating environment.

That is one argument more why Georg von Wright hedges his bet of reason being the hope for the future. The nature mystic may see this, as she can see into the heart of things, the qi of perceiving the ineffable beauty of a leaf. There is a linking of all our past through billions of years with the reality of that leaf. The simplicity of it brings a harmony with all the wildness that we sense and absorb into the inner self. These instincts, innate in all of us, if we can bring them to the light of day, may help answer Wright's plea for instinct, reason, and common sense.

Humanity is striving, with its global consciousness as perhaps never before, to find its secure niche upon Earth. The struggle between forces of exploitation in the name of progress and of adaptation to our natural reservoir of sustenance is quickly escalating. Wright seeks to demythologize the "myth of progress" by recruiting intellectual support to debunk the "false prophet" of scientific materialism.[25]

Given that human beings are (presumably) self-conscious and socially aware, there may be hope that we can modify the basic instincts dictated by our selfish genes to, heedlessly, reproduce ourselves at all costs. It is, to a great extent, the burgeoning population that is at the root of the global environmental crisis. But, for example, if the rest of the world should suddenly attain the levels of energy consumption and subsequent environmental destruction occurring in the United States, the burden of toxic fallout, water depletion, forest destruction, and species extinction will quickly reach globally critical levels. There are already, for starters, the crisis of water shortage and pollution, the focal areas of starvation and malnutrition, global epidemics of AIDS, drug-resistant malaria, and newly emerging viruses such as Ebola and SARS that thrive in overcrowded communities.

## Nature's Revenge

Humanity is now spinning out of the control of its own fate. For thousands of centuries up to our scientific era there has been a well-grounded system of checks and balances in humankind's relationship with her environment. Wars, famines, and epidemics occurred and sooner or later adjusted the population to whatever environmental circumstances prevailed. With present-day technology, the critical point of population size and distribution has been significantly altered.

But there is a mischievous element in nature that has taken up battle with that technology. No sooner have we apparently "conquered" a disease, such as malaria, than both the vectors, mosquitoes, and the causative organisms, trophozoites, adapt, mutate, and attack anew. It is an irony that the loss of biodiversity that E. O. Wilson and others forcibly document is not shared by human pathogens. In their world biodiversity is increasing, thanks to the numerous factors of population dynamics and to the use and abuse of antibiotics. New diseases, food and water crises, human conflicts appear constantly and are increasingly difficult to control. There seems to be no final solution to this ongoing battle.

This battle involves a powerful personal experience. For over fifty years, I have traveled to Asia and Africa, increasingly, as a physician and consultant. I was hard hit by Dengue fever several decades ago, but it took me nearly fifty years to be felled by malaria, the "bad" kind, from *Plasmodium falciparam.*

I know pretty well where I contracted it. Not in my favorite camp, in a forest on the banks of a beautiful river. Mosquitoes and flies were rarely seen there; the ecobalance took care of that. No, I contracted it in a once pristine city, now overcrowded, dirty, and mosquito and rodent ridden. The infection turned out to be drug resistant, and the second-stage chemotherapy that I required, plus the widespread parasitic infiltration of my body, damaged my health for many years.

Was I just plain lucky not to have gotten it before? No; data from the World Health Association (WHO) show that the rise of drug-resistant malaria over those fifty years and the increasing rate of infection in urban areas make me one of the statistics. People I know have died from cerebral malaria.

WHO gave up trying to eradicate malaria from the globe in the 1960s, just as smallpox, not involving a vector such as the mosquito, was being eliminated permanently. The deteriorating problems of urbanization and the breakdown of social and economic conditions overcame the simple logic of eliminating a totally preventable disease. Malaria now affects 300 million people, with 120 million clinical infections, and between 1.5 and 2.7 million deaths a year. It is endemic in ninety-one countries, and the mortality rises steadily, despite all the known methods of prevention and effective treatment.

AIDS accounts for forty million cases in the world with a steadily rising mortality, now at three million per year and five million new infections annually. Again, this is a totally preventable disease with at least a fairly effective treatment.

Where will it all end?

In most societies of the Western developed world, there are new voices of anti-intellectualism, antiglobalism, and anticapitalism that are protesting the direction that humanity is taking. Opposing them are supporters of an increasing hard line of defense of scientific materialism trying to excuse or minimize the significance of the major disasters coming in its wake. These disasters include the progressing greenhouse effect, disappearance of potable water supplies, atmospheric pollution, and the rapid extinction of plants and animals, threatening the ecobalance for hundreds if not thousands of years.

Georg von Wright comes between these extreme viewpoints with a reasonable tone of mind and voice. But the cold intellect of the philosopher is firm: looking ahead it is nearly a given truth that our civilization as we know it may have a short future and that major catastrophe is nearly unavoidable—for it is already beginning. It could have started when these words were written: "Be fruitful and multiply, and fill the earth and subdue it; and have dominion over the fish of the sea and over the birds of the air and over every living thing that moves upon the earth" (Gen. 1:26).

Wright has no immediate solution to his calm, reasoned analysis, except to plea for the return of values to our presently valueless society.

Enlightenment alone will not influence population growth. The "Netherlands Argument" has been used by some to claim that the world can accommodate a population with a per capita density similar to that of the Netherlands, one of the most densely populated, yet one of the cleanest, healthiest, and most prosperous countries in the world. But this is, in fact, a "Netherlands Fallacy." Less than 30 percent of the world's land surface is arable. The lack of available fresh water is even a greater barrier. The world population simply cannot reach that density without utter catastrophe.

But there now appears to be a flattening of the exponential growth curve of humanity. Population scientists speculate that a number of factors are at work: voluntary or mandatory (as in China) limitation of family size, economic factors, and education—but also, as part of human suffering, the litany of starvation, genocide, and epidemic diseases.

Eventually, experts predict, the world population will stabilize at around eleven billion. From there things may go downhill. The English paleobiologist Michael Boulter calculates the eventual extinction of humanity as part of a natural evolutionary process abetted by man-made catastrophe.[26]

The imagination has difficulty projecting changes over long periods of time. One lifetime is generally not enough to feel the changes of our environment. I have at least a seventy-year perspective now and have pointed out changes that I have seen, for the worse in many parts of the world, and for the better in small parts of the developed world. We all need psychologist and ecologist Shierry Nicholsen's "binocular vision" to get the large picture[27] because, as Mitchell Thomashow asks, "How is it that we're on the verge of a sixth megaextinction and so few people seem to know or care?"[28]

Georg von Wright is not far off the mark when he speculates that the end of humanity, from a cosmic viewpoint, is not worth "a pinch of snuff." Many were shocked to think that someone would assert that our "great civilization" could be finite. Yet the shadow of Armageddon has loomed over us perhaps from our ancestor's first fearful sight of a solar eclipse or a fiery comet. The fear of mystery and mortality invites inward thought. Shiva's cosmic dance and Ragnarök came to symbolize and remind us of our collective mortality.

But the astronomer Martin Rees looks beyond the demise of humanity. He foresees the pervasion of the entire solar system by robots and fabricators, human and nonhuman, leaving populations on Earth to weather human extinction. He catalogues the scenarios to include bioerror and bioterror, nuclear catastrophes, new epidemic diseases, and cosmic collisions. He thinks the odds are even that our civilization as we know it will not survive beyond the end of the twenty-first century.[29] Ecopsychologist Theodore Roszak wonders if "Gaia . . . may at some point decide that this so-clever human species is too troublesome a hazard to maintain."[30]

Of greatest threat to our immediate survival as a civilization if not a straggling group of survivors is the daily threat of nuclear incineration. This apocalyptic weapon is now within reach of terrorists as well as rogue countries. Disaster could strike any time by accidental missile launch, by computer malfunction, or by design. We block out of our minds these threats to our survival as well as our sanity.

What can or should we do about it? In *Ecopsychology,* the authors propose a return to our essential animal selves that evolved in the natural world.[31] Our genetic heritage says to reproduce to infinity. Should we care? Yes, certainly for the sake of the environment and social conditions that our offspring will share. Recall that this earth, the homeostatic being called Gaia, is remarkably resilient. The thin biosphere housing all life is a reservoir of water, air, and land. Consider just the greenhouse gas carbon dioxide. As more is released, more is absorbed in water, which acts as a gigantic chemical buffer as well as thermal "sink." The same holds true for other greenhouse products and particulate matter. There are, of course, limits to this buffering and absorbing action. Witness the devastating effects of industrial chemicals released into rivers and lakes, and the massive oil spills along ocean coastlines.

Life has a way of coping up to a point through homeostatic mechanisms. Plants and microorganisms, bacteria and viruses, infest nearly every bit of the biosphere. There are "bugs" and plants (such as fungi) that, in the presence of oxygen, will feed upon and digest almost every organic substance, including fossil oil, and also metabolize inorganic chemicals. Green plants thrive on increasing levels of $CO_2$. As the world temperature increases, so will water vapor, leading to a widened distribution and number of plants, buffering the temperature gradient. But Gaia's tolerance has limits; local droughts, floods, extinctions, and other devastations will inevitably increase as humankind continues to burn, cut, clear, and poison our environment.

There are some hopeful signs, even now, of a reversal of some of this devastation. Many rivers of the industrialized northeastern United States, for the first time in over one hundred years, are supporting the migration of native anadromous fishes such as shad and salmon. The Thames River now has a salmon run. But these signs are relatively few and far between. I will never forget seeing the yellow, polluted rivers draining into the largely empty Aral Sea. Humanity's detritus litters the surface of the oceans. Charles Moore estimates that one-quarter of the world's surface shows visibly an accumulation of plastic debris.[32]

Humanity is presently struggling with the spurious conflict between science and spirit. Witness the burgeoning conflicts concerning evolutionary theory. We have discarded ancient superstitions, and rightfully so, yet we have also discarded the myths and legends that provided a shamanic connection with nature. Scientific knowledge, however, gives us the opportunity for a rational understanding of the cosmos and our place in it. After centuries of technological advances, there are new forces bringing us back to our spiritual senses together rather than in conflict with scientific knowledge.

As Thomas Maxwell writes, "This awakened insight promotes

the healing of our long-standing alienation from the natural world and offers hope for renewal in the midst of widespread cultural deterioration."[33]

The choice is simple and the solution is at hand. The natural human being, guided by his mystic affinity to the biosphere, surely knows.

Gaia is our sacred abode. It is reality. Civilization is abstract.

# 10  THE FUTURE RESTS WITH US

*The West of which I speak is but another name for the Wild: and what I have been preparing to say is, that in Wildness is the preservation of the World.*

THOREAU, "WALKING"

*In the deepest mystical sense, nature is hungry for our prayers. . . . We are like a window of the house of nature through which the light and air of the spiritual world penetrates into the natural world.*

SEYYED HOSSEIN NASR, *THE SPIRITUAL AND RELIGIOUS DIMENSIONS OF THE ENVIRONMENTAL CRISIS*

## Finding the Road

As there are said to be many paths to God, so there are many paths to mystical experience. Much has been written about meditative practice, breathing techniques, yoga, tai chi, and many other exercises that can lead toward *kensho* or individuation or just calmness. But, for many, nothing takes the place of being in the peace and wonder of a natural place. It can be the seashore, a grove next to a stream, a desert, a snow-clad mountain, or a coral atoll. It is there, anywhere in pristine nature, where my spirit spontaneously soars, as it can for most of us. Studies now show that such moments in nature and other "favorite places," the "sites of wild strawberries" that were previously mentioned, are restorative experiences that lead to increased attentiveness, relaxation, clearing of one's mind, subjective vitality, and self-confidence. They are, in fact, healing experiences.[1]

So I go on beating the drum of my theme, joining many others far more experienced and articulate in matters of environmentalism. To really *feel* strongly about our environment, to have a deep emotional connection, we need to revive and disseminate the concept of humanity's spiritual connection to nature. The ecstatic perception of nature, often in solitude, is a rediscovery of the union of the self with all creation.

It is easy to be transported, poetically, with the urge to express these mystical adventures in words. It is natural perhaps to feel that if everyone shared them, the love of nature including fellow humankind would flourish and the world would be a better place.

I seek to bridge the gap of perception between the rationality of science and nature mysticism. Both concern the relationship of humanity with nature; both need to come closer in humankind's thinking in order to increase the understanding and true love of our coexistence with all life. There need be no conflict between the scientific and the mystical connection with nature. When guided by mystic consciousness, scientific knowledge can be a road to reach a deeper understanding of our place in the universe.

As is now abundantly clear, human society is sliding down a slippery slope of environmental destruction and burgeoning population, with associated epidemics of disease, genocide, and starvation. The political assault on carefully erected safeguards of our environment by some government administrations and commercial interests are, in Bill McKibben's words, "So large as to be numbing."[2]

The rate of the present process of environmental degradation is so slow in terms of human life spans, however, that most of us are not aware of it. In my own lifetime, now coming to a close, I have seen the changes in several increasingly troubled urban and rural parts of the world. But it seems as if we have a profound inertia that cannot turn away from continued fatal exploitation of our natural environment.

The psychologist and ecologist Shierry Nicholsen asks how we can hold in our minds both the "infinity of the far future" and the present realities of choice.[3] The climax of our ecocrisis may not be that distant, not much further than a lifetime or two. A spatial perception of time can enable us to perceive its timescale.

Bookshelves in libraries and bookstores are already groaning with the numbers of books on environment and ecocriticism, the majority pessimistic. The time necessary for the evolution of our collective consciousness toward a possibly more enlightened and rational state is not sufficient to address the immediate trends of self-destruction. In a practical sense, we must muster our present resources of environmental consciousness in order to propagate throughout this small world the awareness of our potential fate. Although philosopher Georg von Wright considers our fate to be "not worth a pinch of snuff," mortal beings with instincts of self-preservation and racial propagation must willy-nilly seek solutions.

Yet there are small clues that may help to understand human nature and its deep psychological bond to nature. In natural disasters that destroy life and habitat there are always stories of human beings that sacrifice even themselves to preserve their pet animals, sometimes even plants. These demonstrations of love for fellow life can be projected ultimately to include the attachment to all life, the love of which Stephen Jay Gould wrote, and the identification with nature, which Arne Naess describes in his philosophy of deep ecology.

If we acknowledge, as did Thomas Aquinas, that all our actions are motivated by some benefit to ourselves, we can see how love, the emotional identification with an object, will lead naturally to desire to preserve and nurture, for our projection reflects upon ourselves.

The tingling exaltation of union with a loved one is part of the universal and primal search for union with a cosmic force or deity. Next to the basic instincts for survival, it lies at the very heart of our being, a moral message strongly given by John Muir from his aerie in the Sierra Nevada. The myths of the Greek deities Orpheus and Narcissus, too, may illuminate the erotic parallels between humanity and nature. The mystic love of nature, according to the philosopher Herbert Marcuse, arises from merging the narcissistic love of self with a new erotic relationship with nature.[4] The mystical feeling for nature in all the many forms and degrees is, simply said, love, in a way that could be similar to the religious love of God.

The love of nature is a fundamental requirement for humanity's passage toward reversing the destructive and soon irreversible path of environmental disaster. To put it in a more down-to-earth way, the environmental ethic will not come through the "logical elucidation of new philosophic principles and logistic strictures" but "through a rejuvenation of our carnal, sensorial empathy with the living land that sustains us," according to David Abram.[5] Although it's the feeling part of us that will ultimately make that necessary, life-saving step toward preservation of the biosphere, rationality must enter the equation. Together, they constitute common sense.

Unfortunately, as time drags on, it may be fear alone that will steer that ship away from environmental disaster as the consciousness of humanity awakes from a devastating ecological blow.

The spirituality of nature and solitude, love of life and humanity, and self-awareness is a healing and nurturing state of mind, which environmentalists could promote in the efforts to connect the public with the natural environment. It can be an inherent positive adaptive mechanism, adjusting our often frantic and aggressive behavior to the slow and stately pace of nature's tempo, thus allowing us to maintain a spiritual connection that gives us comfort, peace, and healing.

The subjective world, our inner state, is that of true reality and is tacit. It is immeasurably greater than our span of rational comprehension. It can be compared to the vast sea of the subconscious that James describes, ebbing and flowing on the shores of waking consciousness. This expansion of thought, often experienced in the magical moments surrounded by the quiet vastness of the wild, can enable us to see beyond the boundaries of our immediate world and to perceive the nature of the cosmos.

The ecologist Roger Gottlieb urges that this spiritual connection should not just affect us, but should "inhabit and shape us." An "enzyme of consciousness" could expand environmental awareness in many ways—translating theory to strategy, shifting the focus from physical to biological priorities, exploring the meaning of Nature's divinity as a forum of "eco-theology," which could expand the boundaries of what modern humanity has considered as sacred.[6] At times, this tacit, subjective part of my self seems to surface and engage the sentient world that is all around. I hunger for solitude, seeing, hearing, smelling the trees, plants, the rivers and oceans, mountains and plains and deserts after too long a stay in the sterility of urban surroundings. That hunger is as real as the hunger for food. It seems to be an innate feeling. Wordsworth and W. H. Hudson, born and raised in rural settings at nearly opposite ends of the world, both created beautiful structures of words to sanctify their kinship with the nature that they experienced and loved in their youth. That conditioning, that exposure, particularly in youth, to the blessings of wildness and fellow life is withering as urbanization continues its relentless direction.

## Urbanization: Blessing or Curse?

Many of us are fated to live in cities. They provide shelter, human contact, and the spiritual nourishment of concert halls, theaters, art galleries, museums, and libraries. They are an efficient way of condensing humanity, like ants in an anthill, thus hopefully sparing nature some of the human devastation that has gone on for millennia. City dwellers need not, however, lose their contact with nature. Civic gardens, parks, lakes, and streams, when well designed and preserved, can nurture the yearning for nature that is innate. How will this ideal survive in the uncontrolled, impoverished, sterile, burgeoning global urban sprawl called the "City pox"?[7]

With urbanization proceeding in a seemingly inexorable path, as much as two-thirds of the world's humanity may eventually not know or feel the beauty and comfort of natural environments. The creation and function of the city reflects human purpose and endeavor, but individually we have very little control over our own environment and are often pawns in the urban maze. Many scarcely lift their heads to see the beauty of the sky and space that invest even the meanest metropolis. Environmental memory and biophilia may wither further, and the feelings for responsibility of the preservation and restoration of the environment can fade away.

The uncontrolled sprawl of urbanization is forming a blot not only on our global landscape, but also on the collective mind of humanity. Over two hundred years ago, Wordsworth agonized that "a multitude of causes, unknown to former times, are now acting with a combined force to blunt the discriminating powers of the mind." These forces included "the increasing accumulation of men in cities" with their craving for "extraordinary incident" that needed hourly gratification and a "degrading thirst after outrageous stimulation."[8]

For decades, thoughtful analysts have argued that the headlong consumerist-based path of industrialization must be radically altered. Instead, there have come excuses and explanations couched in pretty words of the impossibilities or necessities of such change. But more and more individuals appear to have become aware of the need for change. The confidence in the present system is waning, and many are liberating themselves from the old mentality of waste and pollution.

The spiritual devastation of the blights of unplanned urbanization, it seems, is the root of much that ails us. There are and have been violent and brutal conflicts in rural areas around the world. Human nature contains a streak of cruelty and brutality that is no less than and may exceed that of most fellow creatures. There is abundant evidence for the nasty and selfish side of our nature. The romantic and idealistic views are often unrealistic. The zoologist Matt Ridley hopes, however, that in the case of humanity, "The roots of social order are in our heads, where we possess the instinctive capacities for creating not a perfectly harmonious and virtuous society, but a better one than we have at present."[9] Deep inside us, as with other social beings, is the instinct for self-preservation that can transcend our mundane search for gratification. That instinct may come down to us from billions of years of pragmatism, knowing that cooperation, not competition, will save the community.

But much depends on what each of us considers our community—family, caste, religion, nation, or the entire human world? With the benefit of enormous hindsight from all the science and history available to us, that instinct can be coupled to rationality and to the structures and strictures of society. A spiritual dimension, too, largely distinguishes us from other life. This morality is our heritage and potential savior. In which direction is it going? Probably to all points of the compass. Wanton cruelty is counterpoised by magnanimous altruism and gentleness, with all degrees of these qualities distributed around the compass rose. Can we steady our errant ship toward a common, humanitarian, and self-preserving goal?

Some of the absurdity and tragedy of uncontrolled urbanization is striking. I visit a historic city in India, which, fifty years ago, was pleasantly laid out with boulevards, parks, and gardens, with clean water and atmosphere. Today, with a fivefold increase in population, it is choking on itself. The sidewalks are not walkable, either from decay or obstruction by innumerable shops, vendors, and parked vehicles. Walking on the streets is a limb-and-life-threatening hazard. To get from place to place, even short distances, vehicles of one sort or other must be used. It is a vicious cycle: the less the walking access, the more the vehicles, belching soot and gases, and, consequently, the further loss of pedestrian possibilities. Lakes and ponds, once sparkling blue, are poisonous green, stinking, and refuse-laden. From a perspective overlooking the city, the choked roads are continuously filled with an immeasurably long line of vehicles, sharply evoking the image of ants on an anthill. Inhabitants tend to look the other way, pointing proudly to sweeping modern landscaped business and residential complexes in the environs, a result of India's economic boom. Will the inner city be abandoned someday, as American industrial cities were a few decades ago?

If cities can be cleaner, wastes recycled, and pollution minimized, then the often ravaged countryside will have the chance to rejuvenate, threatened species recover, and nature to return, slowly, to its wild state. The extreme activism of many "ecocritics" in the green movement may be counterproductive. There is already a polarization of views in large political and economic dimensions. Should not the broader view be to stimulate thinking and to provoke originality rather than espouse militant but unreceived solutions?

There is a powerful positive side to urbanization. As Kellert asserts, "The current lack of meaningful contact with nature in the modern city and suburb reflects a deficiency of imagination rather than an intrinsic flaw of modern urban life."[10] He refers of course to affluent communities that can afford to improve the contact with nature in their urban milieus. For example, I live now in the middle of a highly urbanized city but can find refreshment and solace by a walk to the river and its flanking well-planned parkways.

An "eco-municipality" movement is beginning in scattered communities in Europe, Canada, and Australasia. In Sweden, there are sixty such communities that successfully conserve energy, recycle, and conserve water. Fossil fuel dependence is largely eliminated, including the use of chemicals and plastics derived from oil and coal.[11] A key to these programs is the commitment by the population to drastically change their lifestyle. These changes can serve as models for the power-hungry industrial giants such as the United States, industrialized Europe, China, Japan, and India.

But that is much to hope for under the present conditions of global population pressures and economies. More people mean more demands on energy, food, and water. Great cities have seldom coped adequately with the problems of industrial pollution and water conservation. More food means more cropland, not less. Think however of the struggling chaos of megalopoli in much of the world where economic reality submerges aesthetic value and diesel soot coats the sparse greenery.

Thus the world crisis may not be solved in the short term by technology. A breaking point in Gaia's tolerance is fast approaching.

## Bringing Nature Home

Those lucky enough to have early exposure to life in the outdoors have generally been infected with the spirit of environmental consciousness. Our innate sense of biophilia is in full flower. When we have felt a transcendent experience in nature, we are "hooked" for life. That permanent memory becomes a guide to returning the favor to Mother Nature, to respect, preserve, and restore that which has been damaged or lost through the artificial and destructive actions of humankind.

Depending on our station in life, these ethics can range from living by the simple *primum non nocere* (first do no harm) of the physician's credo to attempting to make sweeping changes to national and international policies. One responsibility that can have long-lasting benefits is the encouragement for the teaching of natural and environmental history and the direct participation of youth into wilderness experiences. As I have mentioned, many programs exist in developed countries and many are beginning in other parts of the world. This learning experience at an early stage will have great benefits for future environmental awareness.

As I have shown, mystical experiences in nature are more likely to occur at younger ages. The psychologists Rachel and Stephen Kaplan studied the impact of an extended and organized nature program on young people, many who came from urban settings. The investigators noted several changes in the group, particularly the "remarkable depth of spiritual impacts" and the "recovery of aspects of mental function that had become less effective through overuse."[12] Perhaps those solitary moments in the wild created the apophatic conditions of mystical feeling that could lead to renewed creativity.

How can such experiences come to urban youth? They may well represent the key to our future. We have seen examples of the innate spirituality of children and their joyous immersion into the bountiful arms of nature. The environmental consciousness of youth may be a principal weapon against the direction the entire world is taking toward consumerism and materialism, a direct antagonist to the preservation and restoration of the biosphere and our collective psyche.

The contact with our natural environment in its majesty, sublime peacefulness or awesome fury, represents, to me, the most enriching path to our inner, natural being whence come inherited, transcendent feelings of union with our biosphere, our planet, and the cosmos.

It is encouraging, therefore, to see organized efforts to bring the spiritual and physical benefits of interacting with the wild. The number of schools and programs on wilderness training and survival, primitive living skills, animal tracking, and other outdoor skills appears to be increasing, even in less developed countries in Asia and Africa. These efforts are still miniscule in respect to the total population, but the impact on our future leaders may lead to increased regional and global environmental consciousness.

The urban life may foster the development of a quick and precocious intelligence but at the cost of eliminating the rich range of experience that should be the heritage of all humanity. Our senses are deprived of their natural stimuli. Recall Kurosawa's epic film about Dersu Uzala and his companion, the Czarist surveyor, who, helpless in the face of nature's forces, is saved by the Kirghiz nomad from certain death in a sudden storm. His instinctive self had been smothered by sensory atrophy. Civilization has trapped many of us into cocoons of our own making, leading us to meaningless internecine conflicts while our own wild selves live underground, dormant and despairing.

Anyone exploring the deep recesses where our Paleolithic ancestors created their art will share the spirit of these artists who were totally deprived of sensory input except for the light of feeble lamps. It must, indeed, have been a sacred and mystical rite to create those paintings, drawings, and sculptures. The representation of fellow animals by *Homo* was a form of religious expression. That bond with nature and fellow creatures has gradually changed over the past twelve thousand or so years. It has evolved instead, particularly in Western culture, into religions that extol images of the human form as sacred, such as the gods of ancient Greece and Scandinavia. Divinity then was bestowed on living human beings, as in Persia and Rome, and ultimately to the martyred Jesus. The concept of Jehovah in man's image, or vice versa, remote from nature, dwelling somewhere in the heavens, completed the divorce of nature from humanity, and established Western theocracies by man, of man, and for man. The earth is the domain of humankind, and we have accomplished much in subjecting it to our will. So successfully, perhaps, have we done so that it may wither away from too much love, the love of exploitation of Mother Earth.

## Needed: The Moral Equivalent of War

The message of hope that this book seeks to convey is the recovery of our universal innate spiritual connection with nature. I have tried to portray the inner peace and healing that come with that spiritual experience, no matter what its source of inspiration, which leads to all the human qualities that we deem to be civilized.

The mysterious, spiritual vibration of being in a certain natural setting, as many in this book have described, may lie at the heart of the deep-rooted, instinctive, and undoubtedly inherited affinity for natural environment and shelter. This is a key to opening the gates of love for nature, the biophilia that is shared, often unknowingly, by all humanity. That love, in turn, is a key to the perception that nurturing the life and resources of this small planet is our main responsibility. The love affair with nature is like a love affair with the most beautiful woman in the world. The heart throbs—the ecstasy is the same; the need to nurture and protect exceeds all else.

Humanity's materialistic treatment of our biosphere has gone on long enough. Our collective head and heart need to be reunited to achieve an ethic for our relationship with the biosphere. Environmental thinkers are raising their voices to be heard. Thomas Berry, among the most respected, writes, "In relation to the earth, we have been autistic for centuries." He urges that "we cease our industrial assault, that we abandon our inner rage . . . that we renew our human participation in the grand liturgy of the universe."[13]

The images that Ansel Adams captured in his large-view cameras are eternal reminders of that ecstatic youthful moment on Mount Clark. Those images have in turn captured the hearts and imagination of possibly millions, a significant role in heightening environmental consciousness.

With 6.8 billion human beings on this earth, there are perhaps only thousands of wilderness activists and millions of ecologically concerned individuals and members of traditional subsistence cultures. That tiny group of environmentalists must communicate to the immensely larger balance of humanity the messages that can convince all to begin to turn away from the slippery slope of biospheric meltdown.[14] Stephanie Mills, the American environmental activist, sees the duty of ecological restoration as the ensuring of the diversity of wildness, which can permit the "wild mystery of evolution" to proceed. Such a woman's movement that came to be called "ecofeminism" has explored some of the deep and sexist conflicts in ideas about human evolution. It has shown how the nurturing spirit of feminism can counter the often destructive, materialistic, and masculine side of humankind.[15]

*Environmental imagination* is the term that the Harvard professor Lawrence Buell uses to describe a process that can "energize" thought and action toward renewed engagement with nature.[16] Awareness may spring vicariously from reading or hearing about what's already in front of most of us. Nature writing serves to bring to our attention not just the beauty, structure, and organization of all natural things, large and small, but also the inroads made by humanity to upset the normally homeostatic and symbiotic biosphere.

But reading about it is never adequate enough to evoke the sharp jab of consciousness that can penetrate into the inner psyche. As John Muir writes about his beloved mountains: "no amount of word-making will ever make a single soul know these mountains."[17] The environmental unconscious defines a state of mind akin to nature mysticism and the related concepts of biophilia, ecological unconscious, ecological identity, and topophilia.[18]

To carry out such a renewal, it seems to me, is to turn to the young people of the world. They are the most receptive to learning, adapting, and spiritual experience. Ecological consciousness is generated in the child's enchanted garden of nature. These ecopsychological currents can continue into adulthood, bringing a natural spirituality that embraces the wilderness experience, expressing it in religion and art, and in cultural and political activism. There is an "ecological ego" that can direct the steps needed to reverse our slide toward environmental disaster.[19]

Schools and colleges everywhere must continue to expand the programs on ecology and environmental sciences. Both "intellectual and visceral journeys" will be necessary to cultivate "biospheric awareness" in the young in order to revive humanity's innate biophilia.[20] In many countries there are flourishing wilderness programs. The Wilderness Awakening School in Washington State is an example. Here the students learn the walking meditation of tracking and the vision quests of the Native Americans, and they emerge enlightened and, one hopes, changed forever in feeling their and our unbreakable link to nature. These modern vision quests foster a sense of self-discovery and self-reliance, and they regenerate from innate sources a deeply imprinted spiritual connection to nature. Such lasting memories can be refreshed by contact with even small bits of nature—a tree, a garden, even a rock.

Major efforts at all levels of society to create more such programs with direct wilderness experience can imbue youth with the knowledge, respect, and spiritual love that Stephen Gould says is the only way to win the battle to save our biosphere. Yet scientists and others, as I have suggested in the introduction, seem to avoid emotional issues when discussing our relationship to the environment. It is embarrassment, perhaps, a personal shyness to bare deep feelings. The naturalist David Orr comments on Gould's aphorism by pointing out that the word "love," much less "emotional bonding" and "fight," are not found in the environmental literature. Perhaps, as Abraham Maslow suggested, the denial of emotions is a defense against being overwhelmed by emotions that can include humility, reverence, mystery, wonder, and awe. Yet it is likely that many individuals move toward careers in biology and ecology after being moved by "an early, deep and vivid resonance between the natural world and us."[21]

Can the spiritual enlightenment from nature experiences lead a person to constructive action to salvage our environment? Can a mystic be a doer as well as a thinker? As I have sought to demonstrate in this book, mystical experience in nature affects a broad spectrum of individuals in a wide range of emotional responses and, ultimately, commitments. Notable examples of American environmental activists and nature mystics are John Muir, Ansel Adams, Aldo Leopold, Bill McKibben, and Henry Thoreau. Yet there are countless unnamed individuals, who do not write books or make speeches, who have felt the magic transformation and who quietly or publicly support and foster environmental conservation. There are no data, but a robust nature mystic can be the next-door neighbor, a member, perhaps, of some environmental or wilderness organization, a hiker, or a hunter.

One personal recollection may illustrate this point. The guide and mountain climber Norman Clyde (1885–1972) was a powerful presence in the Sierra Club. A schoolteacher, he experienced an epiphany early in life when trekking through the Sierra Nevada. He abandoned his profession and chose to live in the mountains for the rest of his life. Although reclusive, prone to solitary mountain ascents at night, achieving numerous first ascents of peaks along the range, he was also an inspiring guide for generations of trekkers and climbers. I recall visiting Norman in his small cabin above Big Pine after a day of trekking. It was incredibly cluttered with gear, yet it displayed a select collection of poetry and classic literature. He was not one to express his feelings, but I sensed a deep spiritual presence akin to that of a *sadhu* who renounces worldly attachment. But Clyde was no *sadhu*. His activities for the Sierra Club and others showed his active dedication to the preservation of our wilderness.

Such an example of an individual is multiplied untold times among vast numbers. But vaster numbers still are virtually trapped in urban jungles, leading "lives of quiet desperation" as Thoreau wrote, to seethe in conflict with fellow human beings, losing those innate tendencies that Wilson termed *biophilia*. Even a brief exposure to untrammeled wilderness is denied them. From such conditions arise so much of the senseless internecine conflict that besets humanity, even in this day of so-called enlightenment.

That wilderness, or its microcosm such as a Zen garden, a stone, a flower, can be a pathway to spiritual involvement with nature, surely the ground for all religion, and the source of total involvement that liberates. The nature mystic does not renounce the world; rather, he or she engages in it.

Religious groups, too, are awakening to the import of the global crisis. An ecological consciousness reminds us that our duty is not just to our fellow beings and to a remote yet immanent God, but also to that which nurtures us all, a part of any divinity, our suffering and fragile Earth.[22]

The second way, equally important, to "cease our industrial assault" is to somehow stop or turn around that giant ship of material "progress" and consumerism. But the inertial momentum of that global behemoth is huge and not easily changed. As Verlyn Klinkenborg points out the scientific data are here. The "true puzzle is human nature."[23] The huge inertia of the mass of humanity for change must be met by something with an equally large counterforce. That something most likely will be the looming environmental disaster. Why have many Americans, the greatest energy users and pollution makers on the planet, refused to face directly the evidence of our role in global warming?

Human life will still go on. We have evolved in an often harsh and unforgiving world and have in turn inflicted our violence upon it. We have experienced unending conflict among ourselves. The violence that we inflict on the planet may result in such disequilibrium that the ultimate consequences are in grave peril of leading to our own demise, at least of society as we know it today, a *Götterdämmerung* for human civilization. The natural human being is innately aggressive but also possesses the need and capacity to search for meaning, which can include the spiritual union with Gaia.

What additional forces can be mustered for the battle to preserve our biosphere? I turn again to the sagacious William James who wrote, nearly one hundred years ago but very much to the point of our present crisis, "What we now need to discover in the social realm is the moral equivalent of war: something heroic that will speak to men as universally as war does, and yet will be compatible with their spiritual selves as war has proved itself to be incompatible."[24]

This battle, selfless, as Krishna taught Arjuna in the Bhagavad Gita, in the transcendent realm of meaning of this great work, was the search for "refuge in the original spirit of man, from which primordial activity extended."[25]

A moral battle is needed, one that involves the virtues associated with war: selflessness, heroism, and energy. The two-million-year-old man exists in all of us, but he can be tamed by our social conscience to confront the faceless enemy of our own creation. That battle is wholly compatible with our spiritual selves, within which we preserve the deep-rooted feeling for our nourishing wilderness—the life, water, air, and soil from where we emerge and to where we will return.

Georg von Wright's pessimistic statement of humanity's future ends by the confession that his faith in reason is his only hope for humankind. He concludes his statement with an epigraph from a poem by Goethe.

> *Noch ist es Tag, da rühre sich der Mann,*
> *Die Nacht tritt ein, wo niemand wirken kann.*

> It is still day and humanity can act,
> When night comes, nothing can be wrought.[26]

Goethe paraphrased a line from the New Testament where Jesus told his disciples, "I must work the works of him that sent me, while it is day: the night cometh, when no man can work" (John 9:4).

It is still day, and there is still time to change course, to renew the emotional bond between nature and ourselves, that fragile bridge in danger of collapse. Let us act to save it now, for when night comes it will be too late.

# NOTES

## Introduction

1. Adams, verbal statement quoted by Newhall in *Ansel Adams*, 16–17.
2. Coleridge, "Anima Poetae," quoted in Laski, *Ecstasy*, 8.
3. W. James, *The Varieties of Religious Experience*, 380–81.
4. Ibid., 515–16.
5. See Cardena, Lynn, and Krippner, *Varieties of Anomalous Experience*, including the chapter by David M. Wulff on mystical experience, for a discussion of the various states of consciousness from the psychological perspective.
6. W. T. Stace views mystical experience in his book *Mysticism and Philosophy* with a cool, pragmatic, and critical eye.
7. Koch, *The Quest for Consciousness*, 6.
8. W. James, *Memories and Studies*, 204.
9. Newberg, d'Aquili, and Rouse, *Why God Won't Go Away*.
10. Stevens, *Wallace Stevens: Collected Poetry and Prose*, 30.
11. Inayat Khan, Lecture series entitled "New Perspectives in Science and Spirituality" delivered at Harvard University, October 21–23, 2001, author's notes.

## Chapter 1. The Beginnings of Nature and Spirit

1. Darwin, *Origin of Species*, 484.
2. Haldane, *On Being the Right Size and Other Essays*, 107.

3. Margulis and Sagan, *Microcosmos,* 14.

4. See Andrew Knoll's lucid review of what we presently know (and don't know) about the early evolution of life in *Life on a Young Planet,* 157.

5. Margulis and Sagan, "The Beast with Five Genomes," 38–41.

6. Tompkins and Bird, *The Secret Life of Plants,* 122.

7. Fechner, *Religion of a Scientist,* 187.

8. Tompkins and Bird, *The Secret Life of Plants,* xiv.

9. Darwin, *The Power of Movement in Plants,* 419.

10. Sinnot, *Cell and Psyche,* 61.

11. Ibid., 48.

12. Ibid., 72.

13. Margulis and Sagan, *Microcosmos,* 152.

14. Peat, *Synchronicity,* 66–67.

15. Richard Feynman observed paramecia as a youngster and gave these thoughtful comments in his delightful *Surely You're Joking, Mr. Feynman,* 92.

16. Popper, "The Place of Mind in Nature," in Elvee, *Mind in Nature,* 45.

17. Jung, "The Structure of the Psyche," in *Collected Works,* vol. 8, 152.

18. W. James, Letter to Henry James, September 17, 1886, *Correspondence,* vol. 2, 50–51.

19. W. James, *The Principles of Psychology,* 152.

20. "The Biosphere and Concepts of Ecology," in *New Encyclopedia Britannica, Macropedia,* vol. 14, 1127–1221.

21. Merbold, quoted in Kelly, *The Home Planet,* unnumbered page. "For the first time I saw the horizon as a curved line. It was accentuated by a thin seam of dark blue light—our atmosphere. Obviously this was not the ocean of air I had been told it was so many times in my life. I was terrified by its fragile experience."

22. Uexküll, *Der unsterbliche Geist in der Natur,* 6.

23. Lovelock, *The Ages of Gaia,* 210. "Our bodies contain a veritable history of life on Earth."

24. Teilhard de Chardin, *The Human Phenomenon,* 68. "Taken as a whole, from the first stages of its evolution, the living substance spread over the Earth forming the features of a single, gigantic organism."

25. Gottlieb, *This Sacred Earth,* 618.

26. A. Stevens, *The Two Million-Year-Old Self,* 5. Stevens quotes Jung: "Every civilized human being, however high his conscious development, is still an archaic man at the deeper levels of his psyche" (3). The prologue of Stevens's book contains a cogent paragraph:

> Rather than stay at home, I would have us journey far into the past and way over the horizon into cultures remote from the traditions of Western psychology. And rather than restrict ourselves to historical parallels from the relatively recent Sumerian, Egyptian, Greek, or Roman past, I would go back much further, back to the hunter-gatherer existence for which our psyches were formed, back to the archetypal foundations of all human experience, back to the hominid, mammalian, and reptilian ancestors who live on in the structures of our minds and brains. To do this is to discover within Jung's two million-year-old person, a 140 million-year-old vertebrate, which supports our finite existence and animates our dreams. (1)

27. Emerson, *Nature* (1836), 13.

28. Wordsworth, "Lines composed a few miles above Tintern Abbey, on revisiting the banks of the Wye during a tour, July 13, 1798," Lines 47–49 in *Selected Poems,* 109.

29. Kellert and Wilson, *The Biophilia Hypothesis,* 422. See also Wilson, *Biophilia,* 1.

30. Jeffries, *The Story of My Heart,* 19.

31. Kellert, *Kinship to Mastery,* 97.

32. Robert Pyle, *The Thunder Tree,* quoted in ibid., 102.

33. Abram, *The Spell of the Sensuous,* 131. For Abram, as the animals, plants, and rivers once spoke to our ancestors, the "inert letters of this page" now speak to us. "This is a form of animism . . . as mysterious as a talking stone."

34. Kahn, *The Human Relationship with Nature,* 7.

35. Shepherd, *Traces of an Omnivore,* 68.

36. I am grateful to David Oswald for permission to use his translation of Rainer Maria Rilke's *Sonnets to Orpheus,* pt. II, st. 14.

37. The affinity of humanity in the direction of wilderness is shown by Helburn also in the examples of zoos, parks, and wilderness expeditions in Helburn, "The Wilderness Continuum."

38. R. Taylor, "Order in Pollock's Chaos."

39. Emerson, *The Journals and Miscellaneous Notebooks of Ralph Waldo Emerson*, 5:137.

40. Gore, *Earth in the Balance*, 264.

## Chapter 2. The Hunter

1. Petersen, *Heartsblood*, 11. Petersen also writes, "Genetics confirms that as a species we have not had enough time in just 10,000 years of agriculture to evolve one iota of change in our collective genomes" (13).

2. Washburn and Lancaster, "The Evolution of Hunting," 299. The authors quote Haldane's comment on the successful and competitive evolution, "that Man is the only creature that can swim a mile, walk twenty miles, and climb a tree" (300). The tiger, however, may come in a very close second. Tigers are known to swim from island to island in the Sunderbans of the Bay of Bengal. See also Corbett's works on tracking the man-eaters of northern India, such as in *Man-eaters of Kumaon*. Paul Shepard in *Encounters with Nature* presents a lucid discussion of our heritage from the primeval nature (69–73).

3. Changeux and Chavaillon, *Origins of the Human Brain*, 75.

4. Ortega y Gasset, *Meditations on Hunting*, 150.

5. Ibid., 152. He continues, "In fact, the only man who truly thinks is the one who, when faced with a problem, instead of only looking straight ahead, toward what habit, tradition, the commonplace and mental inertia would make one assume, keeps himself alert, ready to accept the fact that the solution might spring from the least foreseeable spot in the great rotundity of the horizon." See also Norman Maclean's quotation in *A River Runs Through It and Other Stories*, "All there is to thinking—is seeing something you weren't noticing which makes you see something that isn't even visible" (92).

6. Richard Nelson, "Searching for the Lost Arrow," in Kellert and Wilson, *Biophilia Hypothesis*, 216.

7. Thoreau, "Walden," in *The Portable Thoreau*, 525.

8. Austin, *Zen and the Brain*, 16.

9. Abram, *The Spell of the Sensuous*, 140. In the section "The Language of the Birds," David Abram presents a cogent argument about how our primal sensorium has atrophied.

10. Wilson, *Biophilia*, 104.

11. Nabhan, *Cultures of Habitat*, 9.

12. Murchie, *The Seven Mysteries of Life*, 473.

13. Eddington, *The Nature of the Physical World*, 329.

14. Peat, *Synchronicity*, 222. For a perceptive discussion on some roots for the hunter's trance, read Peat's section "The Tiger and the Forest," 221–25.

15. von Essen, *The Revenge of the Fishgod*, 22–23.

16. Camuto, *Hunting from Home*, 18. He describes in essence the features of the hunter's trance.

17. See Cartmill, *A View to a Death in the Morning*, for a critical distancing from the theory that hunting is a "natural activity."

18. Stange, *Woman the Hunter*, 187. Her book supports the idea that all humanity, no matter the gender, has inherited similar traits and instincts, and, given the circumstances, will make them manifest. The professional hunter's observations are in Yendes, "Contrary to Popular Opinion," 34.

19. Rezendes, *The Wild Within*, 71.

20. Corbett, *Jungle Lore*, 21.

21. Rezendes, *The Wild Within*, 94.

22. Hay, *Mind the Gap*, 116.

23. Dillard, *Pilgrim at Tinker Creek*, 184.

24. V. Nabokov, *Speak, Memory*, 139.

25. Maclean, *A River Runs Through It and Other Stories*, 92.

26. Herrigel, *Zen in the Art of Archery*, 43. His book is a classic of Zen psychology and philosophy.

27. Camuto, *Hunting from Home*, 247.

28. Gill, "Bouldering," 140–41.

## Chapter 3. The Explorer

1. Alter, *Sacred Waters,* 145. Stephen Alter, born in India, undertook a journey, involving months of trekking, to the sources of the Ganges River high in the Garhwal and Kumaon districts of the new state of Uttaranchal.

2. Devereux, *The Sacred Place,* 49. Devereux describes the varieties of natural settings and natural and manmade objects of sacred sites.

3. Matthiessen, *The Snow Leopard,* 115.

4. Nietzsche, *Ecce Homo,* 300.

5. Turgenev, *A Hunter's Sketches,* 445.

6. de Duve, *Life Evolving,* vii.

7. See Adams, *The Soul unEarthed,* for descriptions and sources of several current wilderness programs.

8. Taylor, "Settling for Less," 169.

9. von Essen, *Revenge of the Fishgod,* 63.

10. See Russell Hvolbeck's *Mysticism and Experience* for a further discussion of the impact of nature on mystical experience.

11. Devereux, *The Sacred Place,* 184.

12. Hudson, *Far Away and Long Ago,* 224–25. Stephen Bodio writes in his introduction to Hudson's childhood recollections, "*Far Away and Long Ago* is the best of a rare and wonderful genre: the childhood memories of literate naturalists" (xiii).

13. Chawla, "Ecstatic Places," 23.

14. Melville, *Moby Dick,* 4–5.

15. Tuan, *Topophilia,* 93.

16. Wordsworth, lines 127–34, in *Selected Poems,* 343.

17. Traherne, "My Spirit," in *The Oxford Book of English Verse,* 46.

18. Emerson, *Nature: Addresses and Lectures,* 321.

19. Goethe, *Werke,* Band [vol.] 13, 42. Goethe reviews Ernst Stiedenroth's book *Psychologie zur Erklärung der Seelenerscheinungen* and coins the phrase in praising the author, a scientist, in allowing imagination to participate in the process of creative thought, "without which no art is possible."

20. Skillen, introduction to Bortoft, *The Wholeness of Nature,* ix.

21. Suchantke, *Eco-geography,* ix.

22. Keats, "Fancy," lines 4–7, in *The Complete Poems of John Keats,* 267.

23. Roszak, "Deep Form in Art and Nature," in Coupe, *Green Studies Reader,* 223–26.

24. Emerson, *Nature,* 13. The "transparent eyeball" metaphor provoked considerable discussion and one famous caricature by his fellow transcendentalist Christopher Pearce Cranch (fig. 3.1).

25. Wheeler, "Bohr, Einstein, and the Strange Lesson of the Quantum," in Elvee, *Mind in Nature,* 17–18. "I know of no clue more likely to allow us someday to grasp an understanding of these questions [the origin and structure of the universe] than the quantum" (23).

26. Emerson, *Nature* (1836), 13.

27. Camuto, *Hunting from Home,* 158.

28. Helen Keller had many mystical experiences. See Silverman, *Light in the Darkness,* 15, for a discussion of her mystical experiences and her understanding of Swedenborg.

29. Dillard, "Sight into Insight," in Schrodes, Firestone, and Shugrue, *The Conscious Reader,* 696–97. Dillard comments on the world noise distracting from vital truths:

    > The world's spiritual geniuses seem to discover universally that the mind's muddy river, this ceaseless flow of trivia and trash, cannot be dammed, and that trying to dam it is a waste of effect that might lead to madness. Instead you must allow the muddy river to flow unheeded in the dim channels of consciousness; you raise the sights; you look along it, mildly acknowledging its presence without interest and gazing beyond it into the realm of the real where subjects and objects act and rest purely, without utterance. (697)

30. Buell, *Writing for an Endangered World,* 83. Buell discusses Lopez's "dual accountability" (objective representation versus fabulation) in his piece on how bears stalk seals (92–93). In a revealing aside, Buell writes, "John Stuart Mill, who found solace in Wordsworth's compelling rendition of physical nature, would have been astonished by the stinginess of modern argument that Wordsworth reckoned nature as at best a convenience and at worst an impediment to the imagination"(84).

31. This is a quotation from Thoreau's journal in Hodder, *Thoreau's Ecstatic Witness,* 291.

32. Slovic, *Seeking Awareness in American Nature Writing,* 49.

33. W. James, *The Principles of Psychology,* 396.

34. See Crary's discussion of Goethe's, Kant's, and Schopenhauer's ideas of the role that the senses played in our perceptive and imaginative process in his chapter "Subjective Vision and the Separation of the Senses," in *Techniques of the Observer,* particularly 71–81.

35. Ibid., 142, 145.

36. Thoreau, *The Journal of Henry D. Thoreau,* 155–56.

37. Hofmann, *Insight Outlook,* 7.

38. Swedenborg, *Arcana Coelesta,* par. 4526.

39. Jahner, "The Spiritual Landscape," 32–38.

40. Emerson, *Nature* (1836), 36. Ralph Waldo Emerson, ever the teacher, and thus somewhat grandiloquent as was Lord Chesterfield, wrote essays on many subjects, including his masterpiece *Nature* from which many quotations can be gleaned. Emerson's *Nature,* however, has been a source of confusion, for me at least, which has meant many hours of tedious bibliographical research. There are, in fact, two distinct essays of the same title, written at different times in Emerson's life and of vastly different character.

The first essay, quoted in this chapter, was published in 1836 as a book of ninety-four pages. It was Emerson's first and consists of eight short chapters. According to several biographers and reviewers, it represents the genesis of Emerson's philosophical thesis that later became known as transcendentalism. It is written in a lucid prose with almost naïve enthusiasm, consistent with Emerson's youth.

The second essay, widely read in American literature classes in high schools and colleges, was published in 1844 and was part of a collection of essays entitled *Essays,* vol. 2, of which *Nature* is the sixth and comprises twenty-seven pages. Its prose is more opaque and its character more pedantic.

41. Storr, *Solitude,* 28.

42. Ibid., 37.

43. Lindbergh, *Gift from the Sea,* 24, 32, 33.

44. Csikszentmihalyi, *Finding Flow,* 42.

45. Dickinson, "Spirit in Nature," in *Collected Poems,* 92.

46. Thoreau, *The Portable Thoreau*, 602.

47. Ibid., 630.

48. It is dismaying to read from the new ecocriticism and ecogenderism of attempts to sweep away the sincere but often anthropocentric writings of naturalists like Thoreau. For example, Louise Westling, "Thoreau's Ambivalence toward Mother Nature," in Coupe, *The Green Studies Reader*, 265:

> Male writers down to our time have reiterated Thoreau's version of American pastoral. Hemingway's Nick Adams and Faulkner's Ike McCaslin perform similar escapist nest-building and killing rituals in eroticized landscapes, and gendered responses to Nature motivate environmentally conscious essayists like Edward Abbey and Barry Lopez. Understanding the destructive gender oppositions in *Walden* should help us see that as long as we continue to feminize nature and imagine ourselves apart from the biota, we will continue to enable the "heroic" destruction of the planet, even as we lament the process and try to erase or deny our complicity in it.

49. Emerson, "The Uses of Natural History," in *Selected Lectures*, 13.

50. Emerson, *Early Lectures*, vol. 1, no. 26.

51. Emerson, "The Over-Soul," in *Essays*, vol. 1, *The Complete Works of Ralph Waldo Emerson*, 250.

52. Swedenborg, *Arcana Coelesta*, par. 6319.

53. Thoreau, *The Journal of Henry D. Thoreau*, 5:359, quoted in Slovic, *Seeking Awareness in American Nature Writing*, 24.

54. E. Taylor, *Shadow Culture*, 63.

55. Thoreau, *The Journal of Henry D. Thoreau*, 3:274–75.

56. Hudson, *Far Away and Long Ago*, 224–25.

57. Beston, *The Outermost House*, 10.

58. Eddington, *The Nature of the Physical World*, 321.

59. Muir, *The Wild Muir*, 112–14.

60. Wordsworth, *The Essential Wordsworth*, 108–9.

61. Kellert, *Kinship to Mastery*, 41. Stephen Kellert devotes a chapter to considering the aesthetics of nature, 33ff.

62. Untermeyer, ed., *Modern American Poetry*, 5.

63. Wordsworth, "Tintern Abbey," lines 25–30, in *Selected Poems,* 108.
64. Jonsson, *Inner Navigation,* 321.
65. Griffin, *Animal Minds,* 250.
66. Jung, *Eranos Jahrbuch* (1938), quoted in Laski, *Ecstasy,* 55.
67. Olson, *The Singing Wilderness,* 7.

## Chapter 4. The Warrior and the Athlete

1. Hillman, *Blue Fire,* 180.
2. King, "Globalization and the Soul," 28–30. Teilhard de Chardin is quoted in several of his writings.
3. *Bhagavad Gita,* Karma Yoga, strophe 2.
4. Underhill, *Mysticism and War,* 25.
5. See Murphy and White, *In the Zone.* The authors have assembled 1545 bibliographic entries in their 302-page book. These are catalogued into categories such as mystical sensations of detachment, floating, ecstasy, and unity; altered perceptions of time, size, and light; out-of-body experiences; and extraordinary feats involving exceptional energy. The sheer volume of entries seems to have hampered their ability to unify mystical experiences in athletics to some common basis, a not uncommon problem when writing about any form of mysticism.
6. Cooper, *Playing the Zone,* 38.
7. Benson, *Timeless Healing,* 90. The Harvard physician also studied physiological reactions in mystics including *Sanyasis* and recorded remarkable changes during meditation. These are evidently controlled from the midbrain through blockage of afferent cortical pathways. Murphy and White, *In the Zone,* 138–48, have compared some of these physiological achievements with those of athletes.
8. Bannister, *The Four-Minute Mile,* 1–2.
9. Ackerman, *Deep Play,* quoted in Lipsyte, *Sportsworld,* 280.
10. Andrews, *The Psychic Power of Running,* 82–83.
11. Tolstoy, *Anna Karenina,* 272.
12. Ibid., 273.
13. Herzog, *Annapurna,* 16.

14. Muir, *The Wild Muir,* 92.

15. Jenkins, "Perfume in the Ozone," 29.

16. See Apter, *The Dangerous Edge.* The rewards of dangerous activities can be "a high . . . like no other" and an increased perception of things (40). His list of dangerous sports includes bull fighting, crime, auto racing, auto-erotic asphyxiation, and dueling, among many others—activities many of us would never consider trying.

17. Todhunter, *Dangerous Games,* 71.

18. Hemingway, *Death in the Afternoon,* 216.

19. Crane, *Red Badge of Courage,* 116.

20. Ibid., 148.

## Chapter 5. The Poet and the Artist

1. Emerson, *The Complete Works of Ralph Waldo Emerson,* 3:9–10.

2. Raine, "Nature," 263.

3. W. Stevens, *Wallace Stevens,* 929–30.

4. Burke, *A Philosophical Enquiry into the Origin of Our Ideas of the Sublime and Beautiful,* 57.

5. Ibid., 73.

6. Wordsworth, "Tintern Abbey," lines 55–70, in *Selected Poems,* 109.

7. Ibid., lines 88–111, p. 110.

8. Julian Huxley, *New Bottles for New Wine,* 311. "In the light of evolutionary humanism, however, the connection became clear, though the intellectual formulation given by Wordsworth was inadequate. The reality behind his thought is that man's mind is a partner with nature: it participates with the external world in the process of generating awareness and creating values" (508). Elsewhere in his chapter entitled "Evolutionary Humanism," Huxley states,

> I submit that the discoveries of physiology, general biology, and psychology not only make possible, but necessary, a naturalistic hypothesis, in which there is no room for the supernatural, and the spiritual forces at work in the cosmos are seen as part of nature just as much as the material forces. What is more, these spiritual forces

are one particular product of mental activity in the broad sense, and mental activities in general are seen to be increased in intensity and importance during the course of cosmic time. Our basic hypothesis is thus not merely naturalistic as opposed to supernaturalistic, but monistic or unitary as opposed to dualistic, and evolutionary, as opposed to static. (286)

Note that Huxley nowhere specifies mental activity to be solely that of man.

9. Spurgeon, *Mysticism in English Literature*, 60–67.
10. Wordsworth, "The Prelude: Book One," lines 269–281, in *Selected Poems*, 199.
11. Ibid., lines 288–300, p. 200.
12. A. Huxley, *Wordsworth in the Tropics*, 334ff.
13. Ibid., 340.
14. Oates, "Against Nature," in Halpern, *On Nature*, 236.
15. Ibid., 237.
16. Zaehner, *Mysticism Sacred and Profane*, 35.
17. De Quincey, *De Quincey As Critic*, 442. Thomas De Quincey was a good friend of Wordsworth's and often took long walks with him. He describes the following incident while they were waiting for an overdue mail carriage around midnight:

> At intervals, Wordsworth had stretched himself at length on the high road, applying his ear to the ground, so as to catch any sound of wheels that might be groaning in the distance. Once, when he was slowly rising from his effort, his eye caught a bright star that was glittering between the brow of Seat Sandal, and of the mighty Helvellyn. He gazed upon it for a minute or so; and then turning away to descend into Grasmere, he made the following explanation.... (194)

The quotation in the running text then follows.

18. Stallknecht, *Strange Seas of Thought*, 101ff.
19. Ibid., 12. There seems to be much that connects Wordsworth with William James. In several of his passages Wordsworth's pragmatic and detached revelations of underlying consciousness recall James's conceptual constructions, which will be discussed in chapter 7.

20. Myers, *Wordsworth,* 137.

21. Wordsworth, "Ode: Intimations of Immortality," in *Selected Poems,* lines 202–3, from Recollections of Early Childhood, 191.

22. Ibid., 227.

23. Hodder, *Thoreau's Ecstatic Witness,* 60–61.

24. Emerson, *Nature* (1836), 88.

25. Ibid., 33.

26. Thoreau, *The Journal of Henry D. Thoreau,* vol. 10, 127. October 26, 1857. "The seasons and all their changes are as me. . . . After a while I learn what my moods and seasons are. I would have nothing subtracted."

27. von Essen, *The Revenge of the Fishgod,* 25.

28. Richardson, *Emerson,* 548.

29. Thoreau, *The Journal of Henry D. Thoreau,* 1:74–75. March 3, 1839. We can see why some ecogenderists are incensed by Thoreau's "sexist" literary style.

30. Thoreau, *Collected Poems of Henry Thoreau,* 230–31.

31. Elder, *Imagining the Earth,* 215.

32. Slovic, *Seeking Awareness in American Nature Writing,* 76.

33. Gifford, *Green Voices,* 134.

34. Hughes, *The River,* 51.

35. Ibid., 28.

36. Keegan, *Ted Hughes,* 1214–15.

37. Ibid., 69.

38. See Bryson's characterization of various subsets of nature poetry such as eco- and green poetry in *Ecopoetry,* 5–6. The reference to a conversation with Hughes is on page 79.

39. Martin, *Shadows in the Cave,* 204.

40. David Bohm, *Wholeness and the Implicate Order,* quoted in Martin, *Shadows in the Cave,* 120.

41. Lewis-Williams, *The Mind in the Cave.* In a well-illustrated book, the author presents his theories behind prehistoric art. As others have asserted, he believes that shamanistic practice and primitive spiritualism were the factors leading to the burst of creative energy in Upper Paleolithic humankind. The mystic connection of ancient man to his environment, increas-

ingly masked by "rational" consciousness, survives and warrants nurturing.

42. Hurd, *Entering the Stone.* She describes the psychedelic experiences of a first-time spelunker.

43. See Griffin, *Animal Minds,* for examples of intelligent behavior throughout the animal world that equate to conscious thinking.

44. Martin, *Shadows in the Cave,* 204.

45. See Service and Bradley, *Megaliths and Their Mysteries,* for a survey of these giant rock installations, particularly in Europe.

46. Emerson, *The Journals and Miscellaneous Notebooks of Ralph Waldo Emerson,* 7:186.

47. Emerson, *Nature* (1836), 38.

48. Rowley, *Principles of Chinese Painting,* 20.

49. See Mowry, *Worlds within Worlds,* for a splendid pictorial essay on Chinese scholars' rocks.

50. Rosenblum, *Art of the Natural World,* 39.

51. Hay, *Kernels of Energy, Bones of Earth,* 144. Hay presents the history of many classical representations of the rock in Chinese art.

## Chapter 6. The Healer

1. Walsh, *The Spirit of Shamanism,* 8.

2. Benson, *The Break-out Principle,* 236.

3. Benson, *Timeless Healing,* 225–26.

4. Csikszentmihalyi and Csikszentmihalyi, *Optimal Experience,* 33.

5. Walsh, *The Spirit of Shamanism,* 262. The author reviews the old traditions and demonstrates how modern medicine may benefit. He invokes the need for solitude for psychological and spiritual development (52–55). See also my section titled "Solitude" in chapter 3 of this book, and Anthony Storr's *Solitude.*

6. Berry, *The Dream of the Earth,* 212.

## Chapter 7. The Mystic Ladder

1. H. James, ed., *The Letters of William James,* 2:76–77.

2. Wittgenstein, *Tractatus,* 6:522.

3. Roth, *Original Tao*, 142–43. Nei-yeh comes from early Taoism (400 BC) and describes methods for mystical "inner cultivation."

4. Martin, *Shadows in the Cave*, 107. Further, "Buddhism does not usually claim that the world is a delusion—it is merely understood (i.e. explicitly) normally, in a delusory way" (110).

5. Phillips, "The Genius Machine," *New Scientist*, 30–33.

6. Coleridge, *Biographia Literaria*, 169.

7. Jeffries, *The Story of My Heart*, 18.

8. Martin, *Shadows in the Cave*, 214. He quotes at length passages by Simon Leys in *The Burning Forest* on the origin and concept of *qi*.

9. W. James, *The Varieties of Religious Experience*, 501.

10. Ibid., 380.

11. W. James, *Memories and Studies*, 204.

12. Swedenborg, *Secrets of Heaven*, pars. 5121.2–3.

13. Bergson, *Creative Evolution*, 291.

14. Ibid., 295.

15. W. James, "On a Certain Blindness in Humanity" lecture, in *Talks to Teachers on Psychology*, 855.

16. Maslow, *Religions, Values and Peak Experiences*, 28.

17. Csikszentmihalyi, *Finding Flow*, 251.

18. A prolific nature writer, Diane Ackerman has written a lyric description of her own mystic connection to nature. *Deep Play*, 13.

19. Benson, *The Break-out Principle*, 236.

20. Greenwood's *The Nature of Magic* is a compendium of experiences in various forms of nature or "Earth" religion, including paganism, Wicca, druidism, shamanism, and much dealing with New Age. She explains her philosophy particularly in the introduction (viii).

21. Jamison, *Exuberance*, 24ff. Jamison is a professor of psychiatry at Johns Hopkins. The spectrum of experience covers a vast region of "altered states of consciousness" in which mystical experience has been classified. These together compose the dimensions of human superconsciousness forming the metaphoric mountain up which humanity instinctively strives to climb.

22. Austin, *Zen and the Brain*, 300–305.

23. Wilson, *Consilience*, 261.

24. Russell, *Mysticism and Logic, and Other Essays*, 12.

25. Rolland, *The Life of Ramakrishna*, 33.

26. For a discussion of the Freud-Rolland correspondence, see Parsons, *The Enigma of the Oceanic Feeling*.

27. Freud, *Civilization and Its Discontents*, 2.

> Thus we are willing to acknowledge that the "Oceanic" feeling exists in many people, and we are disposed to relate it to an early stage of ego-feeling; the further question arises: what claim has this feeling to be regarded as the source of the need for religion.
>
> To me this claim does not seem very forcible. Surely a feeling can only be a source of energy when it is itself the expression of a strong need. The derivation of a need for religion from a child's feeling of haplessness and the longing it evokes for a father seems to me incontrovertible, especially since this feeling is not simply carried on from childhood days but is kept perpetually alive by the fear of what the superior power of fate will bring. I could not point to any need in childhood so strong as that for father's protection. Thus the part played by the "oceanic" feeling, which I suppose seeks to reinstate limitless narcissism, cannot possibly take the first place. The derivation of the religious attitude can be followed back in clear outline as far as the child's feeling of helplessness. There may be something else behind this, but for the present it is wrapped in obscurity.
>
> I can imagine that the "oceanic" feeling could become connected with religion later on. That feeling of oneness with the universe which in its ideational content sounds very like a first attempt at the consolation of religion, like another way taken by the ego of denying the dangers it sees threatening it in the external world. I must confess I find it very difficult to work with these intangible quantities. Another friend of mine whose insatiable scientific curiosity has impelled him to the most out-of-the-way researches and to the acquisition of encyclopedic knowledge, has assured me that the Yogi by their practice of withdrawal from the

world, concentrating attention on body functions, peculiar methods of breathing, actually are able to produce new sensations and
diffused feeling in themselves which he regards as regressions to
primordial, deeply buried mental states. He sees in them a physiological foundation, so to speak, of much of the wisdom of mysticism. There would be connections to be made here with many
obscure modifications of mental life, such as trance and ecstasy.
But I am moved to exclaim, in the words of Schiller's diver: "Who
breathes overhead in the rose-tinted light may be glad"! (2–3)

Anthony Storr discusses the conflict within Freud about the "oceanic"
feeling and, in Storr's judgment, the error in Freud's reasoning is that mystical states of mind are merely regressive and narcissistic. His book is, in addition, a splendidly written exploration of the connection between solitude
and the creative personality (*Solitude,* 38–39).

For an exhaustive exploration of the oceanic feeling, with a detailed
analysis of the correspondence between Freud and Rolland, and numerous examples of nature ecstasies experienced by Rolland, see Parsons, *The
Enigma of the Oceanic Feeling.*

28. See Sigmund Freud's letter to his friend Wilhelm Fliess regarding his struggle to write a "Psychology for Neurologists," in *The Standard Edition of the
Complete Psychological Works of Sigmund Freud,* 1:283–85.

29. Jammer, *Einstein and Religion,* 126. "When he [Einstein] was asked, early
in 1921, whether he believed that the soul exists and continues to exist after
death, he replied, 'the mystical trend of our present time, showing itself especially in the exuberant growth of the so-called Theosophy and Spiritualism
is for me only a symptom of weakness and confusion.'

"In 1955, he wrote, 'What I see in nature is a magnificent structure that
we can comprehend only imperfectly, and that must fill a thinking person
with a feeling of 'humility'. This is a genuine religious feeling that has
nothing to do with mysticism" (127).

Jammer, in trying to define Einstein's religious viewpoint, says, "if mysticism denotes immediate intuition of, or insight into, a spiritual truth in a

way different from ordinary sense perception, or the use of logical thinking, Einstein was never a mystic" (132).

I believe that the term *ordinary sense perception* is key to distinguishing Einstein's belief system from that which he considered mysticism. In our discussion of nature mysticism, there is no point of sense perception that exceeds the "normal," at least qualitatively. What mystical experience involves in this context is a vast expansion or enhancement of consciousness, which leads to the sublime and creative moments that have been called ecstatic.

30. The ultimate attribution of Einstein's statements that are discussed here has been difficult but fascinating. It is fairly certain that his original statement (version 1 in the following comparisons) was written in German about 1930 in a short paper titled "Wie ich die Welt sehe," in *Mein Weltbild*. This was then translated into English in 1931 (Jammer, *Einstein and Religion*). Einstein then modified the statement for a phonograph recording in 1932 as part of his *Glaubensbekenntnis* (credo), which is documented in Friedrich Herneck, *Einstein und sein Weltbild*, 100–101 (version 2 in the following comparisons).

The final version has been traced back as far as 1948 in Barnett, *The Universe and Dr. Einstein*. Lincoln Barnett introduces the aphorism by writing, "Einstein, whose philosophy of science has sometimes been criticized as materialistic, once said: 'The most beautiful and most profound emotion we can experience is the sensation of the mystical.' " Barnett continues, "and on another occasion he [Einstein] declared, 'The cosmic religious experience is the strongest and noblest mainspring of scientific research'" (105). The author gives us no citation details. Thus we have a quotation involving the word *mystical* that has been used hundreds if not thousands of times (to judge from searching the Internet) but cannot be directly traced to Einstein's speeches or writings. The only certainty of its veracity as a statement by Einstein is that he, himself, wrote the foreword to Barnett's book. The progression of this statement from its three versions in English and the original German is presented in the following table:

| Version 1 1930 | Version 2 1932 | Version 3 before 1948 |
|---|---|---|
| The most beautiful experience we can have is the mysterious. | The most beautiful and most profound that a person can experience is the mysterious. | The most beautiful and most profound emotion we can experience is the mystical. |
| It is the fundamental emotion, which stands at the cradle of true art and true science. | It is the foundation of religion as well as deeper strivings of art and science. | It is the sower* of all true science.<br>*Source* would be the correct translation it is *Quelle* in German. |
| Whoever does not know it and can no longer wonder, no longer marvel, is as good as dead, and his eyes are dimmed. | Who never experienced that seems to me if not a dead person but then a blind person. | He to whom this emotion is a stranger, who can no longer wonder and stand rapt in awe, is as good as dead. |
| Das Schönste was wir erleben können, ist das Geheimnissvolle. | Das schönste und tiefste, was der Mensch erlben kann, ist das Gefûhl des Geheimnissvollen. | Das schönste und tiefste Gefühl, was wir erleben können, ist die Empfindung des Mystischen. |
| Es ist das Grundegefühl, das der Wiege von wahrer Kunst und Wissenschaft steht. | Es liegt der Religion sowie allem tieferen Strebe in Kunst und Wissenschaft zugrunde. | Es ist Quelle aller wahren Wissenschaft. |
| Wer es nicht kennt und sich nicht mehr wundern, nicht mehr staunen kann, der is sozusagen tot und sein Auge erloschen. | Wer dies nicht erlebt hat, erscheint mir, wenn nicht wie ein Toter, so doch ein Blinder. | Wem dieses Gefühl fremd ist, wer nicht mehr staunen und nicht mehr in Ehrfurcht versinken kann, der ist so gut wie tot. |

31. Lewontin, *New York Review of Books,* October 20, 2005, 54.

32. Honner, "Niels Bohr and the Mysticism of Nature," 243.

33. Buckley and Peat, *A Question of Physics: Conversations in Physics and Biology,* 3.

34. A transcendent passage from Proust, *Swanns Way,* 63–64.

35. Hoffman, *Visions of Innocence,* 34.

36. Ibid., 39.

37. Ibid.

38. Doctorow, *Lives of the Poets,* 27.

39. Louv, *Last Child in the Woods.*

40. Chawla, Ecstatic Places, 22.

41. Public Broadcasting System interview of members of the Kronos Quartet, September 29, 1999.

42. Public Broadcasting System program on Andrew Wiles, October 1998.

43. Nietzsche, *Ecce Homo,* 300. This section of his description of writing *Thus Spoke Zarathustra* stands as a memorable contribution to the creative experience.

44. Leuba, *The Psychology of Religious Mysticism,* 242.

45. Ibid., 240.

46. Greeley, *Ecstasy.* He cites several sources in literature and science to support his thesis that ecstasy is a "dramatically different form of cognition."

47. Thoreau, *The Journal of Henry D. Thoreau,* 1:50–51. Entry of August 13, 1838.

48. Eliot, "Tradition and Individual Talent," in *The Sacred Wood,* 13. First published in *Egoist,* September–December 1919. Eliot continues: "and the more perfectly will the mind digest and transmit the passions which are its material."

49. Danto, *Mysticism and Morality,* 113.

## Chapter 8. Wider Than the Sky

1. H. James, ed., *The Letters of William James,* 2:149–50. To Henry W. Rankin, June 16, 1901. This often-quoted letter summarizes the heart of William James's creation of *The Varieties of Religious Experience.*

2. Ibid., 2:210. June 10, 1901.

3. W. James, *Essays in Philosophy,* 194.

4. W. James, *A Pluralistic Universe,* 169, 289.

5. Ibid., 150.

6. W. James, "A Suggestion about Mysticism," 159.

7. W. James, *The Varieties of Religious Experience,* 377, in the introductory paragraph of the first lecture (XVI) on mysticism.

8. Martin, *Shadows in the Cave*, 6. He cites Polanyi, *The Tacit Dimension*, and constructs many of his ideas about mysticism from this seemingly simple insight.

9. Adler, "William James and Gustav Fechner: From Rejection to Elective Affinity," in Donnelly, *Reinterpreting the Legacy of William James*, 259.

10. Fechner, *Elemente der Psychophysik*, 530. In William James's own copy (now at the Houghton Library at Harvard University), several phrases of Fechner's wave concept are underlined.

11. W. James, *The Will to Believe*, 59. "In this figure a, b, c stand for three organisms, or rather for the total waves of psycho-physical activity of three organisms, whilst AB represents the threshold. In each wave the part that rises above the threshold is an integrated thing, and is connected with a single consciousness. Whatever lies below the threshold, being unconscious, separates the conscious crests, although it is still the means of physical connection" (64). James continues: "One easily sees how, on Fechner's wave-scheme, a world-soul may be expressed. All psychophysical activity being continuous 'below the threshold,' the consciousness might also be continuous if the threshold sank low enough to uncover all the waves. The threshold throughout nature in general is, however, very high, so the consciousness that gets over it is of the discontinuous form" (65).

12. James invokes the oceanic and tidal metaphor in several of his works. In "A Suggestion about Mysticism," 157–58, he presents his concept of Fechner's wave scheme:

> The suggestion, stated very briefly, is that states of mystical intuition may be only very sudden and great extensions of the ordinary 'field of consciousness.' Concerning the causes of such extensions I have no suggestions to make; but the extension itself would, if my view is correct, consist in an immense spreading of the margin of the field, so that knowledge ordinarily transmarginal would become included, and the ordinary margin would grow more central. Fechner's 'wave-scheme' will diagram the alteration, as I conceive it, if we suppose that the wave of present awareness, steep above the horizontal line that represents the plane of the usual 'threshold,' slopes away below it very gradually in all directions. A

fall of the threshold, however caused, would, under these circumstances, produce the state of things, which we see on an unusually flat shore at the ebb of the spring tide. Vast tracts usually covered are then revealed to view, but nothing rises more than a few inches above the water's bed, and great parts of the scene are submerged again whenever a wave washes over them. (157–58)

In another example, in *Human Immortality:*

According to the state in which the brain finds itself, the barrier of its obstructiveness may also be supposed to rise or fall. It sinks so low, when the brain is in full activity that a comparative flood of spiritual energy pours in. At other times, only such occasional waves of thought as heavy sleep permits get by. (17)

James regarded the theory of "threshold of consciousness" with deepest confidence and of great importance to psychology (Bush, "William James and Panpsychism," 322). A poetic New England metaphor of James is seen in *Memories and Studies,* 204:

Out of my experience . . . one fixed conclusion dogmatically emerges . . . that we with our lives are like islands in the sea or trees in the forest. The maple and pine may whisper to each other with their leaves. And Conanicut and Newport hear each other's foghorns. But the trees commingle their roots in the darkness under ground and the islands also hang together through the ocean bottom. Just so there is a continuity of cosmic consciousness against which several minds plunge as into a Mother Sea or reservoir. . . . What are the conditions of individuation or insulation in this mother-sea? We need only suppose the continuity of our unconscious with a mother-sea, to allow waves pouring over the dam. Of course these odd lowerings of the brain's threshold remain a mystery on any terms.

13. W. James, "A Suggestion about Mysticism," 158. James concludes this essay:

I have treated the phenomenon under discussion as if it uncovered tracts of *consciousness.* Is the consciousness already there waiting to be uncovered? And is it veridical revelation of reality? These are questions on which I do not touch. In the subjects of the experience the "emotion of conviction" is always strong, and sometimes absolute. The ordinary psychologist disposes of the phenomenon under the conveniently "scientific" head of *petit mal,* if not "bosh" or "rubbish." But we know so little of the noetic value of abnormal mental states of any kind that that in my opinion we had better keep an open mind and collect facts sympathetically for a long time to come. We shall not *understand* these alterations of consciousness either in this generation or in the next. (158)

How prescient he was!

14. W. James, "A Suggestion about Mysticism," 503.

15. A. Huxley, *Doors of Perception,* 23.

16. Peirce, *Collected Papers,* vol. 7, par. 547.

17. Restak, *Mysteries of the Mind,* 77.

18. Ibid., 86. Restak cites the work of Robert Pollack, who adds, "This wave links the centers responsible for processing sensory information to one another as well as to other centers responsible for unconscious and conscious activities of the mind, in particular the amygdala, the hippocampus, and the frontal cortex, where, broadly speaking, emotional states are generated, long-term memories stored, and the intentions to speak and act generated" (undocumented citation from Robert Pollack, *How the Unconscious Shapes Modern Science*).

19. Zohar and Marshall, *SQ,* 62–63. The author presents her concepts of *SQ,* spiritual intelligence, which in large part embraces my concepts of mysticism, broad as they may be painted.

20. Austin, *Zen and the Brain,* 298.

21. Marilyn E. Marshall, "Gustav Theodor Fechner: Psychological Acrobat," in Brozek and Gundlach, *G.T. Fechner and Psychology.*

22. W. James, *The Principles of Psychology,* 219–78.

23. Ibid., 272–73. James may have studied analytic geometry in his intense, mostly European education, but he expressed the concept of this fairly sophisticated mathematical model in terms easily grasped by the general reader. This is just a further example of the clearness and accessibility of his thinking and writing. Diagrammatic models did fascinate him, and as we

will see, they influenced much of his visual thinking about the "mother sea of consciousness" and Fechner's wave theory.

24. Ibid., 272.

25. Bohm, *Thought as a System,* 131–34.

26. W. James, *A Pluralistic Universe,* 231–32. James considered the threshold of Fechner "as only one way of naming the quantitative discreteness in the change of all our sensible experience" (232).

27. A. Huxley, *Doors of Perception and Heaven and Hell,* 155.

28. Herbert Benson described the scientific basis for the relaxation response in his chapter in *Encyclopedia of Neuroscience,* vol. 2 (Boston: Birkhäuser), 1043–47.

29. Zaehner, *Mysticism Sacred and Profane,* xii–xiii.

30. Vaitl et al., "Psychobiology of Altered States of Consciousness," 100.

31. Ibid., 102.

32. Ibid., 105.

33. Ibid., 108.

34. Mandell, "Toward a Psychobiology of Transcendence," 404.

35. Pert, *Molecules of Emotion,* 133.

36. Goldstein's study on student volunteers is quoted by Levinthal in *Messengers of Paradise,* 178–79.

37. d'Aquili and Newberg, "Religious and Mystical States," 185.

38. Ibid., 187–89.

39. Mandell, "Toward a Psychobiology of Transcendence," 438.

40. Roy, personal communication.

41. Leuba, *The Psychology of Religious Mysticism,* 255ff. "Few of the lesser trance-phenomena are more striking and incontestably wholly physiological in origin than a peculiar appearance of light or brilliance which may be called *photism.* Mystics frequently use the word 'light', but it is not always possible to know whether they use it in a symbolical or in a realistic sense. In a great number of instances, however, the perceptual quality of the experience cannot be doubted" (255ff.).

42. Wordsworth, "The Prelude, 'I walked with nature,'" lines 16–18 in *The Essential Wordsworth.*

43. Nietzsche, *Ecce Homo,* 36.

44. Alcoholics Anonymous, *"Pass It On,"* 121.

45. McKibben, *The End of Nature,* 87.

46. Dean, *Psychiatry and Mysticism,* 10.

47. Hunt, *On the Nature of Consciousness,* 156–59.

48. G. Taylor, *The Natural History of the Mind,* 111 ff. Taylor describes some experiments in meditation: "we see regression to Phase Two [paleomammalian or midbrain function] before our very eyes; colors become more vivid . . . which I interpret as the breakdown of cortically mediated vision in favor of thalamic vision." For those who are interested, this entire chapter on unusual states of consciousness is well worth reading.

49. Austin, *Zen and the Brain,* 241.

50. d'Aquili and Newberg, *The Mystical Mind,* 33.

51. Lewis-Williams and Pearce, "The Consciousness Contract," chap. 2 in *Inside the Neolithic Mind.*

52. Austin, *Zen and the Brain,* 494.

53. Lightman, *A Sense of the Mysterious,* 16–17.

54. Peat, *The Blackwinged Night,* 96. David Peat translates quantum theory for the ordinary reader like myself and takes us on a roller coaster ride to show how such incredible energy can exist in the plenum of the vacuum state. He proceeds to draw parallels with the void of mystic consciousness that I describe. "The total absence—the negation that, at the same time, is a plenum and absolute fullness—is found in the writings of mystics. It is also the vision expressed by artists and musicians alike. All that exists outside the void and in the domain of time is, to some extent, conditioned. For the Buddhist and physicist alike, to be tied to the wheel of time is to be caught up in the eternal web of cause and effect. The void, the negation of all, lies beyond this causality. It is unconditioned, pure potential" (91).

55. Forman, *Mysticism, Mind, Consciousness,* 171–72.

56. d'Aquili and Newberg, "Religious and Mystical States," 185.

57. E. Taylor, "The Spiritual Roots of James's *Varieties of Religious Experience,*" li.

58. W. James, *The Varieties of Religious Experience,* 394.

59. Hamer, *The God Gene,* 11.

60. Merton, *The Ascent to the Truth.* In the chapter entitled "False Mysticism" (59–72), Merton expands on the influences that draw the human psyche

away from mystical contemplation of "the true end and seek(s) the enjoyment of flattering and glorious experiences rather than the perfect gift of
our whole being to God alone." To the influences he lists, I must add, however, those of organized religion, including Merton's own Roman Catholic
Church.

61. W. James, *The Varieties of Religious Experience,* 426.

62. Hunt, *On the Nature of Consciousness,* 189.

63. Morrison, *Spirit in the Gene,* 183. He writes a refreshingly iconoclastic view
of the destructive side of humanity and of our drive toward oblivion. He
misuses, I believe, the word *mysticism,* and he applies the term to a spectrum of feelings and instincts, including fear and hate.

64. W. James, *The Varieties of Religious Experience,* 37ff.

65. Leary, *The Politics of Ecstasy,* 1965.

66. Barnard, *Exploring Unseen Worlds,* 25ff. He discusses James's experiments
at length and concludes:

> This account of James's experiment gives us a glimpse of the
> strength of James's character. We see here not only James's coura-
> geous receptivity to the unknown and the unconventional (as well
> as his openness to ideas that would reverse years of personal philo-
> sophical work), but also his willingness to share this unorthodox
> experience with his academic colleagues. Further, James's com-
> ments on his nitrous oxide experience are also an immensely fertile
> source of insights into the roots of James's later, more developed
> philosophical stance on mysticism. To begin with, this account
> is a clear demonstration of his methodology: phenomenological
> reporting first, followed by an intellectual and ethical assessment.
> We can see also evidence of James's later stress on the emotional
> aspects of mystical experience, as well as the characteristics of
> ineffability, noetic quality, transiency and inner unity that James
> repeatedly associates with mystical experience in his later philoso-
> phy of mysticism. Finally, this account also illustrates the ways in
> which James's repeated emphasis on the theme of reconciliation
> in philosophical work—both the reconciliation between self and
> God that is stressed in the *Varieties* as well as the reconciliation

between mind and matter that was attempted in his later radical empiricism—is intimately connected with his understanding of mystical experience.

67. These comments are quoted by Zaehner, *Mysticism Sacred and Profane*, 114–16. The health guru Andrew Weil, in his book *The Natural Mind*, advocates drug use as a tool to enter other states of consciousness (194–95).

68. Laski, *Ecstasy*.

69. Harris, *Drugged America*, 104ff.

70. Grady, "Medicine Lags against Addiction."

71. Ibid.

72. Ibid., 79.

73. Ibid., 84.

74. Weil, *The Natural Mind*, 195.

75. Ziegler, "Psychedelic Religious Experience," 74–76.

## Chapter 9. Ecocrisis

1. Wilson, *Consilience*, 282.

2. Wilson, *The Future of Life*, 58.

3. www.wikipedia.org/wiki/Asian_brown_cloud.

4. Zwingle, "Megacities," 78.

5. Diamond, *New York Review of Books*, March 25, 2004.

6. Bookchin, "Organic Society," 66.

7. Ibid., 71.

8. Naess, *Life's Philosophy*, 100. He writes: "Human beings do not have the right to reduce the richness and diversity of life. . . ."

9. Roszak, *The Voice of the Earth*, 252.

10. Berry, *Dream of the Earth*, 11. "If we lived in the moon, our mind and emotions, our speech, our imagination, our sense of the divine would all reflect the desolation of the lunar landscape." Also on page 117, ". . . the human psychic structure and our spirituality have been taking shape over all these billions of years . . ." We are surely deeply rooted in the environment from which we arose.

11. von Wright, *Vetenskapen och förnuftet*. This book is based on his lecture

"Images of Science and Forms of Rationality," which was given at a colloquium by the European Science Foundation in Colmar, April 1985. Wright (who died in 2003) was a successor to Wittgenstein as Professor of Philosophy at Cambridge University and was Emeritus Professor at Helsingfors University.

12. Eddington, "In Defense of Mysticism," in *The Nature of the Physical World,* 325.

13. Morris, *The Human Zoo,* quoted in A. Stevens, *The Two Million-Year-Old Self,* 70.

14. Thomas, *The Lives of a Cell,* 107ff. Lewis Thomas reported some observations by the anthropologist C. M. Turnbull in *The Mountain People.*

15. The Zurich psychoanalyst C. A. Meier considered "the unconscious as inexhaustible as nature," that it represented humanity's inner wilderness. "Wilderness and the Search for the Soul of Modern Man," 6.

16. Steven Wofsy writes a comprehensive review of global pollution and warming in "The Great Global Experiment."

17. A balanced book without polemics is needed. This is one: Meadows, Randers, and Meadows, *Limits of Growth.*

18. Sinnot, *The Bridge of Life,* 12.

19. von Wright. *Vetenskapen och förnuftet,* 58.

20. Suzuki and McConnell, *The Sacred Balance,* 174.

21. von Wright, *Vetenskapen och förnuftet,* 58-67

22. Ibid., 64.

23. Stevens, *Roots of War and Terror,* 31.

24. See Bill Moyers's discussion of the political and ecological implication of fundamentalist beliefs in the rapture. "Welcome to Doomsday," *New York Review of Books* (March 24, 2004): 8–10.

25. von Wright, "The Myth of Progress," 132. He continues: "To debunk them is to expose the lack of rational justification for the distorting effects on life stemming from the systems. It is also to urge those who exercise power to consider the value of ends for the attainment of which their acting and doing are the means. It is therefore a plea for a form of rationality that has tended to atrophy under an excessive growth of the instrumental uses of reason. In Weberian terms one could call it a plea for *Wertrationalität* in

a culture which has become obsessed and twisted by a hypertrophy of its capacity for *Zweckrationalität*."

26. See Michael Boulter's *Extinction* for a cogent discussion on evolution and the end of man. The paleontologist Peter Wood brilliantly addresses this "Third Event" of our biosphere in *The End of Evolution*.

27. Nicholson, *Love of Nature*, xi.

28. Thomashow, *Bringing the Biosphere Home*, 10.

29. Rees, *Our Final Hour*, 230.

30. Roszak, *The Voice of the Earth*, 159.

31. Roszak, Gomes, and Kanner, *Ecopsychology*, 15–16.

32. Moore, "Trashed: Across the Pacific Ocean, Plastics, Plastics, Everywhere," *Natural History*, November 3, 2003, 51.

33. Maxwell, "Considering Spirituality, Integral Spirituality, Deep Science and Ecological Awareness," 274.

## Chapter 10. The Future Rests with Us

1. Korpela and Ylén, "Effectiveness of Favorite-Place Prescriptions."

2. McKibben, *The End of Nature*, 69.

3. Nicholsen, *The Love of Nature and the End of the World*, 187.

4. Marcuse, *Eros and Civilization*, 167.

5. Abram, *The Spell of the Sensuous*, 69.

6. Gottlieb, *This Sacred Earth*, 616.

7. Roszak, *The Voice of the Earth*, 217.

8. Wordsworth, Preface to Lyrical Ballads, in *Selected Poems*, 449.

9. The writer and zoologist Matt Ridley documents the best and worst sides of human instincts in *The Origins of Virtue*, 264.

10. Kellert, *Kinship to Mastery*, 205.

11. See S. James and Lahti, *Natural Steps for Communities*.

12. Kaplan, *The Experience of Nature*, 147.

13. Berry, *The Dream of the Earth*, 215.

14. Stephanie Mills writes an impassioned chapter, "The Wild and the Tame," in Burks, *Place of the Wild*, 45.

15. Theodore Roszak presents a historical and analytic discussion of ecofeminism in *The Voice of the Earth*, 233–46.

16. Buell, *The Environmental Imagination*, 2.

17. Muir, *Travels in Alaska,* xviii.

18. Buell, *Writing for an Endangered World,* 275. Lawrence Buell's work is a masterful contribution to the postmodern "hot" literary topic called eco-criticism. Those who wish to know all the other "eco" subjects such as eco-populism, ecogenderism, etc., can find a cogent discussion in this volume as well as in his previous work, *The Environmental Imagination.*

19. Roszak, *The Voice of the Earth,* 321.

20. Thomashow, *Bringing the Biosphere Home,* 192.

21. Orr, "For the Love of Life," 486–87.

22. See John E. Carroll, *Sustainability and Spirituality,* for a discussion on increasing organized efforts by various predominantly Catholic denominations in addressing the ecological crisis through education and spiritual and practical example.

23. Klinkenborg, "Be Afraid. Be Very Afraid," 19.

24. W. James, *The Varieties of Religious Experience,* 367.

25. Bhagavad Gita, Fifteenth Teaching, strophe 4.

26. von Wright, *Vetenskapen och förnuftet,* 150–54.

# BIBLIOGRAPHY

Abram, David. *The Spell of the Sensuous: Perception and Language in a More-Than-Human World*. New York: Pantheon, 1996.

Ackerman, Diane. *Deep Play*. New York: Random House, 1999.

Adams, Cass. *The Soul unEarthed: Celebrating Wildness and Personal Renewal through Nature*. New York: Tarcher/Putnam, 1996.

Alcoholics Anonymous. *"Pass It On": The Story of Bill Wilson and How the A.A. Message Reached the World*. New York: Alcoholics Anonymous World Services, 1984.

Alter, Stephen. *Sacred Waters: A Pilgrimage Up the Ganges River to the Source of Hindu Culture*. New York: Harcourt, 2001.

Andrews, Valerie. *The Psychic Power of Running: How the Body Can Illuminate the Mysteries of the Mind*. New York: Rawson, Wade, 1978.

Apter, Michael J. *The Dangerous Edge: The Psychology of Excitement*. New York: Free Press, 1992.

Austin, James H. *Zen and the Brain: Toward an Understanding of Meditation and Consciousness*. Cambridge, Mass.: MIT Press, 1998.

Bannister, Roger. *The Four-Minute Mile*. New York: Dodd Mead, 1955.

Barnard, G. William. *Exploring Unseen Worlds: William James and the Philosophy of Mysticism*. Albany: State University of New York Press, 1997.

Barnett, Lincoln. *The Universe and Dr. Einstein*. New York: Sloan Associates, 1948.

Barrow, John. *The Artful Universe*. Oxford, UK: Clarendon Press, 1995.

Benson, Herbert. *The Break-out Principle*. New York: Scribner, 2003.

————. *Timeless Healing: The Power and Biology of Belief.* New York: Scribner, 1996.

Bergson, Henri. *Creative Evolution.* New York: Dover Books, 1998.

Berry, Thomas. *The Dream of the Earth.* San Francisco: Sierra Club, 1988.

Beston, Henry. *The Outermost House: A Year of Life on the Great Beach of Cape Cod.* New York: Viking, 1928. Reprinted 1949.

Binet, Alfred. *The Psychic Life of Micro-organisms: A Study in Experimental Psychology.* Chicago: Open Court, 1897.

Bloom, Howard. *Global Brain: The Evolution of Mass Mind from the Big Bang to the 21st Century.* New York: John Wiley, 2000.

Bohm, David. *Wholeness and the Implicate Order.* London: Routledge & Kegan Paul, 1980.

————. *Thought as a System.* New York: Routledge, 1994.

Bookchin, Murray. "Organic Society." In *The Murray Bookchin Reader.* London: Cassell, 1997.

Borchert, Bruno. *Mysticism: Its History and Challenge.* Translated from the Dutch: *Gescheidenis, en uitdaging.* York Beach, Maine: Samuel Weiser, 1994.

Bortoft, Henri. *The Wholeness of Nature: Goethe's Way toward a Science of Conscious Participation in Nature.* Great Barrington, Mass.: Lindisfarne Books, 1997.

Boulter, Michael. *Extinction: Evolution and the End of Man.* New York: Columbia University Press, 2002.

Brockington, A. Allen. *Mysticism and Poetry: On a Basis of Experience.* London: Chapman & Hall, 1934.

Brozek, Josef, and Horst Gundlach, eds. "G. T. Fechner and Psychology." Number 6 in *Passauer Schriften zur Psychologiegeschichte.* Passau, Germany: Passivia Universitätsverlag, 1987.

Bryson, J. Scott, ed. *Ecopoetry: A Critical Introduction.* Salt Lake City: University of Utah Press, 2002.

Bucke, Richard Maurice. *Cosmic Consciousness: A Study in the Evolution of the Human Mind.* 1901. Reprinted with a new introduction by George M. Acklom, 1949. New York: E. P. Dutton, 1970.

Buckley, Paul, and F. David Peat. *A Question of Physics: Conversations in Physics and Biology.* Toronto: University of Toronto Press, 1979.

Buell, Lawrence. *The Environmental Imagination: Thoreau, Nature Writing, and the Formation of American Culture.* Cambridge, Mass.: Belknap Press of Harvard University Press, 1995.

———. *Writing for an Endangered World: Literature, Culture, and Environment in the U.S. and Beyond.* Cambridge, Mass.: Harvard University Press, 2001.

Burke, Edmund. *A Philosophical Enquiry into the Origin of Our Ideas of the Sublime and Beautiful.* 1757. London: Routledge and Kegan Paul, 1958.

Burks, David Clarke, ed. *Place of the Wild.* Washington, D.C.: Island Press, 1994.

Bush, Wendell T. "William James and Panpsychism." Vol. 2 in *Studies in the History of Ideas.* New York: Columbia University Press, 1925.

Camuto, Christopher. *Hunting from Home: A Year Afield in the Blue Ridge Mountains.* New York: W. W. Norton, 2003.

Cardena, Etzel, Steven J. Lynn, and Stanley C. Krippner, eds. *Varieties of Anomalous Experience: Examining the Scientific Evidence.* Washington, D.C.: American Psychological Association, 2000.

Carroll, John E. *Sustainability and Spirituality.* Albany: State University of New York Press, 2004.

Carter, Rita. *Exploring Consciousness.* Berkeley: University of California Press, 2002.

———. *Mapping the Mind.* Berkeley: University of California Press, 1998.

Cartmill, Matt. *A View to a Death in the Morning: Hunting and Nature through History.* Cambridge, Mass.: Harvard University Press, 1993.

Chaisson, Eric. *Cosmic Dawn: The Origins of Matter and Life.* New York: W. W. Norton, 1981.

Changeux, Jean-Pierre, and Jean Chavaillon, ed. *Origins of the Human Brain.* A Fyssen Foundation Symposium. Oxford, UK: Clarendon Press, 1995.

Chatwin, Bruce. *The Songlines.* London: Cape, 1987.

Chawla, Louse. "Ecstatic Places." *Children's Environments Quarterly* 7, no. 4 (1990): 18–23.

Coleridge, Samuel. *Biographia Literarea.* Oxford: Oxford University Press, 1973.

Cook, Reginald L. *Passage to Walden.* Boston: Houghton Mifflin, 1949.

Cooper, Andrew. *Playing the Zone: Exploring the Spiritual Dimensions of Sports.* Boston: Shambhala, 1998.

Corbett, Jim. *Jungle Lore.* New York: Oxford University Press, 1953.

———. *Man-eaters of Kumaon.* 1944. New Delhi: Oxford India Paperbacks, 2005.

Coupe, Laurence, ed. *The Green Studies Reader: From Romanticism to Ecocriticism.* London: Routledge, 2000.

Crane, Stephen. *The Red Badge of Courage.* Boston: Houghton Mifflin, 1960.

Crary, Jonathan. *Techniques of the Observer: On Vision and Modernity in the Nineteenth Century.* Cambridge, Mass.: MIT Press, 1992.

Csikszentmihalyi, Mihaly. *Finding Flow: The Psychology of Engagement with Everyday Life.* New York: Basic Books, 1979.

Csikszentmihalyi, Mihaly, and Isabella S. Csikszentmihalyi. *Optimal Experience: Psychological Studies of Flow in Consciousness.* Cambridge, UK: Cambridge University Press, 1988.

Damasio, Antonio R. *Descartes' Error: Emotion, Reason, and the Human Brain.* New York: Putnam, Grosset/Putnam, 1994.

Danto, Arthur C. *Mysticism and Morality: Oriental Thought and Moral Philosophy.* New York: Basic Books, 1972.

d'Aquili, Eugene, and Andrew B. Newberg. *The Mystical Mind: Probing the Biology of Religious Experience.* Minneapolis: Fortress Press, 1999.

———. "Religious and Mystical States: A Neuropsychological Model." *Zygon, Journal of Religion and Science* 28 (June 1993): 117–200.

Darwin, Charles. *On the Origin of Species.* Vol. 15 of *Works of Charles Darwin.* 1859. Reprint, London: Pickering, 1988.

———. *The Power of Movement in Plants.* 1844. Reprint, New York: New York University Press, 1989.

Dean, Stanley R., ed. *Psychiatry and Mysticism.* Chicago: Nelson-Hall, 1975.

de Duve, Christian. *Life Evolving: Molecules, Mind, and Meaning.* New York: Oxford University Press, 2002.

———. *Vital Dust: Life As a Cosmic Imperative.* New York: Basic Books, 1995.

De Quincey, Thomas. *De Quincey As Critic.* Edited by John E. Jordan. London: Routledge, 1973.

Devereux, Paul. *The Sacred Place: The Ancient Origin of Holy and Mystical Sites.* London: Cassel & Co., 2000.

Dewey, John. *A Common Faith*. New Haven, Conn.: Yale University Press, 1934.

Diamond, Jared. Review of *Twilight at Easter* in *New York Review of Books,* March 25, 2004.

Dickinson, Emily. *The Collected Poems of Emily Dickinson*. 1924. Reprint, New York: Barnes and Noble Books, 1993.

Dillard, Annie. *Pilgrim at Tinker Creek*. New York: Harper & Row, 1974.

———. *Tickets for a Prayer Wheel*. New York: Harper & Row, 1986.

Doctorow, E. L. "Willi." A short story in *Lives of the Poets: Six Stories and a Novella*. New York: Random House, 1984.

Donnelly, Margaret E., ed. *Reinterpreting the Legacy of William James*. Washington, D.C.: American Psychological Association, 1986.

Eddington, Arthur S. *The Nature of the Physical World*. New York: Macmillan, 1928.

———. *Science and the Unseen World*. New York: Macmillan, 1929.

Einstein, Albert. "Wie ich die Welt sehe [How I see the world]." In *Mein Weltbild* [My Worldview]. 1934. Reprint, Frankfurt: Ullstein Materielien, 1980.

Elder, John. *Imagining the Earth: Poetry and the Vision of Nature*. Urbana: University of Illinois Press, 1985.

Eliot, T. S. *The Sacred Wood: Essays on Poetry and Criticism*. 1919. Reprint, London: Methuen, 1972.

Elvee, Richard Q., ed. *Mind in Nature: Nobel Conference XVII*. Gustavus Adolphus College. San Francisco: Harper & Row, 1981.

Emerson, Ralph Waldo. *The Complete Works of Ralph Waldo Emerson*. Edited by Edward Waldo Emerson. 14 vols. Boston: Houghton, Mifflin, 1903.

———. *The Early Lectures of Ralph Waldo Emerson*. Cambridge, Mass.: Harvard University Press, 1959–1972.

———. *The Journals and Miscellaneous Notebooks of Ralph Waldo Emerson*. Edited by William H. Gilman et al. 16 vols. Cambridge, Mass.: Harvard University Press, 1960–1982.

———. *Nature*. Boston: James Munroe, 1836.

———. "Nature." In *Emerson's Essays*. Introduction by Sherman Paul. 1844. Reprint, New York: Dutton, 1971.

————. *Nature: Addresses and Lectures.* New York: T.Y. Crowell & Co., 1900.

————. *The Selected Lectures of Ralph Waldo Emerson.* Edited by Ronald A. Bosco and Joel Myerson. Athens: University of Georgia Press, 2005.

Eriksson, Peter S. et al. "Neurogenesis in the Adult Human Hippocampus." *Nature Medicine* 4 (November 1998): 1313–17.

Fechner, Gustav Theodor. *Elemente der Psychophysik.* Vol. 2. Leipzig: Breitkopf u Härtel, 1860.

————. *Religion of a Scientist.* Selections from Gustav Th. Fechner. Edited and translated by Walter Lowrie. New York: Pantheon, 1946.

Feynman, Richard P. *Surely You're Joking, Mr. Feynman: Adventures of a Curious Character.* New York: W. W. Norton, 1985.

Forman, Robert K. C. *Mysticism, Mind, Consciousness.* Albany: State University of New York Press, 1999.

Freud, Sigmund. *Civilization and Its Discontents.* 1930. Translated and edited by James Strachey. Standard edition. Reprint, New York: W. W. Norton, 1989.

————. *The Standard Edition of the Complete Psychological Works of Sigmund Freud.* Edited by James Strachey. London: Hogarth Press, 1957.

Gifford, Terry. *Green Voices: Understanding Contemporary Nature Poetry.* Manchester, UK: Manchester University Press, 1995.

Gill, John. "Bouldering: A Mystic Art Form." In *The Mountain Spirit,* edited by M. C. Tobias and Harold Drasdo. London: Victor Gollanz, 1980.

Gliedman, John. "Scientists in Search of the Soul." *Science Digest* 90 (July 1982): 7.

Goethe, Johann Wolfgang von. *Werke, Hamburger Ausgabe in 14 Bände.* Munich: Deutcher Taschenbuch Verlag, 1988.

Gore, Al. *Earth in the Balance: Ecology and the Human Spirit.* Boston: Houghton Mifflin, 1992.

Gottlieb, Roger S., ed. *This Sacred Earth: Religion, Nature, Environment.* New York: Routledge, 1996.

Grady, Denise. "Medicine Lags against Addiction." *New York Times* (28 July 1990), Week in Review.

Grant Watson, E. L. *Descent of Spirit: Writings of E.L. Grant Watson.* Edited by Dorothy Green. Sydney, Australia: Primavera Press, 1990.

Greeley, A. M. *Ecstasy: A Way of Knowing.* Englewood, N.J.: Prentice Hall, 1974.

Greeley, A. M., and William McCready. "Are We a Nation of Mystics?" *New York Times Magazine,* January 16, 1975.

Greenwood, Susan. *The Nature of Magic: An Anthropology of Consciousness.* Oxford, UK: Berg, 2005.

Griffin, Donald R. *Animal Minds.* Chicago: University of Chicago Press, 1992.

Haldane, J. B. S. *On Being the Right Size and Other Essays.* Oxford, UK: Oxford University Press, 1985.

Halpern, Daniel, ed. *On Nature: Nature, Landscape, and Natural History.* San Francisco: North Point, 1987.

Hamer, Dean. *The God Gene: How Faith Is Hardwired into Our Genes.* New York: Doubleday, 2004.

Harris, Jonathan. *Drugged America.* New York: Four Winds Press, 1991.

Hartman, Geoffrey H. *The Unmediated Vision: An Interpretation of Wordsworth, Hopkins, Rilke, and Valery.* New York: Harcourt, Brace, 1954.

Hay, John. *Kernels of Energy, Bones of Earth: The Rock in Chinese Art.* New York: China Institute of America, 1985.

———. *Mind the Gap: The Education of a Nature Writer.* Reno: University of Nevada Press, 2004.

Helburn, Nicholas. "The Wilderness Continuum." *Professional Geographer* 29, no. 4 (November 1977): 333–37.

Hemingway, Ernest. *Death in the Afternoon.* New York: Scribner, 1932.

Herneck, Friedrich. *Einstein und sein Weltbild* [Einstein and His Worldview]. Berlin: Der Morgen, 1976.

Herrigel, Eugen. *Zen in the Art of Archery.* New York: Pantheon Books, 1964.

Herzog, Maurice. *Annapurna.* New York: E. P. Dutton, 1953.

Hillman, James. *A Blue Fire.* Selected writings by James Hillman. Introduced and edited by Thomas Moore. New York: Harper Perennial, 1991.

Hobson, J. Allan. *Consciousness.* New York: Scientific American Library, 1999.

Hodder, Alan D. *Thoreau's Ecstatic Witness.* New Haven, Conn.: Yale University Press, 2001.

Hoffman, Edward. *Visions of Innocence.* Boston: Shambhala, 1992.

Hofmann, Albert. *Insight Outlook*. Atlanta, Georgia: Humanics New Age, 1986.

Honner, John. "Niels Bohr and the Mysticism of Nature." *Zygon: Journal of Religion and Science* 17 (September 1982): 243–53.

Horgan, John. *Rational Mysticism: Dispatches from the Border between Science and Spirituality*. Boston: Houghton Mifflin, 2002.

Hudson, W. H. *Far Away and Long Ago*. Introduction by Stephen J. Bodio. 1918. Reprint, New York: Lyons and Burford, 1997.

Hughes, Ted. *River*. New York: Harper & Row, 1984.

Hunt, Harry T. *On the Nature of Consciousness: Cognitive, Phenomological, and Transpersonal Perspectives*. New Haven, Conn.: Yale University Press, 1995.

Hurd, Barbara. *Entering the Stone: On Caves and Feeling through the Dark*. Boston: Houghton Mifflin, 2003.

Huxley, Aldous. *The Doors of Perception and Heaven and Hell*. 1956. 1st Harper Colophon ed. Reprint, New York: Perennial Library, 1963.

———. "Wordsworth in the Tropics." Vol. 2 of *Complete Essays*. 1926–1929. Originally in *Do What You Will*. London: Chatto and Windus, 1925. Reprint, Chicago: Ivan R Dee, 2000.

Huxley, Julian. *New Bottles for New Wine*. New York: Harper and Brothers, 1957.

Hvolbeck, Russell H. *Mysticism and Experience*. Lanham, Md.: University Press of America, 1998.

Inayat Khan, P. V. Lectures entitled "New Perspectives in Science and Spirituality" delivered at Harvard University, Cambridge, Mass., October 21–23, 2001, published in *Spirit of Change: New England's Holistic Magazine,* September–October 2002.

Isselbacher, Kurt J. et al., eds. *Harrison's Principles of Internal Medicine*. 13th ed. New York: McGraw-Hill, 1994.

Jahner, Elaine. "The Spiritual Landscape." *Parabola* 2, no. 3 (1977): 32–38.

James, Henry, ed. *The Letters of William James*. 2 vols. Boston: Atlantic Monthly Press, 1920.

James, William. *Collected Essays and Reviews*. New York: Longman's Green & Co., 1920.

———. *The Correspondence of William James*. Charlottesville: University Press of Virginia, 1992–2004.

————. *Essays in Philosophy*. Cambridge, Mass.: Harvard University Press, 1978.

————. *Memories and Studies*. 1911. Reprint, New York: Greenwood Press, 1968.

————. *A Pluralistic Universe: Hibbert Lectures at Manchester College on the Present Situation in Philosophy*. 1909. Reprint, Lincoln: University of Nebraska Press, 1996.

————. *The Principles of Psychology*. 1890. Reprint, Cambridge, Mass.: Harvard University Press, 1983.

————. "A Suggestion about Mysticism." In *Essays in Philosophy*. 1910. Reprint, Cambridge, Mass.: Harvard University Press, 1978.

————. *Talks to Teachers on Psychology: And to Students on Some of Life's Ideals*. 1899. Reprint, Cambridge, Mass.: Harvard University Press, 1983.

————. *The Varieties of Religious Experience: A Study in Human Nature, Being the Gifford Lectures on Natural Religion Delivered at Edinburgh in 1901–1902*. New York: Longmans, Green, 1902.

————. *The Will to Believe and Other Essays in Popular Philosophy; Human Immortality, Two Supposed Objections to the Doctrine*. 1898. Reprint, New York: Dover, 1976.

James, Sarah, and Torbjörn Lahti. *The Natural Steps for Communities: How Cities and Towns Can Change to Sustainable Practices*. Gabriola, B.C., Canada: New Society Publishers, 2004.

Jamison, Kay Redfield. *Exuberance: The Passion for Life*. New York: Knopf, 2004.

Jammer, Max. *Einstein and Religion: Physics and Theology*. Princeton, N.J.: Princeton University Press, 1999.

Jeffries, Richard. *The Story of My Heart*. London: Constable, 1947.

Jenkins, Thomas M. "Perfume in the Ozone." *Summit*, June–July 1979, 29.

Johnson, Raynor C. *Watcher on the Hills: A Study of Some Mystical Experiences of Ordinary People*. New York: Harper, 1959.

Jonsson, Erik. *Inner Navigation: Why We Get Lost and How We Find Our Way*. New York: Scribner, 2002.

Joseph, R. "The Limbic System and the Soul: Evolution and the Neuroanatomy of Religious Experience." *Zygon, Journal of Religion and Science* 36 (March 2001): 105–36.

Jung, C. G. *The Collected Works of C. G. Jung.* Edited by Herbert Read et al. Princeton, N.J.: Princeton University Press, 1960.

Kahn, Peter H. *The Human Relationship with Nature: Development and Culture.* Cambridge, Mass.: MIT Press, 1999.

Kaplan, R., and S. Kaplan. *The Experience of Nature: A Psychological Perspective.* New York: Cambridge University Press, 1989.

Keats, John. *The Complete Poems of John Keats.* London: Penguin Books, 2003.

Keegan, Paul, ed. *Ted Hughes: Collected Poems.* New York: Farrar, Straus & Giroux, 2003.

Kellert, Stephen R. *Kinship to Mastery: Biophilia in Human Evolution and Development.* Washington, D.C.: Island Press, 1997.

Kellert, Stephen R., and Timothy J. Farnham., eds. *The Good in Nature and Humanity: Connecting Science, Religion, and Spirituality in the Natural World.* Washington, D.C.: Island Press, 2002.

Kellert, Stephen R., and E. O. Wilson. *The Biophilia Hypothesis.* Washington, D.C.: Island Press, 1993.

Kelly, Kevin W. *The Home Planet.* Reading, Mass.: Addison-Wesley, 1988.

King, Thomas M. "Globalization and the Soul: According to Teilhard, Friedman and Others." *Zygon, Journal of Religion and Science* 37 (March 2002): 26–43.

Klinkenorg, Verlyn. "Be Afraid. Be Very Afraid." *New York Times Book Review* (30 May 2004): 19.

Knoll, Andrew H. *Life on a Young Planet: The First Three Billion Years of Evolution on Earth.* Princeton, N.J.: Princeton University Press, 2003.

Koch, Christof. *The Quest for Consciousness: A Neurobiological Study.* Englewood, Colo.: Roberts & Co., 2004.

Korpela, K. M., and M. P. Ylén. "Effectiveness of Favorite-Place Prescriptions: A Field Experiment." *American Journal of Preventive Medicine* 36, no. 5 (May 2009): 435–38.

Krakauer, Jon. *Into the Wild.* New York: Villard, 1996.

Laski, Marghanita. *Ecstasy: A Study of Some Secular and Religious Experiences.* 1961. Reprint, New York: Greenwood Press, 1968.

Leary, Timothy. *The Politics of Ecstasy.* New York: Putnam, 1968.

Leuba, James H. *The Psychology of Religious Mysticism*. New York: Harcourt Brace, 1929.

Levinthal, Charles F. *Messengers of Paradise: Opiates and the Brain*. New York: Anchor Press/Doubleday, 1988.

Lewin, Roger. *Patterns in Evolution: The New Molecular View*. New York: Scientific American Library, 1997.

Lewis-Williams, J. David. *The Mind in the Cave: Consciousness and the Origins of Art*. London: Thames & Hudson, 2002.

Lewis-Williams, J. David, and David Pearce. *Inside the Neolithic Mind: Consciousness, Cosmos and the Realm of the Gods*. London: Thames & Hudson, 2005.

Lewontin, Richard. Review of *The Wars over Evolution*. *New York Review of Books,* October 20, 2005: 54.

Lightman, Alan. *A Sense of the Mysterious*. New York: Pantheon, 2005.

Lindbergh, Anne Morrow. *Gift from the Sea*. New York: Pantheon, 1955.

Lipsyte, Robert. *Sportsworld*. New York: Quadrangle Books, 1975.

Llinàs, Rodolfo R. *I of the Vortex: From Neurons to Self.* Cambridge, Mass.: MIT Press, 2001.

Louv, Richard. *Last Child in the Woods*. New York: Algonquin Books, 2005.

Lovelock, James. *The Ages of Gaia: A Biography of Our Living Earth*. New York: W. W. Norton, 1988.

Maclean, Norman. *A River Runs Through It and Other Stories*. Chicago: University of Chicago Press, 1976.

Mandell, Arnold J. "The Second Second Wind." In Symposium on Psychiatric Aspects of Sports. *Psychiatric Annals* 9 (March 1979): 57–69.

———. "Toward a Psychobiology of Transcendence: God in the Brain." Chap. 14 in *The Psychobiology of Consciousness,* ed. by Julian M. and Richard J. Davidson. New York: Plenum Press, 1980.

Marcuse, Herbert. *Eros and Civilization: A Philosophical Inquiry into Freud*. Boston: Beacon Press, 1955.

Margulis, Lynn, and Dorian Sagan. "The Beast with Five Genomes." *Natural History* 110, no. 5 (June 2001): 38–41.

———. *Microcosmos: Four Billion Years of Evolution from Our Microbial Ancestors*. New York: Summit, 1986.

Marshall, Paul. *Mystical Experiences with the Natural World: Experiences and Explanations.* Oxford: Oxford University Press, 2005.

Martin, Graham Dunstan. *Shadows in the Cave: Mapping the Conscious Universe.* London: Arkana/Penguin, 1990.

Maslow, Abraham H. *Religions, Values and Peak Experiences.* Columbus: Ohio University Press, 1964.

Masson, J. Moussaief. *The Oceanic Feeling: The Origins of Religious Sentiment in Ancient India.* Boston: Reidel, 1980.

Matthiessen, Peter. *The Snow Leopard.* Reprint, New York: Penguin Books, 1978.

Maxwell, Thomas P. "Considering Spirituality, Integral Spirituality, Deep Science and Ecological Awareness." *Zygon* 38, no. 2 (June 2003): 257–76.

McKibben, Bill. *The End of Nature.* New York: Random House, 2006.

Meadows, Donnella, Jorgen Randers, and Dennis Meadows. *Limits of Growth: The 30-Year Update.* White River Junction, Vt.: Chelsea Green, 2004.

Meier, C. A. "Wilderness and the Search for the Soul of Modern Man." In *Testament to the Wilderness.* Zurich: Daimon Verlag, 1985.

Melville, Herman. *Moby Dick, or The Whale.* 1851. 150th anniversary ed. New York: Penguin, 2001.

Mercer, J. Edward. *Nature Mysticism.* London: George Allen, 1913.

Merton, Thomas. *The Ascent to the Truth.* New York: Harcourt, Brace, 1951.

Milton, Kay. *Loving Nature: Toward an Ecology of Emotion.* London: Routledge, 2002.

Mitchell, Dr. Edgar, with Dwight Williams. *The Way of the Explorer: An Apollo Astronaut's Journey through the Material and Mystical Worlds.* New York: Putnam, 1996.

Mitchell, R. G. Jr. *Mountain Experience: The Psychology and Sociology of Adventure.* Chicago: University of Chicago Press, 1983.

Monod, Jacques. *Chance and Necessity: An Essay on the Natural Philosophy of Modern Biology.* 1st American ed. New York: Knopf, 1971.

Moore, Charles. "Trashed: Across the Pacific Ocean, Plastics, Plastics, Everywhere." *Natural History* 112, no. 9 (November 2003).

Morrison, Reg. *The Spirit in the Gene: Humanity's Proud Illusion and the Laws of Nature.* Ithaca, N.Y.: Cornell University Press, 1999.

Mowry, Robert D. *Worlds within Worlds: The Richard Rosenblum Collection of Chinese Scholars' Rocks.* Cambridge, Mass.: Harvard University Art Museums, 1997.

Moyers, Bill. "Welcome to Doomsday." *New York Review of Books* (March 24, 2004): 8–10.

Muir, John. *The Wild Muir: Twenty-Two of John Muir's Greatest Adventures.* Yosemite National Park, Calif.: Yosemite Association, 1994.

———. *Travels in Alaska.* Boston: Houghton Mifflin, 1915.

Murchie, Guy. *The Seven Mysteries of Life: An Exploration in Science and Philosophy.* 1978. Reprint, Boston: Houghton Mifflin, 1981.

Murphy, Michael, and Rhea A. White. *In the Zone: Transcendent Experience in Sports.* New York: Penguin/Arkana, 1995.

Myers, F. W. H. *Wordsworth.* 1880. Reprint, London: Macmillan, 1929.

Nabhan, Gary Paul. *Cultures of Habitat: On Nature, Culture and Story.* Washington, D.C.: Counterpoint, 1977.

Nabokov, Peter. *Indian Running.* Santa Barbara, Calif.: Capra Press, 1981.

Nabokov, Vladimir. *Speak, Memory: A Memoir.* London: Golancz, 1951.

Naess, Arne. *Life's Philosophy: Reason and Feeling in a Deeper World.* Translated by Roland Huntford. Athens: University of Georgia Press, 2002.

Nestler, Eric J., and Robert C. Malencka. "The Addictive Brain." *Scientific American*, March 2004, 78–85.

Newburg, A. B., E. G. d'Aquili, and V. P. Rouse. *Why God Won't Go Away: Brain Science and the Biology of Belief.* New York: Ballantine. 2001.

Newhall, Nancy. *Ansel Adams: A biography. I. The Eloquent Light.* San Francisco: Sierra Club, 1963.

Nicholsen, Shierry Weber. *The Love of Nature and the End of the World: The Unspoken Dimensions of Environmental Concern.* Cambridge, Mass.: MIT Press, 1963.

Nietzsche, Friederich W. *Ecce Homo.* 1896. Reprint, New York: Penguin, 2000.

Niklas, Karl J. *The Evolutionary Biology of Plants.* Chicago: University of Chicago Press, 1997.

Olson, Sigurd F. *The Singing Wilderness.* New York: Alfred A. Knopf, 1956.

Orr, David W. "For the Love of Life." *Conservation Biology* 6, no. 4 (December 1992): 486–87.

Ortega y Gasset, José. *Meditations on Hunting.* New York: Scribner's, 1972.

Parsons, William B. *The Enigma of the Oceanic Feeling: Revisioning the Psychoanalytic Theory of Mysticism.* New York: Oxford University Press, 1999.

Peat, F. David. *The Blackwinged Night: Creativity in Nature and Mind.* Cambridge, Mass.: Perseus Publishing, 2000.

———. *Synchronicity: The Bridge between Matter and Mind.* New York: Bantam, 1987.

Peirce, Charles S. *Collected Papers.* Cambridge, Mass.: Harvard University Press, 1934.

Penrose, Roger. *Shadows of the Mind: A Search for the Missing Science of Consciousness.* Oxford: Oxford University Press, 1994.

Pert, Candace B. *Molecules of Emotion: Why You Feel the Way You Feel.* New York: Touchstone, 1997.

Petersen, David. *Heartsblood: Hunting, Spirituality, and Wildness in America.* Washington, D.C.: Island Press, 2000.

Phillips, Helen. "The Genius Machine," in *New Scientist* 182 (April 3, 2004): 30–33.

Polanyi, Michael. *The Tacit Dimension.* New York: Doubleday 1967.

Proust, Marcel. *Swanns Way.* 1914. Reprint, New York: Modern Library, 2003.

Putnam, Ruth Anna, ed. *Cambridge Companion to William James.* Cambridge: Cambridge University Press, 1997.

Radin, Paul. *Primitive Man as Philosopher.* 1927. Reprint, New York: Dover, 1957.

Raine, Kathleen. "Nature: House of the Soul." *Temenos* 9 (1988): 251–68.

Rees, Martin. *Our Final Hour: A Scientist's Warning: How Terror, Error, and Environmental Disaster Threaten Humankind's Future in This Century—on Earth and Beyond.* New York: Basic Books, 2003.

Restak, Richard M. *Mysteries of the Mind.* Washington, D.C.: National Geographic Society, 2000.

Rezendes, Paul. *The Wild Within: Adventures in Nature and Animal Teachings.* New York: Jeremy P. Tarcher/Putnam, 1998.

Richardson, Robert D. *Emerson: The Mind on Fire.* Berkeley: University of California Press, 1995.

Ridley, Matt. *The Origins of Virtue: Human Instincts and the Evolution of Cooperation*. New York: Penguin Paperbacks, 1996.

Rilke, Rainer Maria. *Sonnets to Orpheus*. Unpublished translation by David Oswald, 2008.

Rolland, Romain. *The Life of Ramakrishna*. 1929. Reprint, Calcutta: Advaita Ashrama, 1984.

Rosenblum, Richard. *Art of the Natural World: Resonances of Wild Nature in Chinese Sculptural Art*. Boston: MFA Publications, 2001.

Roszak, Theodore. *The Voice of the Earth*. New York: Simon and Schuster, 1992.

Roszak, Theodore, Mary E. Gomes, and Allan D. Kanner. *Ecopsychology: Restoring the Earth, Healing the Mind*. San Francisco: Sierra Club, 1995.

Roth, Harold D. *Original Tao: Inward Training (Nei-yeh) and the Foundations of Taoist Mysticism*. New York: Columbia University Press, 1999.

Rowley, George. *Principles of Chinese Painting*. 1947. Reprint, Princeton, N.J.: Princeton University Press, 1970.

Rue, Loyal. *Religion Is Not about God: How Spiritual Traditions Nurture Our Biological Nature and What to Expect When They Fail*. New Brunswick, N.J.: Rutgers University Press, 2002.

Russell, Bertrand. *Mysticism and Logic, and Other Essays*. New York: Longmans, Green, 1919.

Schneider, S. H., and P. J. Boston. *Scientists on Gaia*. Cambridge, Mass.: MIT Press, 1991.

Schrodes, C., H. Firestone, and M. Shugrue, eds. *The Conscious Reader*. 1985. 3rd ed., New York: Macmillan, 1991.

Service, Alastair, and Jean Bradley. *Megaliths and Their Mysteries*. New York: Macmillan, 1979.

Sheffield, Charles. *Man on the Earth: The Marks of Man: A Survey from Space*. London: Sedgewick and Jackson, 1983.

Shepard, Paul. *Encounters with Nature*. Washington, D.C.: Island Press, 1999.

———. *Traces of an Omnivore*. Washington, D.C.: Island Press, 1996.

Silverman, Ray, ed. *Light in the Darkness*. West Chester, Pa.: Chrysalis Books, 1994.

Sinnot, Edmund W. *The Bridge of Life: From Matter to Purpose*. New York: Simon and Schuster, 1966.

————. *Cell and Psyche: The Biology of Purpose.* Chapel Hill: University of North Carolina Press, 1950.

Skea, Anne. *Ted Hughes and the British Bardic Traditions.* 2000. www.zeta.org .au/~annskea/cairo.htm.

Slovic, Scott. *Seeking Awareness in American Nature Writing: Henry Thoreau, Annie Dillard, Edward Abbey, Wendell Berry, and Barry Lopez.* Salt Lake City: University of Utah Press, 1992.

Speth, James Gustave. *Red Sky at Morning: America and the Crisis of Global Environment.* New Haven, Conn.: Yale University Press, 2004.

Spurgeon, Caroline F. E. *Mysticism in English Literature.* 2nd ed. Cambridge: Cambridge University Press, 1922.

Stace, W. T. *Mysticism and Philosophy.* London: Macmillan, 1961.

Stallknecht, Newton P. *Strange Seas of Thought: Studies in William Wordsworth's Philosophy of Man and Nature.* Bloomington: Indiana University Press, 1958.

Stange, Mary Zeiss. *Woman the Hunter.* Boston: Beacon Press, 1997.

Starke, Linda. *State of the World 2003: A Worldwatch Institute Report on Progress Toward a Sustainable Society.* New York: W. W. Norton, 2003.

Stenger, Victor J. *The Unconscious Quantum: Metaphysics in Modern Physics and Cosmology.* Amherst, N.Y.: Prometheus Books, 1995.

Stevens, Anthony. *The Two Million-Year-Old Self.* Number 3 of Carolyn and Ernest Fay Series in Analytical Psychology. College Station: Texas A&M University Press, 1993.

————. *The Roots of War and Terror.* London: Continuum, 2004.

Stevens, Anthony, and John Price. *Evolutionary Psychiatry: A New Beginning.* London: Routledge, 1996.

Stevens, Wallace. *Wallace Stevens: Collected Poetry and Prose.* New York: Library of America, 1997.

Storr, Anthony. *Solitude: A Return to the Self.* 1988. Reprint, New York: Ballantine, 1989.

Suchantke, Andreas. *Eco-geography: What We See When We Look at Landscapes.* Translated and with an introduction by Norman Skillen. Great Barrington, Mass.: Lindisfarne Books, 2001.

Suzuki, David, with Amanda McConnell. *The Sacred Balance: Rediscovering Our Place in Nature.* Amherst, N.Y.: Prometheus Books, 1998.

Swedenborg, Emanuel. *Arcana Caelestia.* 1909. New York: The Swedenborg Foundation, 1968.

———. *Secrets of Heaven.* West Chester, Pa.: Swedenborg Foundation, 2000.

Taylor, Barbara Brown. "Settling for Less." *The Christian Century* (February 18, 1998).

Taylor, Eugene. *Shadow Culture: Psychology and Spirituality in America.* Washington, D.C.: Counterpoint, 1999.

———. "The Spiritual Roots of James's *Varieties of Religious Experience.*" Introduction to section 1 of *The Varieties of Religious Experience.* Routledge Centenary ed. London: Routledge, 2002.

———. *William James on Consciousness Beyond the Margin.* Princeton, N.J.: Princeton University Press, 1996.

———. "William James on Darwin: An Evolutionary Theory of Consciousness." In *Psychology, Perspectives and Practice,* edited by Sheila M. Pfafflin. *Annals of the New York Academy of Sciences.* New York: New York Academy of Sciences, 1990.

Taylor, Gordon R. *The Natural History of the Mind.* 1st American ed. New York: Dutton, 1979.

Taylor, Richard B. "Order in Pollock's Chaos." *Scientific American,* December 2002: 116–21.

Teilhard de Chardin, Pierre. *The Human Phenomenon.* 1955. New edition and translation by Sarah Appleton-Weber. Brighton, UK: Sussex Academic Press, 1999.

Thomas, Lewis. *The Lives of a Cell: Notes of a Biology Watcher.* New York: Penguin, 1974.

Thomashow, Mitchell. *Bringing the Biosphere Home: Learning to Perceive Global Environmental Change.* Cambridge, Mass.: MIT Press, 2002.

Thoreau, Henry David. *Collected Poems of Henry Thoreau.* Edited by Carl Bode. Baltimore, Md.: Johns Hopkins University Press, 1964.

———. *The Journal of Henry D. Thoreau.* Edited by Bradford Torrey and Francis H. Allen. New York: Dover, 1962.

———. *The Portable Thoreau.* New York: Penguin, 1985.

Todhunter, Andrew. *Dangerous Games.* New York: Doubleday, 2000.

Tolstoy, Leo. *Anna Karenina.* 1886. London: Penguin, 1978.

Tompkins, Peter, and Christopher Bird. *The Secret Life of Plants.* New York: Harper & Row, 1973.

Traherne, Thomas. "My Spirit" in *The Oxford Book of English Verse.* 1917. Edited by D. H. S. Nicholson. Oxford, UK: Clarendon Press, 1932.

Tuan, Yi-Fu. *Topophilia: A Study of Environmental Perception, Attitudes, and Values.* Englewood Cliffs, N.J.: Prentice-Hall, 1974.

Turnbull, Colin M. *The Mountain People.* New York: Simon and Schuster, 1972.

Turgenev, Ivan. *A Hunter's Sketches.* 1847–1851. Classics of Russian Literature. Moscow: Foreign Languages Publishing House, n.d.

Uexkuell, Jacob von. *Der unsterbliche Geist in der Natur.* Hamburg, Germany: Christian Wegner Verlag, 1946.

Underhill, Evelyn. *Mysticism and War.* London: J. M. Watkins, 1915.

Untermeyer, Louis, ed. *Modern American Poetry.* 18th ed. New York: Harcourt, Brace, 1962.

Vaitl, Dieter et al. "Psychobiology of Altered States of Consciousness." *Psychological Bulletin* 131, no. 1 (2005): 98–127.

von Essen, Carl. *The Revenge of the Fishgod.* Forest Dale, Vt.: Paul S. Eriksson, 1996.

von Wright, Georg Henrik. *Myten om framsteget* [The Myth about Progress]. Stockholm: Bonnier, 1993.

———. "The Myth of Progress." In *Architecture and Cultural Values.* Report of the 4th Alvar Aalto Symposium. Jyväskylä, Finland: Alvar Aalto Symposium, 1988.

———. *Vetenskapen och förnuftet: Ett försök till orientering* [Science and Rationality: An Attempt at Orientation]. Borgå, Finland: Söderström, 1986.

Walsh, Roger N. *The Spirit of Shamanism.* Los Angeles: Jeremy P. Tarcher, 1990.

Washburn, Sherwood L., and C. S. Lancaster. "The Evolution of Hunting." In *Man the Hunter,* edited by Richard B. Lee and Irvin DeVore, 293–300. Chicago: Aldine, 1968.

Watts, Alan W. *This Is It and Other Essays on Zen and Spiritual Experience.* 1958. Reprint, New York: Pantheon, 1960.

White, John., ed. *The Highest State of Consciousness.* New York: Anchor, 1972.

Weil, Andrew. *The Natural Mind: A New Way of Looking at Drugs and Higher Consciousness.* Boston: Houghton Mifflin, 1972.

Wilson, Edward O. *Biophilia.* Cambridge, Mass.: Harvard University Press, 1984.

———. *Consilience: The Unity of Knowledge.* New York: Knopf, 1998.

———. *The Future of Life.* New York: Knopf, 2002.

Wittgenstein, Ludwig. *Tractatus Logico-Philosophicus.* Translated by D. F. Pears and B. F. McGuinness. London and New York: Routledge (Routledge Classics). (Originally published in German in 1921. First English edition published in 1922.)

Wofsy, Steven. "The Great Global Experiment." *Harvard Magazine,* November–December 2002.

Wood, Peter. *The End of Evolution: On Mass Extinctions and the Preservation of Biodiversity.* New York: Bantam Books, 1994.

Wordsworth, William. *The Essential Wordsworth.* Selected and with an introduction by Seamus Heaney. New York: Ecco Press, 1988.

———. *Selected Poems and Prefaces.* Edited by Jack Stillinger. Boston: Houghton Mifflin, 1965.

Yendes, Albert. "Contrary to Popular Opinion." *Petersen's Hunting,* March 1993, 34.

Zaehner, Robert Charles. *Mysticism Sacred and Profane: An Inquiry into Some Varieties of Praeternatural Experience.* 1957. Reprint, Oxford: Oxford University Press. 1961.

———. *Zen, Drugs, and Mysticism.* New York: Pantheon Books, 1972.

Zajonc, Arthur. *Catching the Light: The Entwined History of Light and Mind.* New York: Bantam Books, 1993.

Ziegler, Michael. "Psychedelic Religious Experience." *Tikkun* 19 (2004): 74–76.

Zohar, Danah. *The Quantum Self: A Revolutionary View of Human Nature and Consciousness Rooted in the New Physics.* In collaboration with Ian Marshall. London: Bloomsbury, 1990.

Zohar, Danah, and Ian Marshall. *SQ: Spiritual Intelligence the Ultimate Intelligence.* London: Bloomsbury, 2000.

Zwingle, Erla. "Megacities." *National Geographic Magazine* 202, no. 5 (November 2002): 70–100.

# INDEX

# Books of Related Interest

**Radical Nature**
The Soul of Matter
*by Christian de Quincey*

**Morphic Resonance**
The Nature of Formative Causation
*by Rupert Sheldrake*

**Plant Spirit Healing**
A Guide to Working with Plant Consciousness
*by Pam Montgomery*

**Moonrise**
The Power of Women Leading from the Heart
*Edited by Nina Simons with Anneke Campbell*

**Original Instructions**
Indigenous Teachings for a Sustainable Future
*Edited by Melissa K. Nelson*

**The Universe Is a Green Dragon**
A Cosmic Creation Story
*by Brian Swimme, Ph.D.*

**The Spiritual Life of Water**
Its Power and Purpose
*by Alick Bartholomew*

**Thomas Berry, Dreamer of the Earth**
The Spiritual Ecology of the Father of Environmentalism
*Edited by Ervin Laszlo and Allan Combs*

INNER TRADITIONS • BEAR & COMPANY
P.O. Box 388
Rochester, VT 05767
1-800-246-8648
www.InnerTraditions.com

Or contact your local bookseller